DISCARDED

The Loyalty Islands

The Loyalty Islands
A History of Culture Contacts 1840–1900

K.R. Howe

The University Press of Hawaii
Honolulu

Library of Congress Cataloging in Publication Data
Howe, K   R
   The Loyalty Islands.

   Bibliography: p.
   Includes index.
   1. Loyalty Islands—History. 2. Ethnology—New Caledonia—Loyalty Islands. 3. Acculturation.
I. Title.
DU670.H68   1977   993'.3   76-50009
ISBN 0-8248-0451-1

© 1977 by K. R. Howe
All rights reserved. No part of this work may be reproduced or transmitted in any form or by any means, electronic or mechanical, including photocopying and recording, or by any information storage or retrieval system, without permission in writing from the publisher.

Simultaneously published by the Australian National University Press, Canberra

Manufactured in the United States of America

for Merrilyn and James Eliot

Contents

Preface		ix
Acknowledgments		xiii
Abbreviations		xv

PROTAGONISTS

1	Loyalty Islanders before 1840	3
2	New Strangers	13

RIVAL CHIEFS, RIVAL FAITHS

3	Mare 1841–1866	21
4	Lifu 1842–1864	35
5	Uvea 1842–1864	46

CHIEFS, CHURCH, AND STATE

6	Lifu 1864–1871	57
7	Uvea 1864–1875	65
8	Mare 1866–1895	71
	Interlude: A Review of Political Change	79

ADVENTURE AND ADVANTAGE

9	Travel	86
10	Trade	101
11	Teaching	117

THE QUESTION OF IMPACT

12	Firearms	134
13	Disease	145
14	Depopulation?	154
	Conclusion	159
	Notes	163
	Bibliography	183
	Index	197

Maps

1	New Caledonia and dependencies	5
2	Mare. Approximate tribal boundaries in the 1850s	23
3	Lifu	37
4	Uvea	48
5	Mare. Si Gwahma control in the 1870s	74

Figure

1	Population of Loyalty Islands	156

Maps drawn by the Cartographic Office, Department of Human Geography, Australian National University.

Preface

European portrayal of South Pacific Islanders has long been coloured by various ideas and emotions. In the second half of the eighteenth century many philosophers, writers, and artists believed that the 'newly discovered' races in the South Seas were living examples of Rousseau's Noble Savage. Early evangelical missionaries, seeing the world in narrow moral terms, and more in tune with the hardships of life in the Pacific, created instead the image of a savage who was ignoble, degraded, brutish. By the mid-nineteenth century poets had again modified the stereotype by taking the freedom of the Noble Savage, combining it with the wildness of his degraded counterpart and fashioning a Romantic savage. The idea that Pacific Islanders, whether they be Noble, brutish, or Romantic, were unable to cope with contact with 'superior' European culture pre-dated later nineteenth-century evolutionary theories which postulated the 'survival of the fittest'. But such theories were seized upon as providing 'scientific' justification and popularised the view: in the second half of the nineteenth century the savage, then, was a mournful creature lying down to die, his race disappearing from the face of the earth as a consequence of losing the struggle for survival with all-powerful Europeans. The early decades of the twentieth century saw a proliferation of neo-Darwinian theories describing and accounting for the dying savage in the Pacific.[1] Today we naturally know that Pacific Island societies did not die out, indeed there is now quite serious overpopulation on some islands. Nevertheless the opinion that

European entry into the Pacific had damaging and in many cases disastrous consequences for the Islanders and their way of life is still popular today. One of the more widely known though scarcely original expositions of this argument is Alan Moorehead's aptly titled *The Fatal Impact: An Account of the Invasion of the South Pacific 1767–1840*: the instant Islanders and Europeans first beheld each other is seen as 'a fateful moment when a social capsule is broken open, when primitive creatures, beasts as well as men, are confronted for the first time with civilization'. Europeans who followed in the explorers' wake —traders, missionaries, and administrators—were 'intruders' ruthlessly transforming island societies 'by firearms, disease or alcohol . . . by imposing an alien code of laws and morals' and so destroying the former 'slow, natural rhythm of life' in the Pacific.[2] The end result, goes the argument, was massive depopulation and, for those Islanders fortunate or unfortunate to enough to find themselves still alive, utter depression and demoralisation in the face of 'civilisation'.

Such present day theories of a fatal impact in the Pacific are more often than not based on unsound historical, anthropological, and demographic scholarship, and, more significantly, on the explicit or implicit notion that 'savages' were witless, incapable of taking their own initiatives (except to lash out like sleeping dogs if kicked too hard by Europeans), and necessarily took a defensive and passive role in their relationship with the supposedly dominant, superior visitors to their shores. Furthermore, the belief that Europeans were vicious invaders is a burden commonly shouldered by 'liberal' writers to assuage feelings of guilt for either real or imagined harm done to Islanders at the hands of their forefathers—a case of inverted racism. Such writers thus frequently reveal more of their emotional and racial view of the world than of the culture contacts they purport to analyse.

That the coming of the Europeans had detrimental consequences for some Pacific Islanders cannot be denied. But current research suggests that, as a generalisation, the 'fatal impact' theory is highly questionable to say the least. For modern Pacific historians and demographers are in the process of painting a very different picture of European impact: the phenomenon of depopulation on a grand scale is now shown to be in large part a myth,[3] and current detailed analyses of many of the Islanders' social, economic, and political developments in the nineteenth and twentieth centuries indicate, in the words of J.W. Davidson, that 'The indigenous cultures . . . were like islands whose coastal regions outsiders might penetrate but whose heartlands they could never conquer'.[4]

Preface

The inhabitants of the Loyalty Islands are among those Pacific Islanders whose culture and way of life have been preserved to a remarkable degree in spite of some 130 years of fairly intensive contact with Europeans and their nearness to a major urban region, Noumea. The reasons why Loyalty Islands society has remained relatively undisturbed and unchanged while at the same time adapting to and utilising European presence, ideas, and technology are to be found in the nineteenth-century contact history of the islands and in the nature of the Islanders' cultural system. This study examines the interaction among and between Loyalty Islanders and Europeans during their first sixty-odd years of contact. Emphasis is placed on the nature of the Islanders' responses and the consequences for their society. It is among the contentions of this study that at least some Pacific Islanders were not basking in idyllic contemplation of their Arcadia before canvas sails appeared over the horizon; that in most of their responses to European presence Loyalty Islanders generally took their own initiatives in an enthusiastic, even aggressive manner such that any socio-political and economic changes, although inspired by Europeans and their technology, were frequently the result of the Islanders' own actions; and that Loyalty Islands culture had great capacity to absorb innovation and change constructively and creatively: the processes of acculturation do not necessarily result in any form of social dislocation.

Many current works which investigate culture contacts revolve around the activities of a single European 'occupational group'—a missionary society, a trading concern, a colonial government institution and so on. The approach adopted here is to place the Islanders firmly at the forefront and to describe and analyse their reactions to the various waves of Europeans reaching their islands. This book is not intended to be a history of traders, missionaries, and administrators on the Loyalty Islands; it is a history of the way in which Europeans and Loyalty Islanders reacted in the contact situation and the consequences for the Islanders. The Loyalty Islands are eminently suited to such an investigation. In one respect they are something of the Pacific in microcosm, for throughout the nineteenth century they were subjected to a constant stream of outsiders—sandalwood traders, beachcombers, whalers, labour recruiters, dealers in island produce, LMS Polynesian teachers, English Protestant and French Catholic missionaries, and French administrators. Furthermore the islands are small enough, and there is adequate documentation, to enable an analysis in some detail of aspects of culture contacts more often approached by historians on a larger scale encompassing greater numbers of participants and larger geographic areas; certain generalisations often made about European impact in the Pacific can thus be tested at a local level. Conclusions drawn from the Loyalty Islands must, however, remain specific, although some parallels with other Pacific islands are apparent.

One of the difficulties of writing about a little-known area of the Pacific is to strike a balance between a chronology and an analysis of events. There are no reliable histories of the Loyalty Islands to which the reader can be referred for people, places, and events.[5] Accordingly, chapters 3 to 8, which deal with the Islanders' responses to missionaries and administrators, and examine the interrelationships among indigenous politics and European religions and nationalities, have been arranged chronologically and on an island by island basis. As there are three islands, each with varying tribal political arrangements, and with different mission organisations and administrators active in various places at different times, attempts to adopt a purely thematic or analytical approach would confuse geography and chronology, and a clear outline of both is essential to an understanding of the Islanders' reactions to these people. Furthermore, it is an approach which, rather than being orientated to follow the often disconnected activities of one or several of these European groups, has enabled the Islanders to be kept to the fore and the pattern and progression of their responses to be followed uninterrupted. With the broad outline of events established in these chapters other equally important aspects of contact—the Islanders' responses to commercial shipping and trade, to religious ideas and missionary education, and to firearms and disease—can safely be dealt with thematically, as in the remaining chapters.

KRH
Massey University, 1974

NOTE

At least half the material consulted for this book is in French. Unless otherwise stated, translations are my own.

Acknowledgments

This study was originally written in the Department of Pacific History at the Australian National University. Many people there gave me valuable assistance: the late Professor J.W. Davidson, Mrs Rosamund Walsh, Mr Robert Langdon, Dr Hugh Laracy, Dr D.T. Tryon, Dr David Lewis, Dr Norma McArthur, and Dr Bronwen Douglas. I am especially grateful to Dr Dorothy Shineberg and Dr Peter Corris for their kind encouragement and ever helpful criticisms. The ANU generously enabled me to study in archives in Europe and New Caledonia and to undertake field work on the Loyalty Islands; my other acknowledgments will follow the route of the research trip. Rome: I am grateful to Father J. Lambert, Father J. Coste, and Sig. A. Cacace at Archivio Padri Maristi. Paris: I wish to thank Professor Jean Guiart of the Ecole Practique des Hautes Etudes, Sorbonne; M. Etienne Kruger of the Société des Missions Evangéliques de Paris; Pastor Raymond Leenhardt for permission to consult documents left to him by his father Maurice; and especially Father M.J. Dubois who allowed me to examine his invaluable collection of documents on Mare while he was working on them himself. Noumea: I am grateful to Archbishop P. Martin and Father M. Laurenge for permission to consult the Archives de l'Archevêché; M. Bernard Brou, M. Joseph Tidjine, M. Charles Hauda, the South Pacific Commission, and especially the Le Pioufle family for their hospitality. Loyalty Islands: for three months my wife and I travelled widely throughout the islands where we were treated with warmth and affection we had never before experienced from strangers. To all those people, unfortunately far too numerous to name, who fed, housed and transported us and who were ever willing to talk about their history and way of life generally, we are deeply grateful. Those deserving special mention are—on Lifu: Pastor T. Wettach, Pastor Jacques Ajapuhnya, M. Hmana Wawalahae, the Passa family, Pastor Simi, Father Tavernier, the Wete family, and M. Marcel and Mme. Eloise Tonne. On Uvea: M. Aizick Wea, Pastor Peteru Ihili, and M. Walep Nacko. On Mare: M. Choucky Cuewapur. I am also grateful to Massey University, Palmerston North, New Zealand for a post-doctoral fellowship which enabled me to prepare this study for publication. Finally, I must express my gratitude to Merrilyn, my wife, for her constant encouragement and assistance on all fronts.

Abbreviations

AAN	Archives de l'Archevêché, Noumea
AMAE	Archives du Ministère des Affaires Etrangères
AMO	*Annales des Missions d'Océanie*
ANM	Archives Nationales, section Marine, Paris
ANOM	Archives Nationales, section Outre-Mer, Paris
ANU	Australian National University, Canberra
APF	*Annales de la Propagation de la Foi*
APM	Archivio Padri Maristi, Rome
BN	Bibliothèque Nationale, Paris
CO	Colonial Office
EP	Ella papers, Mitchell Library, Sydney
FO	Foreign Office
GBPP	*Great Britain: Parliamentary Papers*
JP	Jones papers, Mitchell Library, Sydney
JPH	*Journal of Pacific History*
JPS	*Journal of the Polynesian Society*
JSO	*Journal de la Société des Océanistes*
LMS	London Missionary Society
Min.	Ministre de la Marine et des Colonies. After 1870, Ministre des Colonies.
ML	Mitchell Library, Sydney
Mon.	*Moniteur de la Nouvelle-Calédonie*

NLA	National Library of Australia
ONC	Oceania Nova Caledonia, Archivio Padri Maristi, Rome
OP	Provincia Oceaniae, Archivio Padri Maristi, Rome
PCD	Private Collection of Father M.J. Dubois, Paris
PMB	Pacific Manuscripts Bureau
PRO	Public Records Office
QVP	*Queensland: Votes and Proceedings of the Legislative Assembly*
RC	*Report of the Royal Commission Appointed to Inquire into Certain Alleged Cases of Kidnapping of Natives of the Loyalty Islands*, Sydney, 1869
SMEP	Société des Missions Evangéliques de Paris
SSJ	South Sea Journals, London Missionary Society Archives
SSL	South Sea Letters, London Missionary Society Archives
SSO	South Sea Odds, London Missionary Society Archives
SSR	South Sea Reports, London Missionary Society Archives
VMA	Villa Maria Archives, Sydney

Protagonists

1
Loyalty Islanders before 1840

The three main islands of the Loyalty Islands group, Mare, Lifu, and Uvea, lie along a line parallel to and about 60 miles east of New Caledonia. All three, as well as a scattering of islets between Mare and Lifu, are formed of raised coral, heavily covered in bush, and from a distance at sea appear as low horizontal streaks of green in contrast to the vertical profile of their mountainous neighbour. Uvea is an atoll, reputed to be one of the most idyllic in the south seas, with low-lying habitable land stretching 30 miles around the eastern side of its lagoon. Both Lifu and Mare were originally atolls but have since risen well above sea level. Lifu, 37 miles long and 25 miles across at its widest point, and Mare, 25 by 20 miles, have large flat central plateaus, the dried out remains of their lagoon beds, and are bordered by higher coastal rims which once formed the outline of the atolls. The rims are sharply terraced on both their plateau and seaward flanks where ancient shorelines were worn into their coral as the islands rose: Lifu has been elevated in four clearly defined stages and Mare in five with its coastal rim, the highest land in the group, reaching to 350 feet above sea level. Uvea and Lifu are made purely of coral, but Mare also has small basalt outcrops at Rawa and Peorawa, thought to be the remains of mountain tops formed in the Miocene era and around which coral polyps built their reefs.

Approaches by sea and access to the shores are generally difficult. Uvea's lagoon provides a reasonable anchorage and the glistening lagoon beach, stretching almost the entire length of the main islands, allows for easy access. But Uvea's east coast and the coastlines of Mare and Lifu are choked by dangerous inshore reefs with a backdrop of rugged coral cliffs making landing hazardous, if not impossible, in all but a few places. There are no reliable anchorages on Lifu or Mare though vessels on Lifu can shelter from prevailing easterly winds in Sandalwood Bay, where boats can unload onto rocks at Chepenehe and onto small beaches at Eacho and Dueulu; landings are also possible at the inlets at Mu and Luengoni, and on the fine beach at We, but only in the calmest weather. On Mare ships can lie protected from the easterlies in the bays at Ro and Tadine where landings are made directly onto rocks, and also at the tiny sandy inlets at Netche and Mebuet.

The land surface is a mass of grotesquely twisted, dried coral which made travel extremely difficult over all but tracks worn by generations of bare feet. There are no rivers or streams on such porous ground and natural supplies of fresh water were very scarce and found only at the bottom of the deepest grottos. Before Europeans taught the Islanders to dig wells with the aid of metal tools, the only man-made source of fresh water was in holes cut into the base of coconut trees where rain water trickled. Soil is dry, thin, and usually confined to some inland areas where it lies in pockets among coral rocks, yet it is excellent for growing yams, the staple food. Inspite of the dry coral surface and lack of topsoil the bush is thick and luxuriant, especially around the seashore and over the coastal rims. Groves of coconut trees are dotted throughout Mare and Lifu and virtually cover Uvea. The central plateaus of Mare and Lifu are overgrown with scrub and secondary growth, the result of ages of plantation clearing fires. Generally the plateaus are featureless, even monotonous, except for several spectacular grottos like giant fist holes punched deep into the coral, and, as if to balance them, some huge cylindrical upthrusts of coral resembling medieval fortresses. The most notable of these is *titi* rising 160 feet above the plain at La Roche on Mare.

The climate is extremely pleasant, for the islands are out of the humid malarial zone. Average temperatures range from 22°C on Mare to 24°C on the more northerly Uvea with overall seasonal variations of less than 6°. Because there are no mountains to attract and capture banks of cloud, rainfall is lower than in New Caledonia and averages less than 60 inches a year. The general salubrity, however, is sometimes spoiled by droughts,

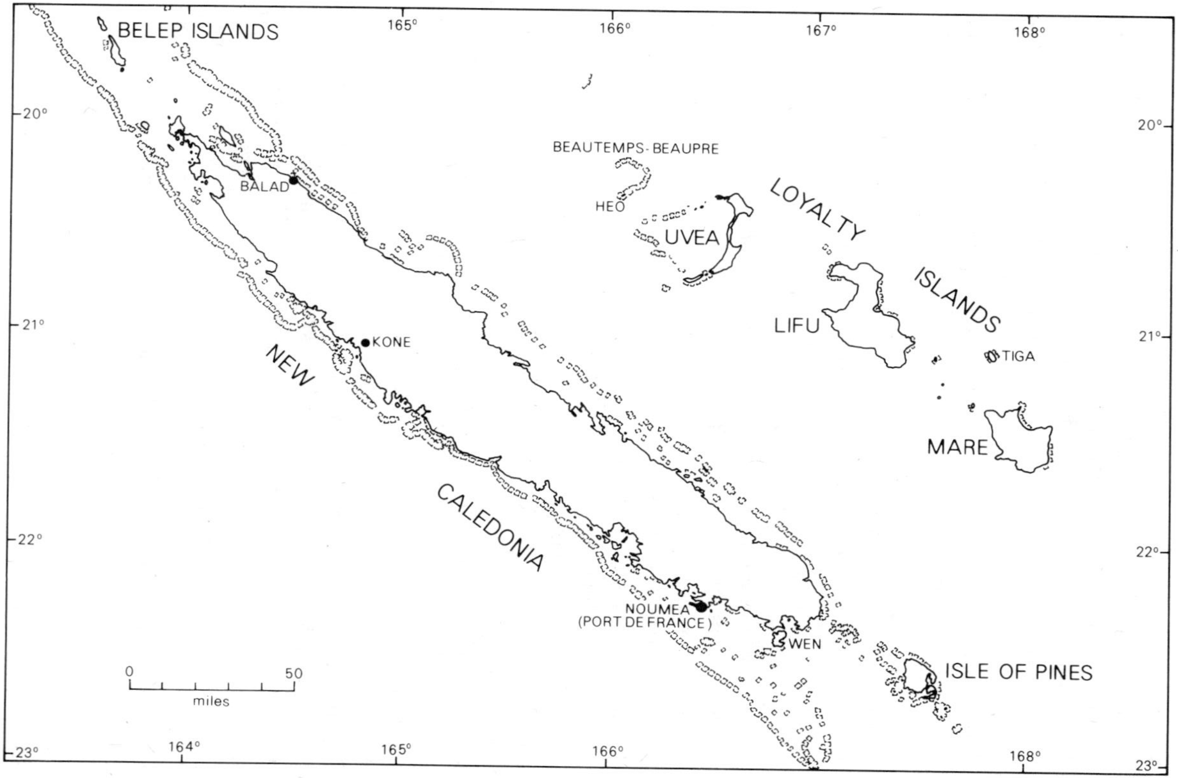

MAP 1   New Caledonia and dependencies

and the occasional tropical cyclone especially in the December to March 'summer' season.

Lacking safe anchorages and reliable supplies of fresh water and having a topography completely unsuited for European agriculture, the Loyalty Islands were useless for extensive European settlement; and the course of nineteenth-century culture contacts was significantly influenced by this consideration.

The people of Melanesia originated from the region of the South China Sea and over thousands of years travelled down the Melanesian island chain, reaching New Caledonia at least 3000 years ago.[1] The Loyalty Islands were probably settled contemporaneously with New Caledonia but, although generally following New Caledonian cultural patterns, Loyalty Islanders developed some of their own racial and cultural characteristics. They became more attuned to a maritime environment than the New Caledonians and were celebrated sailors[2] because of their need to voyage to and from the mainland to barter for such essential items as stone for tools. Certain New Caledonian agricultural techniques, notably terraced irrigation, were irrelevant on the Loyalty Islands, thus encouraging further adaptation and change. Differentiation between the two peoples was also heightened by other than ecological factors. The Loyalty Islands were the landfall for innumerable Polynesians blown westwards from their homelands by prevailing winds, and as Mare, Lifu, and Uvea extend across New Caledonian latitudes they received many more strangers than the mainland. Polynesians were usually peacefully integrated into the communities and were commonly given positions of some status by local chiefs, who regarded them as *enehmu*, or favourites,[3] in return for a monopoly of whatever intellectual or technological skills the migrants possessed: Tongans, for example, were renowned as canoe builders.[4] The earliest European travellers all noted the prevalence of Polynesian racial characteristics among the populace and met recent arrivals from Tonga and Samoa.[5] In particular the northern and southern regions of Uvea were found settled by descendants of Wallis (Uvea) Islanders who had voyaged there in the latter half of the eighteenth century.[6] There were also numerous instances of local migration among the Loyalty Islands, New Caledonia, and the Isle of Pines.[7]

Through generations of intermarriage most Loyalty Islanders, apart from recent arrivals from New Caledonia, were readily distinguishable from other Islanders in the south-west Pacific. A.W. Murray, one of the first missionaries to land on Mare, described the inhabitants as having a much less revolting appearance than the natives of the New Hebrides. . . . They are a different race from any I have before seen. Their countenances have a more European cast than those of any of the islands to the east. There is no appearance of the negro about them. Generally their expression of countenance is mild and pleasant, and they are on the whole a fine interesting looking people.[8]

An early sandalwood trader, Andrew Cheyne, thought that the people were 'equally savage with the Isle of pine Natives', but that their features showed 'rather a milder, and more pleasing appearance'. He continued:

> The Men both old and young go entirely naked, and the only dress worn by the Women is a fringe about 3 inches wide tied round the body, and which does not cover their nakedness—the unmarried women and young girls go entirely in a state of Nudity. The natural colour of the hair of both men and Women, can hardly be ascertained—for they are in the habit of dying it with lime—which gives it a White, Red, or Brown appearance according to the taste of the individual. . . . Circumcision is not practised here, as at the Isle of Pines.[9]

Later Europeans went into great detail describing the racial traits of the Loyalty Islanders, pointing out their uniqueness in Melanesia and stressing their Polynesian features.[10] 'The Loyalty Islanders', wrote one, 'more closely resemble the Tongans, and the Polynesians generally, than the races of Melanesia'.[11]

The pre-European population cannot be determined with any accuracy but at the time of the first reliable missionary censuses in the 1860s, Mare had 4300 people, Lifu 5700, and Uvea 2500.[12] They lived in small villages scattered throughout the islands, some on the coast, others inland. Their dwellings were, as they still are, carefully constructed conical huts made from grass, pandanus, and coconut tree fronds. On Uvea many of the huts were square, perhaps reflecting influences of Polynesian migrants. To Europeans the inhabitants led a difficult existence, short of fresh water and labouring long and hard on their subsistence plantations in the interior.[13] Even missionaries, notorious for dismissing Pacific Islanders as idle creatures, were pleasantly surprised by the Loyalty Islanders' vigour: 'They had', wrote one, 'a less relaxing climate . . . and a soil which needed hard work to make it supply them with food; and they had thus been trained in habits of energy and industry'.[14] After cutting and burning an area of bush and scrub, clearing the soil and tilling it, they planted taro, sweet potatoes, and above all yams, which formed the bulk of their food. Small quantities of bananas and sugar cane, as well as coconuts, supplemented their diet.

The Uveans also ate quantities of fish and shellfish from their bountiful lagoon but there was little fishing on Mare and Lifu because of the dangerous coastlines and the extreme depths of water close inshore. There was little division of labour, the women participating with the men in all but the heaviest tasks—such as cutting down bush. A wife was a 'beast of burden; she goes fishing, works the land, she fetches water and wood', noted a bemused Frenchman.[15]

Economic life involved more than subsistence agriculture: it was necessary to journey frequently to New Caledonia and the Isle of Pines to barter for certain essential and ceremonial items. A series of socio-trading routes formed a rough semi-circular pattern centred on Lifu. Mareans and Lifuans sent a variety of artefacts southwards to the Isle of Pines and southern New Caledonia: shell necklaces and bracelets, pandanus mats, decorated gourds, and small packets of strong filament which was woven into fine mesh nets for catching small school fish—these were known as 'white' articles. In return they were given cord made from flying fox fur, ceremonial jade axes, jade necklace beads (most of the jade originating from the island of Wen), and a variety of other stones for tools—these were 'black' or 'dark' articles.[16] Uveans and Lifuans sent shell trinkets as well as chiefs' daughters to the north and central east coast of New Caledonia—for Loyalty Islands women, especially Uveans of Polynesian descent, were prized above all others as wives by New Caledonian chiefs. In exchange New Caledonians exported stones and large tree trunks because the Loyalty Islands, although heavily timbered, lacked trees suitable for the construction of the large double canoes used for inter-island travel.[17]

The Loyalty Islanders believed that their existence was affected and ultimately controlled by ubiquitous spirit-beings—the spirits of the dead, represented by the dead person's fingernails, tufts of hair, bones, and teeth, all carefully protected and carried about in small packets, and spirits of supernatural origins which fell into two classes.[18] Some had regulative functions in the temporal world, such as responsibility for the fertility of women and crops, the weather, the health of the people, and their success in fishing and warfare, and were represented by natural forms such as trees, rocks, areas of bush, villages, burial grounds, and various birds and animals. The Islanders also possessed small figures carved from wood, and naturally shaped or roughly carved stones, the most important of which were the *haze*. The more perceptive missionaries noted that such artefacts were not idols: 'They generally look to some spirit beyond the image or stone before which they bow'.[19] Other spirit-beings, having no physical representation, existing in human or phantom form in the Islanders' imaginations, were malevolent and held responsible for death and destruction. There was no hierarchical arrangement of any of the spirit-beings, and no concept of a supreme one; each was a separate and independent entity. All were capable of benefiting or harming the Islanders and much of a person's everyday existence was concerned with rituals to appease hostile forces or perhaps set them onto enemies, and to solicit the aid of regulative spirits. Although priests and sorcerers held most sway with the spirit world, nearly all individuals claimed some degree of supernatural influence, usually based on the relics and ever-present spirits of ancestors.[20] Living in a constant and intimate relationship with the spirits, the Islanders felt themselves under surveillance no matter what they did or where they went. Theirs was a cosmological view, making no distinction between religious and secular matters but concerned to explain, and perhaps to regulate, the forces of cause and effect; they made no attempt to explain the existence of their world or to hold to any metaphysical absolutes. In its general characteristics their system of beliefs seems to have followed the broad outlines of many other Melanesian religions.[21]

There are a variety of languages on the Loyalty Islands. Nengone is the common language on Mare and Dehu on Lifu. Both islands also had their own 'respectful language', Miny on Lifu and Iwateno on Mare, used only for addressing chiefs and 'nobles'; only fragments of these two languages survive today. Uvea has two separate languages, Iai, the Melanesian tongue, and Uvea, spoken by the Wallis Island descendants, which has retained its Polynesian morphology and syntax but has also borrowed considerably from Melanesian languages. All the languages of the Loyalty Islands (except Uvea) are typically Melanesian though less complex than the languages of the Solomon Islands and the New Hebrides.[22]

Possibly as a result of Polynesian influences, the socio-political organisations on the Loyalty Islands had several characteristics more commonly found in the eastern Pacific than in Melanesia. Society was hierarchical and fairly rigidly stratified, chiefly positions were normally hereditary, and status at all levels was ascribed rather than earned competitively as in Big-man communities typical of many areas in the Solomon Islands and the New Hebrides. And although having much in common with the social structures found on New Caledonia, Loyalty Islands society had some of its own distinctive characteristics.[23]

Each individual belonged to a patrilineal, exogamous, and patrilocal clan which was in essence an extended family.[24] Unrelated persons or groups, perhaps migrants or remnants of another clan routed in battle, could also join existing clans. Each clan had its totem and legends of its past which usually owed more to fertile imagination than to fact. The clan chief was, in theory, the oldest male directly descended from the clan's founding couple, but in practice he usually came from the strongest line—which may or may not have been the original one—in the clan. He was regarded as the 'first born' to symbolise the real or supposed link with the clan's forefathers; he was also the clan's 'father', its members his 'children'.

Most clans belonged to an alliance with others, paying a common allegiance to a 'great chief' who was normally the chief of the strongest clan in the group, and forming tribes or great chiefdoms. Whereas clan chiefdoms were based on proclaimed kinship ties, great chiefdoms were political arrangements forged by conquest or by peaceful diplomacy. Given the high incidence of immigration and general mobility of the population in pre-European times, the political divisions of the islands were often in a state of flux; warfare was endemic as ambitious leaders campaigned to extend their political and territorial control. Provided a chiefdom remained a cohesive entity, leadership was, apart from exceptional circumstances, hereditary with succession normally going to the eldest son who gradually assumed chiefly duties when aged about twenty.[25] Each great chief traced his origins back to mythical rather than historical events and sought to create a long and glorious past for himself, often taking 'dynastic' titles to indicate a lengthy real or imagined line of succession. Deference to these men was complete: on Mare and Lifu they were addressed in Miny and Iwateno, and on all islands their followers grovelled on all fours if moving in their presence. No one ever stood while a chief was speaking, only a select few had the right to touch his body or his personal possessions, and only he could eat certain foods, such as tortoise meat, and the eyes, heart, and breast of a slain enemy. Early European visitors considered that the great chiefs were strutting, tyrannical autocrats but these observers failed to perceive that the great chiefship was a position of trust and carried with it responsibility for the well-being of the chiefdom. Furthermore, there were well-established checks to a leader's arbitrary and irresponsible behaviour.

There was, for example, rigorous separation of political authority and ownership of land. Proprietary rights were vested in the clan and no chief had rights to land other than those due to him as a clan member. Even clans defeated in battle retained their land but paid tribute, usually in yams, to the conquering chief.²⁶ Another effective check to despotism was a great chief's council of elders consisting of clan chiefs and important priests—the 'nobility'. All policy decisions affecting the tribe were discussed with the chief in council in an attempt to reach a consensus of opinion.²⁷ The elders were reputed to present their views boldly and few great chiefs refused to heed their advice on important matters.²⁸ The councils had considerable influence in deciding whether or not a chief's eldest son was worthy of succession and, if he was not, could choose another son, a nephew, or indeed any one else.²⁹ Great chiefs, especially those of Lifu, also had to consider the opinion of the 'masters of the soil'—descendants of the original inhabitants who long ago lost direct political control by conquest or by having given the chiefships to newcomers, but who still retained most of the privileges of their forefathers and claimed the right to depose great chiefs. Although without formal authority they were considered divine men because of their ancient and mythical links with the totems and spirits of the land and were regarded with aweful respect.³⁰

Numerous dignitaries or 'ministers' surrounded the great chiefship, forming a vast administrative hierarchy of spokesmen, diplomats, war ministers, personal servants, guards, specialist labourers, priests and sorcerers.³¹ Such a retinue not only aided the chief with the affairs of his chiefdom but, if necessary, could act as a further counterweight to chiefly despotism. The great chiefs were there less to command than to serve as a centre of cohesion for the administrative networks of the chiefdom and to be an object of affection.³² This is not to suggest chiefs were powerless; they did have very considerable influence but had neither the right nor the means to impose unpopular measures upon their followers.

Relationships among all individuals in the hierarchy of a great chiefdom were ceremonially delineated and political obligations were expressed in the annual presentations of the season's first yams. The young tubers were offered first to the heads of families, then to the clan chiefs, and were passed up through the pyramidal ranks of dignitaries and nobles, each person adding to the gift, until it finally reached the great chief. He in turn gave yams as expressions of respect and affection to certain individuals, particularly the masters of the soil.³³

While socio-political structures varied in size and subtleties of composition in each locality, Loyalty Islands society viewed as a whole consisted of a number of rigidly stratified hierarchies, each under a great chief. It was a society whose members placed great emphasis on the role of the nobility, a characteristic particularly marked on Mare and Lifu by the respectful languages.³⁴ And it was a society which was neither static nor particularly stable, but one with a long history of immigration, warfare, and continual change in areas of political control: Europeans were by no means the first strangers to make landfall, bringing with them new ideas and techniques and contributing to socio-political and economic change. Just as chiefs had long been adept at accommodating immigrants and exploiting their presence and skills, so too did they attempt to turn the arrival of Europeans to their advantage.

2
New Strangers

The Loyalty Islands' low profile kept them hidden from Cook, who was the first European to see New Caledonia, and from d'Entrecasteaux following soon afterwards. The first recorded sighting was in 1793 when the store-ship *Britannia* sailed past the west coast of Mare on a voyage from Sydney to Djakarta.[1] Three years later the store-ships *Fancy* and *Providence*, plying the same route, landed very briefly on Mare and Lifu. The logkeeper, running short of paper, merely noted that the Islanders were 'friendly and honest'.[2] Dumont d'Urville roughly charted the three islands in 1827 and 1840 but never set foot ashore.[3] It is probable that there were other late eighteenth- or early nineteenth-century sightings or landings by Europeans, for there are at least two recorded oral traditions of brief European presence on Mare and two on Lifu;[4] one of these might have been the ill-fated La Perouse before he sailed further north and was wrecked on the reefs of Vanikoro. The Islanders almost certainly had further direct and indirect knowledge of Europeans from Polynesians who had drifted westwards since explorers, missionaries, and traders had reached the eastern Pacific and from contact with northern New Caledonia and the Isle of Pines—two areas visited by Europeans before the 1840s: d'Entrecasteaux, for example, met a canoe load of Uveans at Balad in 1793.[5]

The lure of sandalwood and the challenge of a new mission field attracted traders and evangelists to the Loyalty Islands in the 1840s. Members of the LMS visited the islands throughout the 1840s and early 1850s to land Polynesian teachers who were trained to introduce Christianity and 'civilisation' to the 'benighted' inhabitants. This technique of evangelisation by proxy had been used to advantage in areas of Polynesia and was thought to be an admirable way of penetrating Melanesia without exposing European missionaries to the rigours of its climate and the alleged ferocity of its inhabitants. As the Society soon learned, the Loyalty Islands were out of the malarial zone and the people were generally eager to accept newcomers. By the early 1850s the teachers had completed their pioneering duties and several important chiefs were actually demanding European missionaries. In response the LMS settled permanent missionaries on Mare in 1854, Lifu in 1859, and Uvea in 1864. Other chiefs, who were mortal enemies of those associated with the LMS, had meanwhile called upon the French Marist Mission for assistance, and priests established stations on Uvea in 1857, Lifu in 1858, and Mare in 1866. The French Catholic and English Protestant missionaries, bitterly divided by longstanding religious and national prejudices, were inextricably involved in the Islanders' own turbulent politics as rival chiefs adopted rival faiths and, with the missionaries' encouragement, indulged in 'religious wars'.

Of lesser significance for the Islanders was Bishop Selwyn's Melanesian Mission which took an interest in them in the 1850s. Selwyn's innovative policy was to take Melanesian youths to spend a summer at St Johns College in Auckland receiving religious instruction and then to return them to their islands where they would become 'little centres of light to their own people'.[6] The scheme was a failure on the Loyalty Islands, for reasons to be discussed, as were his and Patteson's two attempts to set up posts staffed by a European missionary.

The French government annexed New Caledonia and its dependencies (including the Loyalty Islands) in 1853 but did not intervene in Loyalty Islands affairs until the 1860s when it felt compelled to try to end religious and national rivalries and tribal fighting. The Noumean administration, although eager to establish effective sovereignty over the islands, had no intention of creating a permanent administrative structure. It lacked the necessary resources and, more importantly, the islands were useless for any large-scale economic exploitation, unlike New Caledonia with its farming potential and its extremes of mineral wealth. Apart from a military expedition to Lifu in 1864, French government presence on the Loyalty Islands was generally limited to one representative and occasional visits by commissions to investigate disturbances. The French were unable to bring about political stability among the chiefdoms or put an end to religious

New Strangers

and national conflicts until the 1870s on Uvea and Lifu and 1895 on Mare.

Commercial interest in the Loyalty Islands began with sandalwood traders from Australia in the 1840s. They made at least forty-six visits before the aromatic timber was depleted by the 1850s[7] and, until the trade in the south-west Pacific petered out in the early 1860s, continued to call at the islands to barter for provisions and hire Loyalty Islanders as crews. Noted for their seamanship and willingness to labour for Europeans, the Islanders played a major role in maritime commerce in New Caledonian waters and beyond. The entrepreneur Henry Burns operated a large sandalwood cleaning station on Uvea from 1856 until 1861; other English captains took Loyalty Islanders on pearl diving and bêche-de-mer expeditions around the Solomon Islands and New Guinea; and in the 1850s and 1860s English, French, and American whalers built shore stations, employed local labour, and frequented the Loyalty Islands' leeward coastlines in search of schools on their annual migrations. But by far the greatest number of vessels calling at the islands belonged to traders operating out of Noumea (since its founding in 1853) in search of island produce for the flourishing New Caledonian expor trade. From 1857 until 1885, for example, they made over 1000 trips to the Loyalty Islands.[8] This trade continued into the twentieth century and from its inception employed almost exclusively Loyalty Islands' crews. Most of the vessels, although licensed by the French administration, were owned by Englishmen, and throughout the nineteenth century New Caledonian commerce was dominated by English entrepreneurs.

In the 1860s the Loyalty Islands also became a focal point for ships recruiting labourers for the Queensland sugar plantations. There are thirty-nine voyages on record,[9] and at least 1000 Loyalty Islands men worked in Australia for three-year terms.[10] From the 1870s and 1880s the French hired Loyalty Islanders, as they continue to do to this day, to labour on the huge open cast mines in the mountains of New Caledonia.

While coastal and overseas contact with Europeans was considerable, the Islanders had relatively few Europeans living amongst them; nevertheless there were more than usually resided on a Melanesian island during the early contact period.[11] The Loyalty Islands may have been unique in this respect for, in line with their long-standing policy of accepting and integrating Polynesian migrants, the communities usually received Europeans hospitably, and for much the same reason: to benefit from the newcomers' skills. In the 1840s and 1850s the Islanders were host to at least five beachcombers, a dozen or so runaway whalers and escaped convicts, and numerous castaways including the entire crews of the *Sarah* and *Castlereagh*, wrecked in Sandalwood Bay in 1849. But the majority of settlers throughout the century were resident traders, men who ran small stores, bought and sold island produce, and sometimes chartered or owned schooners on the Noumea-Loyalty Islands run. The names of at least twenty-seven such traders have been recorded.[12] Most were integrated to a greater or lesser extent into the local societies where they lived in the Islanders' manner and were highly esteemed; at least half of them married daughters of chiefs. European settlement reached its peak about 1870 when the total population, including missionaries, numbered sixty-three.[13] There was some decline after this date: LMS missionaries and their families began to leave, and commercial competition, combined with crop failures and market collapses, drove some traders away. At the end of the century only missionaries and the long-established settlers were allowed to remain when the French closed the islands to further European settlement and declared them a 'Native Reserve'.

European contact with the Loyalty Islands was fairly intensive, in spite of their smallness and unsuitability for European settlement. Furthermore a considerable number of Islanders experienced life amongst Europeans on sailing ships, Queensland plantations, and New Caledonian mines. Both at home and overseas Loyalty Islanders were exposed to a wide spectrum of European society—one which was predominantly male, but not exclusively so, for there were the wives of the LMS missionaries and of several resident traders, and ample opportunity to observe, and perhaps have closer relations with, European women in Australia and New Caledonia.

All these Europeans made different demands upon the Islanders—from the missionary who wished to impose a rigid legalistic and moral code, to the beachcomber who was satisfied to live with an Island woman; from the trader attempting to barter for a cord of sandalwood, to the labour recruiter seeking to remove a young man from his island home. But whatever their requirements, all European visitors exposed Loyalty Islanders to a vastly different technology, novel activities, and alien concepts: if they were not the first strangers to set foot on the islands they were certainly the most culturally removed. How the Islanders responded to two European interest groups—missionaries and administrators—is the subject of the following six chapters.

Rival Chiefs, Rival Faiths

By the mid-1860s both LMS and Marist missionaries had established permanent stations on all three of the Loyalty Islands. Virtually the entire populations had been 'converted' by one or other mission, each island being divided into clearly defined spheres of English Protestant and French Catholic influence. An explanation of the missionaries' rapid success and of the religious divisions of the islands involves an examination of the tribal arrangements at the time of first regular contact with Europeans and of how great chiefs and other aspirants to power sought to apply certain mission institutions and the religious and national hostilities between the two mission societies to their own politics. The Christianising of the Loyalty Islanders, as well as the patterns of mission settlement and influence, were the products of chiefs willingly accepting and utilising the missionaries, not of the missionaries choosing how and where they wished to operate amongst the communities. The nature of the chiefly structure, together with pre-European precedents for assimilating and making use of newcomers, was fundamental to the success of the Christian missions on the Loyalty Islands—a success that was virtually unique in Melanesia for most of the nineteenth century and in dramatic contrast to ill-fated missionary endeavours in the New Hebrides and Solomon Islands. There the demanding terrain and unhealthy climate, the multiplicity of languages, the inhabitants' hostility towards strangers, and the comparative rarity of large chiefdoms with well-entrenched hereditary leaders through whom the missionaries might safely and effectively operate, resulted in hardship, failure, and sometimes tragedy for the pioneer evangelists.

For most Loyalty Islanders to support either the LMS or Marist Mission and become a Christian was a decision initially made for them by their great chiefs, who chose the faith they believed could best help them regain, defend, maintain, or extend their authority. Some of these leaders, through association with either the Protestant or Catholic missionaries, achieved unprecedented power within their own chiefdoms and sometimes beyond, with their followers enjoying the material and other benefits that came from mission settlement in their areas. The division of the islands into regions of Catholic and Protestant influence was, however, more complex than a division along boundaries of inimical chiefdoms, for the new religions aggravated existing and created new intra-chiefdom hostilities. Ambitious men, often clan chiefs, saw opportunities to break former allegiances within great chiefdoms and sought support from the mission opposed to the interests of their superiors in order to establish and aggrandise their own distinct influence and attract as many followers as possible. Political organisations on each island were significantly altered by Islanders exploiting mission presence. Such developments contrast with the popular image of black-clothed evangelists manipulating hapless 'natives' and destroying existing socio-political institutions, along with other aspects of indigenous culture.

This exploitation of religious, national, and political rivalries was not solely the preserve of the Islanders. The relationship between chiefs and missionaries was often a symbiotic one: if a chief saw the chance of increasing his status by choosing one or other mission, the mission he accepted might similarly benefit. As one LMS missionary, referring to a Lifuan great chief, explained: 'Having secured the favour of the king, you were not only safe, but the gospel became popular, and multitudes attended the services who would not have dared to be present, if the king had expressed his disapprobation'.[1] Both Marist and LMS missionaries were well aware that much of their appeal lay in their mutual antagonism rather than in their respective doctrines. The war between Protestant and Catholic Islanders, wrote an LMS missionary, 'is not a religious one, it is an old feud, but being at enmity on land and chiefs' matters, each party has chosen to be opposite in religion also'.[2] A Marist missionary explained that 'Catholics and protestants live apart, have few relations with each other; it is less the religion than questions of chieftships and territories that divide them'.[3] But just as the Islanders were quick to pick up and shrewdly utilise the religious and national differences between the missions, the missionaries too were adept at understanding the fundamentals of the Islanders' political aspirations and took an active part in them, for success or failure in establishing, consolidating, and extending their missions depended almost entirely upon the political fortunes of their local patrons. Although both Catholic and Protestant missionaries habitually condemned the Islanders for fighting amongst themselves and preached the doctrine of Christ as 'Prince of Peace', nevertheless they were always ready to encourage armed aggression by 'Christian soldiers' to force recalcitrant Islanders to obey a mission-supporting chief and to battle with warriors belonging to the opposing mission. Neither the Islanders nor the missionaries, then, were unconsciously or helplessly manipulated by one another. Both generally displayed an ability to appreciate, if not always to capitalise successfully on, the realities of European rivalries and tribal politics. Missionary activities began first on Mare, then on Lifu, and finally on Uvea—the order in which they will be examined.

3
Mare 1841–1866

Mare was notable among the three islands for its turbulent pre-history. According to reliable indigenous tradition, considerable numbers of migrants from New Caledonia, Lifu, and Polynesia were accepted by the original inhabitants, *eletok*, but were denied any political authority. At the beginning of the nineteenth century the disaffected migrants and descendants of migrants took matters into their own hands and massacred a great many of the *eletok*.[1] The violent processes of regrouping clans and redividing the island into great chiefdoms had not been long under way when regular European contact began in 1841. The southern and eastern regions were split into numerous warring and politically unstable tribes, whereas the northern area was becoming increasingly dominated by the Si Gwahma tribe led by the Naisiline family.[2] Great chief Yiewene Naisiline had conquered the neighbouring Si Waeko tribe (which was henceforth incorporated into his Si Gwahma chiefdom) and ruled from the eastern shores of Northern Bay to just north of Tadine. Fortunately for him and his successors most of the Europeans visiting Mare came to this area because of the anchorage afforded by Northern Bay and the sheltered landing places in the coves at Netche and Mebuet; the exposed, reef-encrusted eastern and southern coastlines kept tribes in these regions virtually isolated from direct European contact for over twenty years.

The LMS missionaries, having first sighted Mare while sailing from Tana to the Isle of Pines the previous year, put into Northern Bay in 1841.

Those aboard the *Camden* were at first apprehensive of the barren-looking coast but were astounded when two canoes put out through the reefs and one of the paddlers cried out: 'I know the true God'.[3] Taufa, as he was called, had been blown from his home island Nuiatoputapu in the Tongan group some years previously and now, along with a number of other recent Polynesian arrivals, lived with great chief Yiewene as his *enehmu*. It was not unprecedented, therefore, for Yiewene readily to agree to protect two Samoan teachers whom the missionaries wished to leave with him, and he added them along with their European utensils to the retinue of Polynesians in his household at Netche. The missionaries were delighted with their reception, for although they thought the Mareans were 'deeply degraded' being 'quite naked' and living 'doubtless also in misery and wretchedness', they were 'in a remarkably prepared state for the reception of the Gospel, so peaceable and apparently so little attached to any system of false religion.'[4]

Throughout the 1840s and early 1850s the LMS vessels made almost annual voyages to Mare to land Rarotongan and Samoan teachers.[5] Sandalwood traders too were constant callers throughout the 1840s.[6] Having a virtual monopoly on anchorages and landing places Yiewene and his Si Gwahma tribe did very well in their transactions with these visitors, much to the disgust of other Mare chiefs. So jealous were those in the southern regions that when a vessel did brave the reefs and put men ashore in Si Ruemec territory the local chief, according to the LMS teachers, 'commanded his people to kill them all at once; saying all the ships and property had gone to the other district now let it be revenged'. Yiewene immediately wished to punish those responsible for the ensuing massacre of the boat's crew for 'he considered himself now as related to the foreigners on acct. of his relation to them the Teachers'. The Samoan teachers, however, prevented him from sending warriors and he and his people 'wept that they might not go & be revenged'.[7]

Yiewene was portrayed by the LMS missionaries as a crotchety old savage, eager enough to accept Polynesian teachers but only to exploit their possessions and technical skills. He paid little heed to their evangelising, in spite of his promises to the missionaries on their brief visits and, on his orders, so too did most of the tribe. Services which the teachers initially conducted in his house soon had to be moved elsewhere 'owing to the noise and confusion on the . . . premises', and henceforth only a small number of Tongans made up the congregations.[8] Ta'unga, a Rarotongan teacher, complained:

MAP 2 Mare. Approximate tribal boundaries in the 1850s.
Based on a map by John Jones enclosed in Jones to LMS, 23 April 1858.

> Jeiue treated us kindly with regard to bodily needs, but he was not partial to the message of God. He would not behave properly on the Sabbath, and the people followed him in his wicked ways, saying evil things to us. He and I quarrelled many times. I tried to persuade him to believe but he flatly refused.[9]

Only once did Yiewene consider that the new doctrines might be of some use: during an epidemic which swept across the island he called upon the teachers' God to repel the disease-making spirits; when the sickness continued unabated his initial scepticism of Jehovah's existence was confirmed.[10]

Although Yiewene enjoyed the benefits of regular and peaceful shipping contacts, he was easily persuaded by some Isle of Pines visitors who, flushed with their recent successful sacking of the brig *Star*, encouraged him to attack a sandalwood vessel as a shortcut to greater riches. His attempt to take the *Brigand* failed although ten of her crew were killed. Shortly afterwards his warriors captured the *Sisters* and killed all eleven crew members not, it seems out of greed this time but because the captain had allegedly taken to Yiewene with a rope's end during an argument over prices for sandalwood. Having stripped the vessel and set it alight, Yiewene's men amused themselves by flicking gunpowder from one of the *Sisters*' barrels onto a fire. To achieve more spectacular results they threw in handfuls until, inevitably, a spark landed in the barrel and five Islanders perished in a great explosion. The powder barrel incident had significant repercussions for the Naisiline chiefship for one of those killed was Menedoku Bula, Yiewene's youngest son and heir.[11] Relationships with the traders remained cordial from then on because the Si Gwahma chief and his people realised the advantages of peaceful trading and were, in any case, becoming increasingly fearful of retaliation by Europeans for the deaths of crew members of the *Brigand* and the *Sisters*.[12] Tribes in the south maintained their hostile feelings towards Europeans: a party of seven runaway convicts from Norfolk Island landed at Medu and five were killed instantly: the remaining two managed to flee inland and were protected by a party of Si Gwahma warriors.[13] Mare gained the reputation of 'massacre island', although sandalwood traders still tried their luck and the LMS missionaries persisted with their now unpromising mission field. The chronicler of their 1846 visit dejectedly noted:

> ... since the last visit of the vessel no visible progress has been made in the work,—that by the command of the chief none of the people go to the services. ... A Tongan family in the neighbourhood are the only individuals

who regularly attend worship, and some of the chief's sons occasionally go, but it appears they are always scolded for doing so by their father. . . . On the whole his [Yiewene's] conduct has been kind, but he always got angry when they the teachers introduced religious conversation. The sons say that they are much restrained by their father, and that it will be a good thing when he dies, for then they will be able to do as they desire.[14]

The aging Yiewene died of dropsy in 1848 and, according to the LMS missionaries, told his sons with his dying gasps that he had been wrong to oppose 'The Word of Jehovah . . . let the heathenism of our family die with me'.[15] His youngest surviving son, Yiewene Kicini Bula, described by Captain Erskine the following year as a 'fine boy of thirteen or fourteen',[16] was appointed successor, and during his minority two older brothers, Naisiline Alakuten and Naisiline Nidoish acted as regents.[17] The latter two immediately attended the instructions of the LMS teachers, not, as the missionaries liked to imagine, because of the pious exhortations of their dying father, but because for some time they had perceived the political advantages of associating themselves closely with the new religion. Freed from their father's restraints they immediately exploited the institutions of Christianity and the presence of the teachers to secure their own positions and to assume more intensive control over the everyday activities of their people. Utilising the teachers' technological skills, the two Naisilines had built for themselves whitewashed limestone cottages surrounded with neat gardens and picket fences, and ordered their people to construct huge churches at both Ro and Netche. The Sabbath was rigorously observed, attendance at services was compulsory, classes for baptism were commenced, nudity was covered, and polygyny publicly abandoned, all under the watchful gaze of the Naisilines.[18]

LMS commitments elsewhere were too taxed to allow European missionaries to settle on Mare, even if the situation was so favourable. Still jealously regarding Mare as its own, the Society was dismayed when the Anglican Melanesian Mission from New Zealand was attracted to the island. Selwyn first landed on Mare, in Si Gwahma lands, in 1849 when his schooner *Undine* was accompanied by Erskine's HMS *Havannah*. Three young men sailed back with him to Auckland. Selwyn returned briefly in 1850 and 1851, each time landing and taking off students and being met with 'noisy joy'. He marvelled at the progress of Christianity, stemming, he admitted, not from his own efforts but from the inspiration of the LMS Polynesian teachers. At both Ro and Netche they had encouraged the Islanders to build large chapels, each one packed with 500 eager listeners:

'every knee is bent during the prayers—every voice joins in the responses', he reported approvingly. Among the Si Gwahma people there were, he believed, 'probably more Christians than anywhere in these seas'.[19]

Relationships between the LMS and the Melanesian Mission rapidly became embittered over the question of which mission should work on the island.[20] Much to the disgust of the LMS, Selwyn adopted a new tactic, perhaps to pre-empt the LMS, and landed William Nihill, a missionary from New Zealand, at Netche. Although dying of consumption Nihill worked tirelessly, translating religious texts into Nengone and printing them on a small press, conducting services, taking a census, and collecting insects, plants, and shells. Everywhere he went in Si Gwahma territory he was treated with the utmost respect: 'The natives supply us with food in abundance, yams, etc. at all times, fowls very frequently, pork occasionally. They treat us just as they do their own chiefs, attending to our wishes, saluting us etc.' The religious fervour of the people amazed him:

> These people spend more time in worship & religious exercises than any I have ever known. I do not know what time monks in religious houses are supposed to spend in common worship, but every Sunday these people devote seven & a half or eight hours to public worship during the whole of which time, broken up into five parts, they are either *hearing* prayer, or reading, or a sermon, or being catechized, or singing. Everything is conducted with the greatest solemnity & decorum, and I am quite anxious & perplexed because I fear that this can not last, and that without God gives these simple converts greater share of grace to keep them steadfast than is usually vouchsafed to men, there must be a falling away. Religion has become the business of their lives, & without their mode of life is changed, and something given them to do, they cannot, I fear, withstand the temptations which their easy mode of life must continually expose them to, when the novelty has worn off.[21]

But the religious enthusiasm was restricted to Si Gwahma lands: throughout the rest of Mare the Islanders looked and behaved just as they had when the Europeans first arrived. He made one foray into their territory to try to 'enlighten' such 'heathen' but everywhere he went the chiefs refused to accept his teachings, for Christianity was considered to be the religion of the Si Gwahma people, their enemies; to accept it was unthinkable for it would be a sign of submission to them.[22]

Nihill died at Netche in 1854 and his death, together with the arrival of two permanent LMS missionaries some months previously, effectively ended Melanesian Mission influence on Mare. Although its mission vessel made four more visits during the 1850s to take off and return scholars, there were no further attempts to establish a permanent station. Selwyn's ambitious scheme of taking Islanders to Auckland was admirable on paper but largely impractical when put to the test, and fared just as badly on the Loyalty Islands as elsewhere in Melanesia. From 1849 until 1858 he took 120 Islanders from the south-west Pacific to St Johns; thirty-nine of these came from the Loyalty Islands (twenty-two from Mare, three from Tiga—a small island between Mare and Lifu—thirteen from Lifu, and one from Uvea).[23] Apart from the difficulties in travelling such vast distances each year, Auckland's summer climate was too cold for many of the boys, and numbers died. Of those who returned to the Loyalty Islands none contributed significantly to mission work. They had neither the material wealth nor technological skills of the LMS teachers, nor did they have any significant standing in their own communities, and their well-known conceit on their return was scarcely likely to impress their countrymen.[24]

The LMS redoubled its efforts to supply permanent European missionaries for Mare, not only because of Selwyn's work there but because of the incessant demands by the Islanders themselves. The two Naisilines felt that they had exploited the Polynesian teachers to the full; further progress, they believed, depended upon procuring as many permanent missionaries as possible. An LMS missionary enthusiastically described his visit to Mare in 1853:

> It would seem as if the old and usual order in such matters were reversed in the case of this people—instead of our going to them to compel them to come in, they have to use their utmost effort to compel us to go to them, and teach them the way of life and salvation.[25]

Finally, in 1854, the Society landed John Jones and Stephen Creagh at Netche, a village of plastered cottages with a church and large houses ready for them and their families: 'Seldom or ever has it been the lot of missionaries to commence their labours under circumstances so favourable, among a people so prepared to receive them'.[26] Jones settled at Ro and Creagh remained at Netche. With his aggressiveness, initiative, and stern self-righteousness Jones quickly overshadowed the gentler, more studious Creagh and became the spokesman for the mission on Mare with the unofficial LMS headquarters at Ro, in spite of the great chiefship at Netche.

Their mission was, in their terms, an instant success: by 1855 the entire population of the Si Gwahma region, about 3000, was considered Christian and the missionaries delighted in reporting that their flocks were clothed, clean, reading from books, and in sending off impressive figures for congregations and church membership. The mission stations themselves, with their vast missionary houses, store sheds, forges, printing presses, and workshops, bore ample testimony to the rapid consolidation and prosperity of the mission.[27]

The relationship between the Si Gwahma chiefship and the missionaries was one of mutual exploitation—the chiefship was strengthened through association with the LMS mission, and the missionaries' followers increased in numbers and behaved with due decorum because the chief so decreed. Just before the two missionaries arrived, the teenage Yiewene Kicini Bula died and his infant son was declared great chief; until he was old enough to assume command Naisiline Alakuten was appointed regent.[28] But he was quickly overshadowed by the more energetic Naisiline Nidoish, who was noted for his ambition and for his arrogant and officious nature. He had designs not only on the Si Gwahma chiefship but dreamed of one day ruling the entire island. He saw his opportunity in steadfastly supporting Jones and Creagh, and for over thirty years the interests of the LMS mission and Naisiline Nidoish were virtually inseparable—the extension of the Si Gwahma chiefship went hand in hand with the extension of Protestantism on Mare.

Within a year of their arrival Jones and Creagh declared a series of 'dispensations' designed 'for the rule of this land, for the punishment of evil doers, for the dread and terror of the hearts of men who are obdurate and unbelieving'. Such offences as theft, adultery, failure to attend church, and failure to obey chiefs and missionaries were punishable by hard labour, imprisonment, and chaining for months on end. Together with the missionaries Naisiline Nidoish organised a 'police force' of young toughs who roamed about seeking out and punishing 'miscreants'.[29] Armed with the new laws, and a means of effectively enforcing them, Naisiline Nidoish assumed almost absolute authority. He and the missionaries decided policy for the tribe, ignoring the councils of nobles. A new hierarchical administrative structure headed by Naisiline Nidoish and the missionaries emerged. Beneath them were the Polynesian teachers and the Mare pastors, who gradually took over the duties of the Polynesians. The Si Gwahma region was divided into church districts, each one presided over by a Mare pastor who arrogated many of the functions of the local clan chiefs. Villagers had to build huts and supply food, which was prepared and cooked by clan chiefs' daughters, for the pastors. On Sundays the local pastor's police detachment marched the whole village off to church. The pastors also controlled ranks of church officials—chapel keepers, organisers, overseers—followed by the church members and the 'listeners'. Many of the nobility found that their traditional positions were seriously threatened by the new administration but, as they lacked any effective means of gaining popular support to oppose its institutions, most of them readily supported the innovations. Members of the nobility often became the most ardent supporters of Christianity, seeing in its doctrines and customs a means of maintaining their former entrenched positions within the social hierarchy. The new administrative structure thus paralleled and to a considerable extent assimilated the pre-Christian political stratification of the chiefdom. The notable difference between the old and the new hierarchy was, however, that all controls were now applied directly from the top: the chiefship became a despotism. Anyone who dared to question or challenge Naisiline Nidoish was likely to be imprisoned. Even Jones and Creagh, who were well aware that the success of their mission on Mare depended upon his support, nevertheless privately expressed reservations about his officiousness. 'His believing that it was his duty to exercise authority in the church as well as out and his firmness almost amounting to obstinacy made the case more difficult', commented Jones, who also accused him of indulging in 'arbitrary government and sometimes is the cause of serious unpleasantness both to the people and ourselves'. Some members of the Si Gwahma referred to him in a derogatory manner as 'The Law'.[30]

It is highly unlikely, however, that such changes in the chiefdom could have taken place had the majority of the Si Gwahma people been actively opposed to them. The influence of the mission and Naisiline Nidoish was based on more than just coercion. Christianity and its trappings quickly became a dominant popular force in the north-west of Mare. There was a genuine and even aggressive enthusiasm for wearing clothes, church going, singing hymns, reciting catechisms, learning to read and write, and participating in church feast and sports days. Baptism and church membership added to all individuals' dignity and competition was keen for the necessary instruction. The mission was also closely identified by the Islanders with the technological apparatus of the European world. Metal implements such as fish-hooks, saws, and axes introduced in their hundreds by the mission lightened the burdens of everyday living. The extensive mission stations at Ro and Netche were a source of delight and prestige to the

Christian Mareans. Naisiline Nidoish's own house was marvelled at not only by his own people but by many European visitors. One described it as

> ... quite a palace compared with the usual run of Western Polynesian native abodes. It is a stone house of two stories, with French windows which open out to a verandah and balcony in front. The interior fittings, such as the staircase, are not quite complete, and several of the rooms are still unfurnished. the furniture is of plain deal; and upstairs, or rather, up the ladder, is a great four-posted bed.[31]

Such developments indicated to other Europeans a level of 'civilisation' unprecedented in the south-west Pacific. English vessels flocked to Northern Bay or anchored off Netche, bringing with them untold material prosperity for Naisiline Nidoish's people, who exported their island produce to the rapidly expanding Noumean market and signed on as short-term crew members.[32]

The more aggressively the Si Gwahma tribe associated itself with Englishmen and Protestantism the more the Islanders throughout the rest of Mare, although amazed and deeply impressed by the revolutionary happenings in the north-west, were determined to maintain their own unchanged identity. One visitor commented:

> What struck me was the great difference at once discernible in the Heathen and Christian Natives as they stood together—the former naked with painted bodies and weapons in their hands, the latter clothed and the countenance altogether different it is most remarkable how the reception of the Gospel changes and softens a fierce and savage expression.[33]

The proximity of the 'heathen' lands was a constant challenge to Jones and Creagh, and with their Polynesian teachers they made periodic journeys southwards. They were invariably received in a peaceful manner, the Islanders crowding about eager to find out more about these two men who had brought such changes to the north of their island. At night they sneaked up, said Creagh, 'to see if we slept like themselves: they could not fancy we did as we were enveloped in blankets'.[34] Little heed was paid to what the missionaries said about the new religion, for the people were far too concerned with the trade the missionaries brought: 'nothing pleases them more to barter, & nothing displeases them more than to hear anything about religion'.[35] But although rejecting the missionaries' message the southern and eastern tribes never doubted its power or that the missionaries were men of supernatural influence. If any of these Islanders visited Netche or Ro and were enticed into a church they were terrified that some evil would befall them for trespassing 'on what they considered Sacred ground'. Those who stayed on during a service trembled wide-eyed in the pews and only when they came out did they 'breathe freely' again. Nor were goods ever stolen from the missionaries on their southern visits: the Islanders pointed at an article and asked, 'Is it not sacred?'[36]

The great chiefs readily acknowledged the material and technological advantages of becoming a Christian, and agreed that the prospect of living in peace would be 'good',[37] yet they could not be induced to accept the new religion. Jones and Creagh learned, as Nihill had before them, that political considerations were the mainstay to their objections: acceptance of Christianity would mean deference to the Si Gwahma whose chief would, they not unreasonably assumed, send his teachers and dreaded policemen to overthrow their authority.[38]

Hostility between Naisiline Nidoish and the southern great chiefs increased throughout the later 1850s and the missionaries were forced to stop sending deputations of teachers after two had been killed. Naisiline's first battle, however, was with the neighbouring Si Achakaze on his eastern flank. Relations between Si Gwahma and Si Achakaze were generally friendly and some of the Si Achakaze had accepted Christianity and made frequent pilgrimages to Ro and Netche. But Gocene, the great chief, and the majority of his people, were determined to maintain their independence from Naisiline Nidoish, much to his annoyance. In 1860 he and Gocene quarrelled over a woman and the Si Achakaze attacked and killed five members of a Christian deputation. Creagh explained that Naisiline Nidoish, in his Christian charity, had not the slightest desire for revenge, but thought that the 'heathens' should be taught a lesson to prevent future trouble. 'Mr Jones and myself', wrote Creagh, 'think this would be a good step. Something decided must be done to intimidate these hardened heathen & to prevent a repetition. . . . We trust & pray that God will protect these poor people who wish to do right'.[39] Naisiline Nidoish's men murdered five of the Si Achakaze and the Si Gwahma chief asked Gocene 'as a climax . . . what they thought now of the God of the Christians, whom they had despized'. Gocene's answer was to kill five of the Si Gwahma after which he and his people fled to Menaku where they ensconced themselves high up in the coral cliffs. Naisiline Nidoish attacked at night, leading his warriors with the battle cry, 'Naisiline the chief of Jehovah', a modification of his former cry, 'Naisiline the son of Jewessi'. The Si Achakaze were soundly defeated, though Gocene managed to escape with a spear sticking through his throat. Jones and Creagh were delighted: 'The Christians are encouraged having *right* & *light* on their side'. One Si Gwahma warrior acted, they said, 'very scripturally' for he emulated David and cut off the head of a fallen enemy.⁴⁰

The Si Gwahma victory in the name of the Christian god had a profound effect upon surrounding tribes, and the great chiefs of the Si Nerech, Si Med, and Node ri kurubu thought it prudent to accept the new religion lest they suffer the same fate as the Si Achakaze. Not surprisingly mission reports were enthusiastic about so many 'heathen' now sitting 'at the feet of Jesus', although, as Jones was well aware, 'their hearts are not converted'.⁴¹ Naisiline Nidoish immediately despatched his teachers and policemen and effectively ruled half of Mare. Such was his reputation that the great chiefs Wanakami of the Si Ruemec and Jomae of the Si Gurewoc, together with a small minority of their followers, also agreed to accept teachers,⁴² but Naisiline Nidoish's influence was as yet tenuous in these regions.

To add to his triumphs his *de facto* position within the Si Gwahma tribe was legitimised in the early 1860s. When Naisiline Alakuten died in 1858 Naisiline Nidoish was technically regent for Yiewene Kicini Bula's infant son, and when the child died in 1861 Naisiline Nidoish was considered by the majority of his people as the great chief of the Si Gwahma. The missionaries, hastening to make capital from the fact that he could no longer be accused of usurping the chiefship, and also hoping to consolidate his recent territorial gains, crowned him 'King of Mare' in 1862.⁴³ But their attempts to found a 'missionary kingdom' in the western Pacific were premature for there were still too many tribes bitterly opposed to Naisiline Nidoish, and some leaders of these tribes turned elsewhere for help.

The Marist Mission located small stations on Uvea in 1857 and Lifu in 1858 but the priests were in far too precarious a position to enable them to extend their mission southwards to Mare. The Catholic mission on the Isle of Pines, however, was well consolidated, for by 1857 virtually the entire population had been 'converted' and long standing socio-trading ties between the Isle of Pines and the south of Mare, particularly with the Si Medu tribe, provided a natural line of communication for the priests.⁴⁴ Many of the Si Medu visiting the Isle of Pines in the later 1850s saw the possibilities of requesting French Catholic missionaries to help them ward off the encroaching influences of the English Protestant missionaries and Naisiline Nidoish. The most enthusiastic advocate for a Marist mission on

Mare was the baptised Waikosone, who claimed the great chiefship of the Si Medu. He made several voyages to the Isle of Pines in the early 1860s to encourage the priests to settle on Mare.[45] The Marists were hesitant for they were aware that Waikosone's activities created considerable unrest on Mare: Naisiline Nidoish threatened to kill any Catholic, whether Islander or European, who set foot upon the island, and several of the great chiefs in the south and east were deeply concerned by the political implications of having a Catholic mission in their midst. More seriously, Waikosone's tribe, with a population of about 250, was divided into two hostile factions, one led by Waitheane, who challenged Waikosone for the leadership and was opposed to his association with the Marists. Waikosone was fortunate to have as his ally Sinewami, great chief of the Si Gureschaba, the most powerful tribe in the south and east largely because of the natural fortress—the impregnable sheer-sided *titi*—above its principal village (now La Roche). With Sinewami's assistance Waikosone defeated Waitheane, and the priests felt that the way was clear to land on the island.[46] In 1866 Prosper Goujon, priest on the Isle of Pines since 1848, sailed there by canoe. Landing at Medu he crossed to La Roche to meet both Waikosone and Sinewami and on his arrival was shown into a large hut wherein he found a rough altar bedecked with crucifixes and religious paintings brought previously from the Isle of Pines.

Though Sinewami welcomed Goujon enthusiastically, he had no wish to turn Catholic at Goujon's or Waikosone's urging. His great worry, he told Goujon, was to know exactly how Naisiline and the other great chiefs would react: he suspected they might join together and destroy him. For days he hesitated, consulting his advisers, his followers, and neighbouring great chiefs. It was not so much their counsel that decided him to wear the Catholic medal, but the arrival of Si Gwahma warriors in a threatening mood convinced him that only with the aid of the priests could he maintain his independence. Following his example 100 of the Si Medu and the Si Gureschaba immediately declared themselves Catholics. Tabe, who had recently assumed the great chiefship of the Si Gurewoc, was similarly threatened by Naisiline Nidoish's warriors and, fearing for his independence, reversed his father Jomae's policy of supporting the Protestants and took the medal also.

Goujon met other chiefs, most of whom told him that, if Waikosone, Sinewami, and Tabe came to no harm supporting the Marists, they too would join the church. Altogether, Goujon spent three months on Mare, and returned to the Isle of Pines well satisfied with his newly won support based mainly on the Si Medu followers of Waikosone and the Si Gureschaba. Of Waikosone and the Si Gureschaba he wrote: 'He led us to the most evil, dark tribe, the most backward, the most distant, but the most influential and the most central with regard to the pagans'.[47] Towards the end of 1866 permanent Marist missionaries, François Beaulieu and Jerome Guitta, established a post at La Roche.

The lines of battle were now clearly drawn. Naisiline Nidoish in association with the LMS mission had extended his chiefdom to encompass the north-western half of Mare as well as having a handful of teachers among the Si Ruemec; to combat further encroachment the Si Gureschaba, Si Medu, and Si Gurewoc (except for a few dissidents among the two latter tribes) were firmly committed to supporting the Marists. Each mission made plans to 'convert' the other's territory with the aid of Mare warriors, and their respective supporters aimed to consolidate and extend their chiefdoms by exploiting mission presence.

4
Lifu 1842-1864

Unlike the *eletok* of Mare the original inhabitants of Lifu shared authority with immigrants. Lifu was consequently a much more politically stable island at the time of first regular contact with the West. Where Mare's chiefdoms were numerous, small, and often fragmented, Lifu's were larger and well consolidated. The two dominant great chiefdoms were Wet led by Gwiet, and Losi led by Bula. Their relations were marked by continual hostility but neither chiefdom was able to conquer the other and there was a long-standing balance of power. The small independent great chiefdom of Gaitcha, ruled by Zeula, was wedged between Wet and Losi forming a buffer state; in the 1840s it was allied to Losi and at enmity with Wet.

Early sandalwood traders who learnt of Lifu's existence from the Mareans initially put into the tiny inlet at Mu, residence of the aged and blind great chief Bula of Losi. Bula enthusiastically welcomed Europeans and was delighted when a young crew member, Charles Bridget, deserted the schooner *Munford* in 1842. The chief immediately offered him protection, and Bridget became an *enehmu* along with a group of Tongans. He remained with Bula for five years and was known widely among the traders as 'Cannibal Charley'.[1] The anchorage at Mu was a difficult one, full of sunken rocks, exposed to easterlies, and so small a vessel had 'hardly room to Swing'.[2] Most sandalwood traders preferred the sheltered waters of Sandalwood Bay, much to Bula's annoyance, but here they were liable to find themselves involved in conflicts between Wet and Gaitcha.

In 1842 Andrew Cheyne anchored off Dueulu, principal village of Gaitcha, and in so doing antagonised Gwiet whose land encompassed most of the bay and who was determined to monopolise trade with Europeans. Cheyne spent several trying days bartering with Zeula's people and at the same time warding off canoe loads of Gwiet's warriors 'all painted black for War, and armed with Spears, clubs, Tomahawks, Slings & Stones'. His crew were frequently assailed by 'These Bloodthirsty Villains' boarding 'like wild Bulls' and had to drive them off with bayonet charges and, towards the end of their stay, cannon fire.[3] Captain Simpson also became involved in tribal politics in Sandalwood Bay two years later. He anchored off Chepenehe and was hospitably received by Gwiet whom he described as fifty or sixty years old, 'short stature, grisly beard, dark restless eye deep sunk in his head, thick bushy eyebrows, rather a wooly head of hair.'[4] He also wore a large lock of hair on one side of his head which he vowed never to cut until he had killed his arch rival Bula. Zeula, meanwhile, was jealous of Simpson's dealings with Gwiet and glowered across the Bay. The captain did finally send a boat to Gaitcha in search of wood, and with near disastrous results. One of its crew, accidentally hit by a Gaitch man, fired his musket into a crowd gathered on the beach. The enraged Lifuans were eager to attack, but Simpson, similarly enraged, quickly punished the seaman and managed to placate Zeula with scarlet cloth and an old cuirass. A relieved Simpson commented: 'the different tribes may be at variance with each other, in the case like the present, any of them are but too glad to make it an excuse to commit depredations on the whites, as a retaliation for the outrage'.[5] With such divisions amongst the Lifuans in the north of the island, those outsiders wishing to settle usually remained at Mu with the peaceable Bula. In 1842 he welcomed two Samoan teachers from the Si Gwahma tribe, his allies on Mare. Eager to live up to his reputation for hospitality in order to attract as many ships as possible to his half of Lifu, he took them into his household and supported their teachings. Almost immediately thirty to forty people attended their services.[6] The LMS checked on its new mission field in 1845 and reported:

> . . . a number are gathered together on the side of nominal Christianity. They still fight, however, have night dances, pray to their ancestors, and add to all the worship of God. A change has of late come over the chief Bula; he has given up cannibalism. Formerly he has had sixteen cooked bodies laid before him at a meal, now he will not touch human flesh, and threatens death to any of his family who ever again tastes of it.[7]

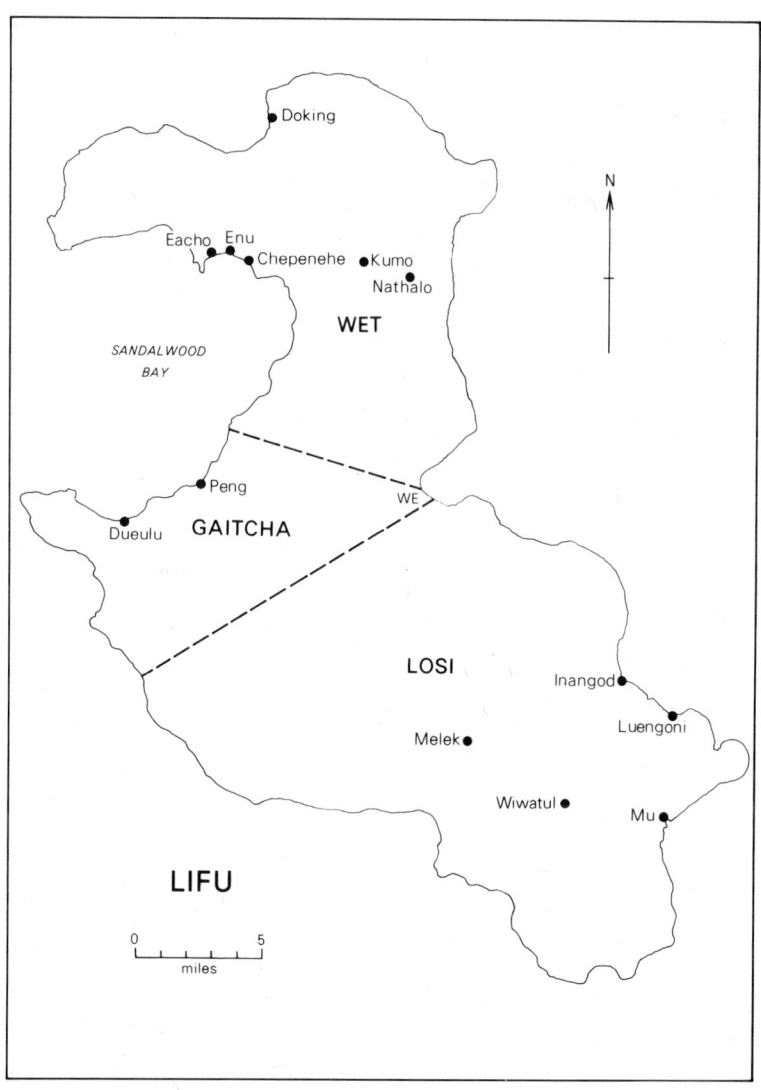

MAP 3   Lifu

Bula was eager to reassure those on the mission vessel of his good intentions towards the teachers and any missionaries who might settle at Mu. His spokesman told the missionaries:

> In all past generations Lifu has had a good name. Lifu has always been kind to strangers. You see these Tongans sitting here? Go on shore, and you will see the graves of their fathers who were drifted hither, and lived and died among us. Go on shore, and you will see the children of Tanna men. The fathers are all dead and buried, but the children live. We have always been kind to white men too. Do not be suspicious. We are not going to take a bad name for a good one.[8]

The following year visiting LMS missionaries reported that 'even *now* missionaries might, not only without danger but with almost sure success, live among the people. The power and authority of the chief are very great, and are at present decidedly in favour of the introduction of the Gospel'.[9]

Bula died in an epidemic shortly after the mission vessel departed and all evangelising and trading in Losi ceased during the ensuing civil war. The exact cause of the conflict cannot be determined but it seems likely that rival claims to the chiefship were a major factor.[10] The LMS teachers, Bridget, and James Reece—a sandalwood agent working at Mu—fled to Mare, and Bula's sons took refuge with their friends in Gaitcha. Fighting dragged on for three years, not affecting Gaitcha and Wet, before rival clans were reconciled and Bula's eldest son, also called Bula, assumed the great chiefship of Losi. Keenly aware of the benefits the two Naisilines on Mare were receiving from their association with the LMS teachers, the young Bula invited back those who had earlier fled. When the LMS missionaries again voyaged to Lifu in 1852 they were amazed at the external signs of Christianity and 'civilisation' at Mu. Bula had erected a large coral-block and concrete chapel complete with pulpit, reading desk, and 'neat venetian blinds', and he and the teachers, ably led by Fao, were housed in whitewashed plaster cottages surrounded by gardens, gravel paths, and white picket fences. The villagers were all 'more or less clothed' and 700 regularly attended services. Lifu, the missionaries enthused, was 'one of the finest and most inviting field for missy labour among the islands on which our teachers are at work throughout Western Polynesia'.[11] Those at Mu continually demanded that the LMS establish a permanent station. Retorted one young chief angrily: 'Say not *some* day! . . . I do not like to hear that word *some day*! Why not say, *to-day*? Why not one of you stay?'[12] When the people learned that Jones and Creagh had arrived on Mare in 1854 demands for '*their missionary*' grew 'louder and louder': whenever the mission vessel called at Mu it was surrounded by crowds of up to 3000 clamorous Islanders, almost the entire population of Losi.[13]

The teachers' influence spread rapidly throughout Bula's chiefdom. Fao was eager to move onwards into Wet and Gaitcha and he set up a post at We, strategically situated on the boundaries of the three chiefdoms yet still safely in Bula's territory at the southern end of the beach.[14] Both Zeula and Ukeneso, who was chief after his father Gwiet died, saw Bula and his new allies as a serious threat to their independence. They had no intention, therefore, of allowing the teachers upon their soil. As an LMS missionary later explained:

> Ukenezo was by no means disposed to embrace the religion of his great enemy Bula, although many of his subjects were. He, too, had heard of the "power of Jehovah;" and, like many others, seemed far more impressed by this attribute than by the tale of His love and the gift of His Son. They felt that the latter might be mythical, but that there was no mistaking the former: they considered that they had had indisputable evidence of the superiority of Pao's God over any they possessed. But then He was the God of their enemies. Had Pao landed on their side of the island he would doubtless have been received by Ukenezo as he had been by Bula; but, coming as the friend and teacher of his enemies, he not only looked upon him as one of them, but as the chief cause of his defeat in their late wars; and declared that he would club and cook him whenever he got the opportunity.[15]

But in spite of the chiefs' objections the teachers managed to exploit rivalries within Wet and Gaitcha and establish footholds there. In 1856 Wainya, chief of the Wainya clan which lived at Chepenehe, rebelled against his great chief and accepted some teachers. The implications were plain enough: Wainya was one of the most ambitious and influential clan chiefs in Wet, ranked next to Ukeneso and was married to his sister.[16] By virtue of his geographic position he had built up considerable expertise in dealing with English traders and had benefited materially from their visits. Ukeneso, on the other hand, was a weak, timid man and, as the chiefship was based 7 miles inland at Nathalo, he had gained little from the shipping. By becoming a Christian and utilising the teachers' presence Wainya hoped to consolidate his position further and stand independent from Ukeneso, even to the point of becoming the effective ruler of Wet.

John Jones, the LMS missionary from Mare, toured Lifu in the same year. He met Ukeneso who told him that he was determined to remain a 'naked savage' even though many of his people were deserting him for Wainya. He added, however, that if Jones could send a missionary to live with him at Nathalo he would become a Christian at once; but he had 'no disposition' to accept Polynesian teachers.[17] Jones wrote pleading letters to the LMS begging them to send at least four missionaries. He believed it was possible that, if Bula, Zeula, Wainya, and Ukeneso each had a missionary, the whole of the island would opt for Christianity at once. Whereas mission expansion on Mare, he argued, was limited by tribal fighting and 'chiefs without number', Lifu was politically stable with only four principal chiefs.[18] The LMS was unable to send even one missionary.

The teachers' breakthrough in Gaitcha came in 1857 when Zeula died leaving a nine-year-old son as his heir. An ambitious 'secondary chief' immediately denounced the young boy and claimed the leadership for himself. The teachers were quick to support the usurper and he in turn took the opportunity to strengthen his position with their assistance.[19]

Ukeneso and the supporters of the young Zeula were horrified at the rapid infiltration of their lands by the LMS teachers and the associated challenges to their status and authority by rebellious lesser chiefs. At the urgings of Bazit, one of their Uvean allies who had accepted a Marist priest in 1857, they too sent out invitations to the Marist Mission.[20] The Marists were eager to send representatives, for they were aware that it would only be a matter of time before the LMS sent permanent missionaries to bolster the gains already made by its teachers. And they were well aware too of why Ukeneso wanted them; Poupinel explained that the chief

> . . . hoped that by having some [Catholic] missionaries, he would be protected by the French against the ambition of a subordinate chief who wished to supplant him. The chief of Kepenehe was supported by the catechists, who wished to give him authority over the first chief, who was not amenable to their religion.[21]

Xavier Montrouzier was chosen to lead the Lifu mission mainly because, as he put it himself, of his 'belligerent nature'. He saw the situation on the island as 'desperate'; Lifu was to be his 'Sebastopol' where he would 'battle with the Protestants'.[22] The then Commandant of New Caledonia, Major Jules Testard, fully supported the idea of a Catholic mission on Lifu, for he hoped it would be a counter to the increasing English commercial and religious influences there.[23] He personally sailed on the warship *Styx*, which deposited Montrouzier and his fellow missionary François Palazy at Eacho in Sandalwood Bay in 1858. Most of the Lifuans present, and especially those a short distance away at Chepenehe, were terrified at the sight of the warship flying the French ensign. The Polynesian teachers had long been haranguing their congregations on the wickedness of French governments, claiming that administrators would soon cross from New Caledonia to take their land and destroy the authority of their chiefs, and that Catholic priests were the French government's spies and envoys, besides being heretics.[24]

Even Ukeneso was fearful enough and needed some urging to board the vessel. He wanted the two priests to return immediately with him to Nathalo, but Montrouzier refused and pointed out how they had to stay near the coast where they could be in contact with European ships. Ukeneso begrudgingly agreed to let them remain at Eacho for the meantime and then scuttled back to Nathalo in case the Chepenehe Protestants assailed him. The priests were left to themselves and sat dejectedly in a squalid little hut, hungry, thirsty, and not daring to move away in case someone sneaked out of the bush and stole their property. Ukeneso had shown them a nearby grotto with fresh water somewhere in its depths but neither Montrouzier nor Palazy had the nerve to descend the thick vines which hung 60 or 70 feet down the sheer-sided hole.

> For the natives, who have no clothes to wash, nor pots to boil, it means little to them if there is water or not. Instead, they drink coconut juice and suck sugar cane; if they wish to bathe, they go to the sea. But it is not the same for us, accustomed to another way of life, and having other needs.[25]

Five days after he had left them, Ukeneso plucked up the courage to return and built a larger hut for the missionaries. On its completion the two priests held their first service on Lifu but were dismayed that they had to speak English to make themselves even vaguely understood. And they were disgusted that their listeners' vocabularies consisted of 'mostly dirty words rather than expressions appropriate for discussing spiritual ideas'.[26]

Slowly gaining confidence, Montrouzier and Palazy made tentative forays inland. Within six months they had small huts built for them at Nathalo and We (in Wet), and also at Dueulu where the supporters of the young Zeula gave them a warm welcome. From their headquarters at Eacho they made periodic visits to these places, staying a few days in each. Montrouzier was pleased with their progress: 'The mission goes well. The obstacles are disappearing, the prejudices fall, the natives see that the protestant catechists have abused their credulity and they are coming to us'.[27] Several children were baptised, though in secret and under the pretext of giving medical aid, in case the Islanders objected violently, and there were some 600 'listeners' out of a total population of almost 6000. But the priests were unhappy. Both men hated the Lifu landscape, their poverty, and the hardships of day to day living.[28]

Selwyn and Patteson hoped to overcome some of the Melanesian Missions problems by transfering its school from Auckland to one of the islands. They chose Lifu because it was close to the New Hebrides where they planned to collect their scholars, and it had the reputation of already being a 'Christianised' island. Furthermore, the Mission had called into Mu several times in the early 1850s and Patteson could speak the language reasonably well, having learnt it from Lifuans taken to St Johns. There was now an additional reason: the Marists had a foothold on the north of the supposedly Protestant island.

Patteson took twelve New Hebrideans to Mu, only weeks after the Marists landed at Eacho. He was confident the school there would be a great success and excited at the prospect of dwelling amongst the Islanders for several months. Trying to live a Romantic ideal, he took ashore with him nothing but tea and ships' biscuits, intending to live on local food consisting, as he imagined, of yams, coconuts, pigs, fowls, turkeys, fish, and turtle meat: 'I have no doubt I shall live very well'.[29] But his four-month sojourn at Mu was a sad disillusionment. There was an unvarying, and to him oppressive diet of yams and coconuts, and little fresh water. His Lifuan hosts thrived on such food, but the New Hebrideans were wont to complain: 'Lifu people very kind, but no water, no bread fruit, no banana, no fish. Very good to go to New Zealand'.[30] Where Selwyn and Patteson believed that the New Zealand environment hindered the Islanders' training, it was precisely the prospect of going to New Zealand that attracted many young men to the mission, for in Auckland they could experience some of the novelties of the white man's world. At Mu Patteson had little time for teaching so involved was he in organising food supplies for his scholars, and the Mission later admitted that his school 'did not prove very successful'.[31]

Patteson met the Marists priests and to the surprise, and doubtless disappointment of the Lifuans, they treated each other with courtesy and respect. Patteson thought that Montrouzier was a 'gentleman' but took exception to his view that 'he could force upon the Lifu people whatever he pleased, the French Government having promised him any number of soldiers he may send for to take possession, if necessary, of the island', and to his 'frequent introduction of the words "man of war" into all discussions'.[32] Patteson impressed upon the Lifuan Protestants the dangers of antagonising the priests in case they did call on the Noumean administration,[33] and scorn and abuse of the priests did abate, at least for a time, probably as a result of Montrouzier's intransigence and Patteson's counsel.

Late in 1858 Montrouzier was transferred to New Caledonia. He believed his contribution to the Marist Mission on Lifu had been to establish a beachhead in a land of Protestants and to have intimidated the more outspoken Protestant teachers. He had also baptised, in secret, twenty-six Lifuans, twenty of whom were, he was convinced, already in Heaven. But of the 750–800 Lifuans who supported the Marists he was honest enough to admit that 'What they desired was not knowledge of the truth, it was guns and above all the alliance of the French to crush the protestants, who . . . wished to proselytize by armed might'.[34] With his departure the mission lost all momentum. His replacement, Jean-Baptiste Fabvre, was unable to travel because all his shoes wore out on the rough coral tracks, and only one mission ship visited Eacho for the next ten months. The two men lacked materials to improve their huts or build chapels, and were forced to live on a diet of yams when their own supplies ran out.[35] Presenting a spectacle of dejection, misery, and virtual isolation in the bush at Eacho, they were scarcely likely to impress the Lifuans or be of much assistance to the hapless Ukeneso, who was scared to travel beyond the confines of Nathalo.

The LMS, which had been unable to provide missionaries for Lifu when begged to do so by the Lifuans, quickly reviewed the situation when it learned that two opposition mission societies were on the island. It is hard to judge whom the Society saw as posing the greatest threat—the Marists or the Melanesian Mission. One of the LMS secretaries thought that Patteson would spread only 'evils' amongst the Lifuans: 'It is a lamentable circumstance that in their efforts for the Evangelization of the Islands of the Pacific, the Society's Agents have in some instances met with no less serious obstruction from the professed friends of the Gospel than from its avowed enemies'.[36] In 1859 several thousand Lifuans watched the arrival of Samuel MacFarlane and William Baker in the LMS mission vessel *John Williams*, long since nicknamed by the Lifuans 'no missionaries'.[37] The island was divided into two mission districts: Baker and his family went to Mu and MacFarlane and his family settled at Chepenehe. Their arrival could not have been in greater contrast to that of the Marists the previous year. At Mu the Bakers were at once 'comfortably lodged in a neat plastered six-roomed cottage, which the teachers gave up for their residence', and at Chepenehe 'The willing crowd picked up the things from the boat as soon as it touched the beach, and trunks, casks, and cases flew up to the teachers' house, in at the door, and were laid down in whichever of the seven rooms Mr MacFarlane pleased to direct'.[38] By the end of the first day, wrote MacFarlane, 'all our goods were landed, and cups and saucers were rattling, and the tea-pot steaming'.[39] The Marists watched dumbfounded from their hut at Eacho.

MacFarlane, a witty, articulate, and supremely arrogant Scotsman, who quickly dominated the other LMS missions on the Loyalty Islands, gloried in the accord the Lifuans paid him and the setting up of his home comforts:

> We have never been troubled with the feeling that because we are missionaries we ought to deny ourselves of easily-acquired conveniences and comforts; indeed, it has always been our endeavour to have things as neat, clean, and convenient as possible: trying to raise the natives to us, rather than descend to them.

On looking across the bay, he disdainfully acknowledged the existence of the two priests living, he observed, 'in miserable houses, remarkable only for their filth and disorder'.[40]

The Protestant mission on Lifu developed as rapidly as had its counterpart on Mare. The Islanders eagerly built store-houses and workshops for the missionaries, and erected large churches; each mission station was set amidst acres of cleared ground, surrounded by high coral-block walls. Thousands pledged their allegiance to the mission.[41] Like Naisiline Nidoish's people on Mare, the Lifuans under Bula and Wainya displayed tremendous enthusiasm for the church. The vast majority did so willingly and spontaneously but, as on Mare, there was no place for those who were reluctant to follow the masses. MacFarlane drew up a series of laws, similar to those promulgated by Jones and Creagh on Mare, which applied Christian principles 'to social life . . . to substitute them for the ferocity and revenge by which all classes had been previously influenced'. Policemen were appointed in villages throughout the island 'to investigate minor offences and impose suitable fines or punishment, whilst the supreme court was held at Mu'. Even MacFarlane had to admit that the police were 'more vigorous than just in enforcing their five laws, or rather their own ideas, for their little code became ludicrously elastic sometimes'.[42] Both Bula and Wainya benefited greatly from their close association with the LMS missionaries and, like Naisiline Nidoish, assumed powers which were probably unprecedented. Bula not only became a despot within his own chiefdom of Losi but effectively ruled the whole island with Wainya as his second in command in Wet and Gaitcha.

To help counteract Protestant dominance the Marist Mission sent further missionaries in 1860. But the priests continually changed their areas—from Eacho to Nathalo to Dueulu—and some were recalled leaving only Lubin Gaide and Jean-Baptiste Fabvre by 1862. Such mobility and change of personnel added to the difficulties of their already unsettled lives and prevented them from forming close ties with their local supporters. The priests' mood of discouragement persisted: they lacked food, had little communication with their Noumean superiors, and their poverty was 'proverbial in all the Vicariate' of New Caledonia.[43] Unlike the LMS missionaries they were slow to pick up the Lifuan languages, and in despair they watched MacFarlane and James Sleigh (who replaced Baker at Mu), who ate and lived very well with their wives to care for them, and the aggressive LMS system with its 'phalanx of catechists, with its books, with its schools, with its material resources . . . . The Catholic work advances slightly and slowly'.[44] Out of a total population of almost 6000 the Marists had a total of only 600 supporters at Eacho and Nathalo and 150 at Dueulu; and they thought that less than half of these were 'Christians'.[45] The remaining population was Protestant.

Where MacFarlane referred to the 'ludicrously elastic' interpretation of his Mission's laws, the Marists labelled it an 'inquisition'. Bula's policemen became increasingly fanatical in their opposition to Ukeneso and Zeula; and their Catholic followers were sometimes tortured and forced to labour for Protestants. Neither Ukeneso nor those looking after the young Zeula were able to retaliate, for their supporters were hopelessly outnumbered. 'The policemen', wrote Gaide, 'believed they were above the great chief [Ukeneso], and became tyrants'.[46]

By 1860 the Bula chiefship in association with the LMS had achieved supremacy throughout the island. Ukeneso's attempts to offset Bula's authority and that of the rebellious Wainya by calling for Marist missionaries had achieved little; he had already lost popular support, except at Eacho, Nathalo and Dueulu, and the Marist Mission was lacking in effective personnel and resources. But the prospect that he and the Marists would soon be completely at the mercy of Bula, Wainya, and the LMS was soon to result, as Montrouzier had earlier threatened, in the forceful intervention of the French government.

5
Uvea 1842-1864

The Marist Mission, although losing the initiative to the LMS on Mare and Lifu, achieved dominance on Uvea. As on the other two islands the division of the Uvean population into two opposing religious camps is largely explicable in terms of pre-European tribal arrangements and of the Islanders' local politics.

Uvea was originally populated by Lifuans from Gaitcha and Wet and migrants from New Caledonia.[1] By the mid-eighteenth century the island was roughly divided into two main chiefdoms. Great chief Bazit at the village of Weneki controlled the northern region, Ohwen, and great chief Taume ruled over the southern half, the districts of Fayawe and Muli, from the village of Fayawe.[2] Two subsequent migrations provided the basis for the tribal divisions of the island in the nineteenth century. In the latter half of the eighteenth century some Wallis Islanders were building a canoe for their chief when a stone broke from its axe lashing and injured the chief's son. The working party, led by Nekelo, Dumai, Beka, and the Tongan Pumali, were terrified of retribution and fled to sea. Their canoe drifted some thousand miles to the south-west and landed at the north of Uvea on the small island of Uneis.[3] Bazit readily accepted the castaways, for he saw that they might make valuable allies in his wars with Taume to the south. There were no women among the migrants, who intermarried with the original inhabitants and adopted most of their customs, although they retained much of their own language.[4] Beka and his followers remained on Uneis while Nekelo later settled at Heo, and Dumai and Pumali, either by conquest or at the invitation of Taume, made their permanent home on the island of Muli.[5] Soon after the Wallisians had arrived on Uvea a number of New Caledonians from Kone landed in the district of Fayawe. In a series of wars their leader, Whenegay, defeated Taume and built up a powerful chiefdom centred on the village of Fayawe.[6] By the 1840s Ohwen was still led by the Bazit family. Within this region there were a number of chiefdoms ruled by the Melanesians Owa at Onyat, Imwene at Bazit's village of Weneki, and the recent Polynesian arrivals Beka of Uneis and Nekelo of Heo. All these chiefdoms, similar to great chiefdoms in that each comprised a number of clans, had varying degrees of autonomy from Bazit although they had a greater or lesser system of formal or informal ties with him such that Ohwen was a region of considerable political coherence clearly distinct from the rest of the island.[7] Erskine met Bazit and Nekelo, who acted as a 'war minister' for Ohwen in the later 1840s. The latter he described as a 'sombre-looking man . . . having tattooed on his chest, in large Roman characters, "*Nicolo, King of Ware*" '. Bazit, not to be outdone, had 'Basset' engraved on his chest.[8] Whenegay's descendants still held sway over the southern half of the atoll, except for the small island of Muli where the Polynesian Dumai was chief and the Tongan Pumali played a lesser role.[9] Cheyne described Whenegay in 1842 as

> . . . in the lowest grade of Savage Ignorance and a Cannibal—yet there was something straightforward about him—which I had not before met with at any of the other Islands—and which led me to think he might be trusted. It was evident to me that he had great power over the Natives—and sufficiently able to protect any vessel that might visit his place. . . . The Kings name is Whiningay—he is about 45 years of Age, nearly 6 feet high, well made with rather a Wild and Daring expression of countenance—has Elaphantiasis in his right Leg, and holds his present rank through having been a great Warrior.[10]

Bazit and Whenegay were the bitterest of enemies, each striving for dominance of the atoll. It was these two men, and their successors, who in large part decided the pattern of the Islanders' reactions to European, and especially missionary, presence.

Sandalwood traders reached Uvea's lagoon in 1842 where, in spite of tribal fighting, bartering was usually peaceful providing ships' masters stayed clear of local politics.[11] And as both the northern and southern regions were equally accessible to vessels, neither Bazit nor Whenegay was

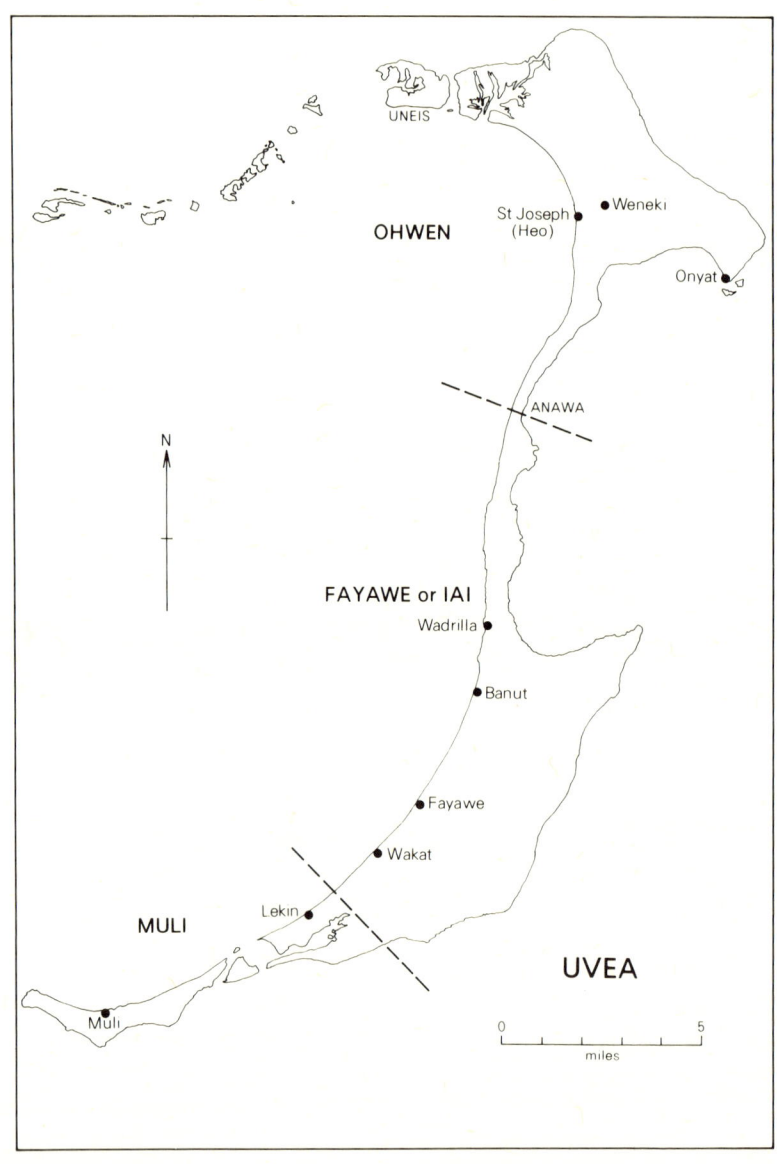

MAP 4   Uvea

deprived of the goods offered by the traders for wood, unlike the chiefs to the south and east of Mare. Tribal hostilities came to an end in the late 1840s apparently as a result of Whenegay's death.[12] His son Jokwie assumed the chiefship of the Fayawe region, and peace continued until 1856. At the beginning of that year Nekelo either was killed or died of natural causes and warfare with the south was renewed as a consequence. Under the pretext of arranging a peace settlement Jokwie was enticed to Ohwen where he was assassinated, and the tribal fighting assumed more serious proportions.[13] The Whenegay chiefship made strenuous efforts to gain a more formal alliance with, and hopefully assistance from, Europeans. Seeing the advantages that Bula, Wainya, and Naisiline Nidoish had received from the LMS, Jokwie, just before his death, had asked Creagh on Mare for teachers. By mid-year there were two Marean teachers in the village at Fayawe.[14] That same year the sandalwood entrepreneur Henry Burns fortuitously established a large sandalwood station at Fayawe, where he spent the winter months until 1861. Burns's presence was of great significance for the people of the district not only because of the material prosperity his station brought them, but because Jokwie's son was a minor and Burns was appointed regent. As he later explained:

> When I returned to the island in 1856, there was no head to the tribe, the king having been killed in fight; he had an only child, who was but two years of age, and his brother who was a sort of regent was imbecile, the power was therefore placed in my hands.[15]

> The people had every confidence in me. I was the king there. We had a regular code of laws for our government, established by myself and the chiefs. I am sorry to say I have not a copy of them, as they with my journals were lost when I went to England. The people looked to me to settle all their disputes . . . . If I said anything it was right.[16]

Burns's appointment may well have been in the tradition of offering the leadership to a newcomer whom the elders thought capable of benefiting the chiefdom. However, he held the position only for a short time for in 1857 Ombalu, another brother of the deceased Jokwie—and apparently no 'imbecile'—was regent.

Bazit and the young Nekelo, who assumed the chiefship at Heo on his father's death, were dismayed to see the Whenegay chiefship so closely associated with English traders and the LMS mission and, in a now thoroughly predictable pattern, invited Marist missionaries from north-eastern New Caledonia.[17] In 1857 Jean Bernard and François Palazy settled at

Heo, or St Joseph. Fighting between the north and south immediately intensified as French Catholic and English Protestant influences aggravated the long-standing feud. The LMS made its first visit to Uvea the following year to land Polynesian teachers to reinforce the mission conducted by the Marean teachers. There had been little visible progress by these men in the two years they had been at Fayawe mainly, the missionaries believed, because of the district's obsession with its war against the north. And although the people were eager enough to accept the Polynesian teachers the fighting was their overall concern.[18] The priests too were pessimistic about their chances of ever having influence in the south: the Fayawe people, they explained, 'remain true to the sentiments of their ancient hostility: perhaps also they are afraid of appearing to submit to the chiefs of the . . . [northern] tribe, if they accept . . . [the Catholic] religion'.[19] Nevertheless the priests did make gains through their threats to call for a French warship.[20] The turning point for their mission came with Commandant Testard's visit to Uvea in the *Styx* when he and Montrouzier collected Palazy on their way to Lifu in 1858. The priests impressed upon the Commandant the necessity for a station at the village of Fayawe, the centre of hostile English influence. Testard immediately sailed there and 'demanded' that the Fayawe people allow the Marists to settle in their village. No one dared to object, said Bernard, for 'the fear of the warship was stronger than their faith'. Bernard and Eugène Barriol, who replaced Palazy, 'took the opportunity to go there immediately to found an establishment beside the Protestant one'.[21] Barriol took up residence at the new station but was soon disillusioned. He had great difficulty in learning the Iai language and was continually abused by the villagers and the Marean and Polynesian teachers. Furthermore, at both Fayawe and St Joseph the priests had few resources: they ran short of food and water and had great difficulty in gathering wood and other essential materials for their huts and chapels. A young Brother sent to help them was a hindrance for he 'detested' life on the atoll and vomited every time naked women crawled passed him on all fours to enter or leave a hut.[22] No mission vessel arrived for over six months, and Bernard complained that they had been 'abandoned in the wilderness'.[23]

In spite of the priests' inability to impress the Islanders with material wealth, support for the mission increased in both regions. By 1859–1860 the principal chiefs in the north, Bazit, Imwene, Nekelo, Beka, and Owa gave at least tacit support to the Marists, and the entire population of about 1000 attended services.[24] In the south several of the lesser clan chiefs in the Wakat-Lekin areas asked the priests for assistance to help them put down challenges to their authority by ambitious young men supported by the Protestant teachers.[25] But the breakthrough for the Marists in the south came when all 300 residents on the island of Muli decided to support them; their great chief Dumai saw his chance to emphasise his independence from the Whenegay chiefship,[26] and there were, in addition, strong sociohistorical ties between the Wallisian descendants on Muli and those in the north. Some people from the village of Fayawe told Barriol: 'Father your prayer is best, we wish to accept it, but as it comes from . . . [Weneki] we are ashamed . . . you must come yourself and take the principal chiefs by the hand and everyone will follow'.[27] However, at least 200 from the Fayawe district, with a population of 1000, decided to support the Marists.[28] In addition to political reasons for changing their allegiance, some of the Fayawe people were worried about the French warships: 'They said', recorded Barriol, 'perhaps with truth, that if we kill the missionaries, that . . . [the French] will take our country'.[29] The priests well knew that few of these people had 'changed their pagan life' and were Catholic 'only in words', but, they rationalised, better that than their becoming Protestants.[30]

As the Marist Mission gained momentum and the numbers of Protestant teachers were annually increased, violence between Catholic and Protestant supporters regularly broke out. Hostility between the northern and southern regions came to an end as the Islanders became more preoccupied with factional squabbling in their own areas. The Fayawe region was particularly disturbed because of the presence of Barriol, surrounded by large numbers of Protestants, and because the regent Ombalu had none of the authority of the former Whenegays to maintain order. One European traveller commented: 'thanks to a crowd of petty chiefs without influence, anarchy is permanent'.[31] The northern region too became unsettled when in 1860 the Marists attempted to draw up a code of laws to consolidate their support before the Protestant teachers had time to make their way there. Bernard and Bazit called together the principal chiefs and in Bazit's name promulgated laws for compulsory attendance at church services, strict observance of the Sabbath, and the prohibition of polygyny and the dissolution of marriages.[32] The implications of such laws upon the political structure of Ohwen were potentially profound, for they gave Bazit the opportunity to interfere in the internal affairs of the other chiefdoms—a right he did not normally have. However, every chief except Owa of Onyat, who was determined that his authority should not in any way be weakened by Bazit, reluctantly agreed to accept the laws.³³ The Protestant teachers and catechists at Fayawe quickly supported Owa's stand and declared him an independent chief without any obligation whatsoever to Bazit. Owa pledged his support for the Protestants and symbolically broke his ties with Bazit by returning a fibre belt Bazit had once given him. Within a few hours Protestants from Fayawe flocked to Onyat and erected a grass chapel next to the Catholic one. Bernard and Bazit accused Owa of rebellion and warriors destroyed his entire village and drove the inhabitants south to Wadrilla, where they took refuge.³⁴

When a permanent Protestant missionary arrived in the village of Fayawe in December 1864 he was in an unenviable position. The Marist missionaries, although they had achieved very little in their attempts to evangelise the Islanders, had no schools, and were still materially poor,³⁵ had, nevertheless, the support of most of the Uvean population. In conjunction with Bazit and Nekelo they had an iron grip on the people of Ohwen and no Protestant teachers or supporters dared travel into the area; everyone on Muli and most of the people in the Lekin-Wakat region as well as some 200 in Fayawe itself followed the priests.³⁶

Chiefs, Church, and State

By the mid-1860s both Marist and LMS missionaries had been able to establish stations on each of the Loyalty Islands and 'convert' the inhabitants largely because chiefs were eager to apply certain mission institutions as well as the missionaries' national and religious prejudices to their own politics. After 1864 the situation became more complex than a simple interaction between rival chiefs and rival faiths: the French government, based in New Caledonia, intervened in Loyalty Islands affairs.

France annexed New Caledonia in 1853. The proclamation referred to 'New Caledonia and its dependencies' and although not specifying the latter, it was generally understood that they were the Loyalty Islands. Until 1864 French administrators in Noumea (or Port de France as it was known until 1866) had no wish to concern themselves with these economically insignificant islands but became increasingly disturbed by events there. They were alarmed at the tribal fighting between English Protestant and French Catholic supporting Islanders and at the growth of English religious and commercial influence so close to New Caledonia causing, wrote one Governor in 1860, 'considerable prejudice. The natives are more English than French. A vigorous occupation alone will establish there our supremacy. But it takes men, and money'.[1] Seriously short of both, the administration saw the settlement of Marist missionaries as 'the only way to extend . . . [French] influence'.[2] By the early 1860s, however, the intensification of religious, national, and tribal hostilities called for more positive action from the government, and chiefs and missionaries who had hitherto been concerned with one another now had to come to terms with a major, and finally dominant, European influence.

The French administration was unable to 'pacify' the Islanders and missionaries immediately. Its policies lacked direction and decisiveness. Because the islands were of no economic significance and because the administration lacked resources and finance, actual government presence was minimal. Apart from stationing a commandant and some soldiers at Chepenehe on Lifu in the 1860s and a lone resident who lived there from 1870, the only other French officials to set foot on the islands usually stayed only a matter of days, and more often hours. The French were further hindered by antagonistic Islanders and missionaries. The LMS missionaries in particular severely limited the range of the New Caledonian governors' actions. The mission's effective propaganda network throughout Australia and England gave wide publicity to the politico-religious troubles, blaming them on the Noumean administration. The LMS also brought strong pressure to bear upon the local administration by channelling protests through the British Foreign Office to a sympathetic Paris government. Officials in Paris had no desire to quarrel with England and warned their officials in New Caledonia not to persecute the Protestant Islanders or the LMS missionaries for fear of 'international consequences'. The Noumean administration was unable to take severe reprisals against the Loyalty Islanders, as it did without qualms against the New Caledonians; nor could it simply expel all the LMS missionaries. Not until the 1870s on Lifu and Uvea and the 1890s on Mare could the government bring about peace and political stability and an end to the religious and national rivalries by gradually exiling the more troublesome Islanders and finally removing several of the more militant missionaries. It is no coincidence that Lifu, the most politically stable of the three islands in the 1840s, was the first to regain this state whereas Mare, in a post-revolutionary turmoil when Europeans first arrived, was the last to do so—suggesting that the processes and progress of 'pacification' owed as much to the nature of political arrangements existing at the time of first regular contact with Europeans as to the manner of European intervention.

Although the French administrators finally secured the obedience of the Islanders and the missions, they never managed to erase the strong undercurrents of the Islanders' anglophilia, which still exist today. By 1900 the government's presence and strength was more potential than actual, and, as long as there was peace amongst the Islanders and missionaries and no challenge to French sovereignty, the government was content not to interfere in island life.

6
Lifu 1864-1871

The island of Lifu came first to the attention of the French administration when the Protestant Lifuans' zeal exceeded their discretion. Encouraged by the LMS missionary MacFarlane, Bula's and Wainya's police roamed throughout the chiefdoms of Wet and Gaitcha terrorising Ukeneso's and the young Zeula's Catholic followers. Even Europeans were not safe: a visiting Irishman who refused to attend a Sunday service at Chepenehe found himself bound and gagged, while the master of a trading vessel was held for two days at Mu until he paid 'harbour dues'.[1] Ukeneso, who had called upon the Marist missionaries to aid him in 1858, now sent out urgent appeals to the Noumean administration. On his behalf a Marist missionary from Noumea, Jean Bertrand, interviewed Governor Charles Guillain. He claimed that MacFarlane had over 200 policemen throughout Lifu who ostensibly maintained 'the divine laws' but who made no distinction in practice between temporal and spiritual matters; Ukeneso and Zeula were 'no longer masters of their own land' for MacFarlane had the police punish anyone who obeyed their commands instead of the new laws. 'Things at Lifu are at the point where the politics of the Chepenehe autocrat must oppress us or our supporters fight a war to the death, or the Governor comes to make the despot see reason'.[2]

Several months later, in May 1864, Guillain gazetted the Loyalty Islands as a 'military district'[3] and sent a commandant and twenty-five soldiers to close down all LMS schools and stop the distribution of its religious propaganda. They set up camp at Enu, midway between Eacho and Chepenehe, where the French tricolour was raised for the first time on the Loyalty Islands. MacFarlane described Ukeneso and his followers 'rejoicing at the arrival of the soldiers, whom they regarded and represented as their *enemus [enehmu]* . . . come at their request to punish the disobedient and obstinate Protestants'.[4] Hundreds of Protestants flocked to Chepenehe, 'enraged and using menacing language'. MacFarlane had 'some difficulty in prevailing upon them to abandon their intention of, as they said, sweeping the soldiers into the sea'.[5] The French commandant hastily reported to Guillain that the Lifuans had risen en masse, and that his government was facing an 'insurrection' which only 'severe measures and an energetic front' could put down. The people of Chepenehe, he went on, 'are entirely imbued with English ideas'; the word French, or wee-wee (*oui-oui*) was synonymous with Catholic: when asked what religion they professed, they replied 'English' or 'Britannia'; and most could speak English. He thought MacFarlane was the real great chief of the island with his own hierarchical system of authority—under him came Bula, Wainya, Polynesian teachers, police, and catechists. He was, said the official, 'their supreme missionary . . . the representative of God on earth; he had communication with the eternal' (MacFarlane would not have disagreed). The commandant concluded: 'the island of Lifu is an immense machine whose wheels run smoothly under the direction of the English minister at Chepenehe and his catechists. It is a vast exploitation of the credulity of an entire people to the advantage of MacFarlane and his associates'.[6]

Guillain and 198 soldiers arrived at Enu in June. They marched into Chepenehe where Guillain mounted a platform and prepared to address the villagers. But they had long since fled, which Guillain interpreted as an act of rebellion against French authority. As soon as he departed, they poured back and spent the evening dancing around the Protestant church, screaming abuse at the soldiers at Enu and firing muskets into the air in a mood of defiant bravado.[7] Guillain's subsequent attempt to surround the village resulted in bloodshed. Three of the more extreme Protestants shot a soldier, whereupon the troops charged the villagers with bayonets, including those attending a church service: two soldiers and four Lifuans died and 'many' Protestants were wounded.[8] Meanwhile, a group of soldiers whom Guillain had ordered to march overland from Mu, approached Chepenehe. Fleeing villagers ran headlong into them and, described MacFarlane, 'set up a shout for vengeance, and, heedless of consequences, fell upon them with their clubs and tomahawks'.[9] Five Islanders were shot, and five soldiers wounded. Those Protestants who managed to escape from the French were given shelter by the Catholics at Nathalo—the beginning of a rapprochement between former enemies that was to grow throughout the 1860s.

Guillain declared a state of siege and proclaimed martial law. The LMS mission was closed down and MacFarlane confined to his house. The Governor justified his actions:

> ... under the cover of the protestant religion strangers have sought to denationalize the population of the Loyalty Islands, and force several of the chiefs to arrogate powers which alone belong to the Governor . . . .
>
> ... the natives of the village of Chepenehe tribe of Houet [Wet], and those from several parts of Leussi, repudiating their obligations towards the colonial authority, fomented disorder and revolt among the other people of the island of Lifou.
>
> ... since our arrival at Hiacho and in spite of the appeals we have made to rebellious chiefs, they failed to attend to our orders and so persisted in their rebellion.[10]

For several weeks Guillain conducted 'mopping up' operations. Troops were sent inland to follow up rumours of planned attacks and destroyed Protestants' huts, but there was no further violence. The great chiefs and most of the Islanders quietly submitted. He 'reinstated' Ukeneso, whom he considered a 'thoughtless and lazy man', as great chief of Wet. Wainya was deposed and his brother, who had long supported the Marists, was 'elected' as chief of Chepenehe. Bula was confined to Losi, had to dismiss his police, and was forbidden to indulge in 'politics' with the LMS missionaries. Zeula, Bula, and Ukeneso were to be 'intermediaries between . . . [French] authority and their subjects' and were to hold the positions of great chiefs only as long as they obeyed the government's instructions. The Polynesian teachers were expelled and, until further instruction, all LMS and Marist Mission activity was suspended.[11] Guillain was satisfied with his expedition: 'Lifu is conquered'.[12] At the end of the month he returned to Noumea leaving behind a detachment of soldiers under a commandant. In November the state of siege was lifted, but the soldiers remained.

The effects and implications of the 1864 expedition to Lifu were shrouded in controversy as each European group—the French administrators and Protestant and Marist missionaries—sought to maintain and justify what influence it could.

The LMS mission was initially forced to a standstill and the missionaries replied with an outburst of righteous indignation. MacFarlane was just the man to lead them into battle against the French. As he wrote to a friend who suggested that the island might turn Catholic now the government had intervened:

> What! beat a retreat! And before French men too! Ah, Sir, I see you don't know me yet. My 'energetic temperament' may and hope will lead to introduce the gospel to other lands still shrouded in heathen darkness.... You need not entertain any fears for the cause of Christ on Lifu. No restrictions which the French are able to place upon me can impede very much the progress of truth and knowledge on this island even if I were silenced tomorrow. My presence, influence, and advice would I am sure baffle all attempts which might be made to turn the natives from the simple truths in which they have been trained.[13]

He organised a massive propaganda campaign, or his 'paper war' as he liked to call it. He had voluminous correspondence with Guillain and the Lifu commandants, and with the LMS, which organised deputations to the British government.[14] The Foreign Office passed on the complaints to Paris through normal diplomatic channels[15] and sympathetic French ministers acted quickly. They charged Guillain for acting with 'excessive vigour' and challenged his right to suppress the LMS mission.[16] The French ambassador in London informed the LMS of 'his regret at the occurrences complained of' and assured the Society that 'the most stringent order had been sent to prevent a renewal of them'.[17] In January 1865 Napoleon III wrote to the LMS:

> I have received the memorial which you addressed to me relative to the measures recently taken in the Loyalty Islands by the Governor of New Caledonia. I am writing to Commandant Guillain to censure any measure which would impose a restraint upon the free exercise of your ministry in those distant lands. I feel assured that, far from raising any difficulties in the way of the representatives of French Authority, the Protestant mission, as well as the Catholic, will seek to diffuse among the natives of the archipelago the benefits of Christianity and civilisation.[18]

The LMS missionaries declared to the last that behind all Guillain's measures on Lifu lay Christianity's 'dazzling caricature, Popery',[19] but through either ignorance or unwillingness to admit it they never mentioned that, with Guillain's arrival in New Caledonia in 1862, the relationship between the Noumean administration and the Marist Mission had soured. French society throughout the nineteenth century was periodically convulsed by the conflict between ultramontane Catholicism, largely stripped of the political power it held before the revolutionary period, and the dominant forces of anti-clericalism. In the 1840s and 1850s, however, the Paris governments were generally prepared to support French Catholic missions in the Pacific because they could help consolidate and extend French influence.[20] Until Guillain's governorship the New Caledonian administrators, although not always in sympathy with the Marists' religion and mission policies and indeed sometimes hostile to them, all saw the Marist Mission as a necessary counter to English influence, especially on the Loyalty Islands.[21]

But Guillain was an ardent anti-cleric and clashed openly with the Marists, accusing them of meddling in state affairs and coercing and creating divisions among the New Caledonians, deploring what he considered their intolerant and bigoted notions. For their part the Marists saw him as a dangerous socialist and fanatical anti-cleric, an 'emissary of the Anti-Christ, the friend of pagans' who wished to 'destroy the Catholic religion; to establish a phalansterian doctrine . . . '.[22] Until Guillain's departure in 1870 he and the Marists campaigned bitterly against one another.[23] The priests on Lifu were therefore in a difficult situation. Although opposed to the Governor they were dependent upon his intervention to protect them and Ukeneso in the face of Protestant violence. But Guillain's aim, as the Marists realised, was not to protect their mission but to put down influences hostile to French sovereignty.[24] Delighted that French soldiers had arrived, the priests were nevertheless dismayed at the fighting at Chepenehe and accused Guillain of excessive violence.[25] Guillain in turn criticised the priests for not having sent him more detailed information on the Lifuan situation and for not having organised a party of Catholic Islanders to aid the soldiers.[26] The Marists in fact suffered more as a result of Guillain's expedition than did the LMS missionaries. Until Guillain received his reprimand from Paris the priests, like the LMS missionaries, were forbidden to preach, teach, have catechists, or distribute literature, and their followers, along with the Protestants, were forced to labour for the soldiers at Enu. But where MacFarlane ignored the French and secretly held schools and distributed books, the Marists had neither the courage nor resources to do so. Seeing MacFarlane blatantly disobeying the Governor's orders, they came to the conclusion (wrongly) that Guillain was working for the LMS missionaries,[27] and they maintained a running battle with him and the commandants until 1870. Fabvre in particular treated Guillain with the utmost contempt and wrote abusive comments about his officials.[28]

As well as having to deal with antagonistic LMS and Marist missionaries, Guillain also had the task of gaining the loyalty of the Lifuan people. Obedience from the majority was never in question after June 1864 and it was maintained by a system of *corvées* which required the great chiefs to send up to 100 men at a time to build quarters for the soldiers at Enu. Both Marist and LMS missionaries railed against the use of forced labour and wrote of the general atmosphere of subjugation. Lifuans initially fled into the bush whenever they learnt of the commandant's approach.[29] Guillanton, commandant from 1865 to 1869, attempted to win some popular support by reviving night dances which the missionaries had long since prohibited, but he never managed to achieve any genuine rapport with the Lifuans, and only brought upon himself a further outburst of LMS propaganda, including accusations that the dancing led to the 'vilest of immorality in which Sodomy . . . [was] conspicuous'.[30] The Lifuans generally showed an 'extreme docility' towards the commandants,[31] many perfecting a hypocritical servility. MacFarlane noted: 'To bamboozle the Commandant is already beginning to be regarded as a merit by some of the fast young men'.[32]

The French officials' main concern was to control the Protestant teachers and the great chiefs. Teachers could only be appointed with their great chief's and the commandant's approval and were forbidden to preach outside their own districts.[33] Guillain's policy towards the great chiefs was one of conciliation and punishment. Bula, Ukeneso, and Zeula were taken frequently to Noumea where they stayed with Guillain and were treated royally.[34] But none of the chiefs responded as Guillain anticipated. Bula's 'insolence', his 'surly behaviour', and his unwillingness to order his men to labour for the French earned him a year in Noumea where he was made to attend a government school. It was Ukeneso, the great chief who had been so pleased to see the soldiers arrive in 1864, who caused the French the most trouble. Although reinstated as great chief of Wet, he found the commandants' regulations as abhorrent as those of the LMS police. Like Bula he was slow to supply men for the *corvées*, and 'insolent', and he too spent a year in Noumea under close supervision. Zeula was similarly sent to Noumea for disobeying instructions.[35]

The seemingly interminable squabbling among the French administrators, Protestant and Marist missionaries, and the Lifuans came to a sudden halt at the beginning of the 1870s. Guillain returned to Paris and his replacement adopted a far more moderate attitude towards both mission societies. The military post on Lifu was abandoned and the island became an 'arrondissement' under a Resident, instead of a 'military district'. *Corvées* ceased and with them the issue that had most frequently brought the administration and the great chiefs into conflict. Resident Caillet, who arrived in 1870, lived alone at Chepenehe and had 'nothing to do except guard the flag, he never concerned himself with the natives and their affairs' on Lifu.[36] As long as the Islanders did not fight amongst themselves, and the missionaries acknowledged French sovereignty, they were left to their own devices. Caillet was instructed to impress upon the Lifuans that the government 'wished to have neither a military establishment, nor an administrative establishment in the archipelago'. The French, wrote Caillet, wished to leave untouched the 'traditional hierarchical structure' of the three great chiefships, and as long as the Lifuans governed themselves peacefully, no attempt would be made to interfere or impose any European administrative structure.[37]

The LMS mission lost much of its revolutionary impetus with the departure of the abrasive MacFarlane in 1871. In 1865 he and his wife had entered the deserted Catholic church at Nathalo and rummaged about. The two were caught red-handed and the ensuing Marist outrage gave Guillain his chance to turn the tables on MacFarlane, forcing the LMS to recall him.[38] James Sleigh remained at Mu and other English missionaries lived at Chepenehe until 1920, but all were more peaceable than MacFarlane. On the Marist side the impetuous Fabvre remained until his death in 1883, although old age and illness moderated his views. Both missions had amicable relations with the Noumean administration and increasingly friendly relations with each other.

Each of the European groups had partly achieved its aim and had been partly compromised by the other interests. English Protestantism remained the dominant mission influence with the allegiance of some 6000 Lifuans,[39] but it had been unable to remain independent of French control and could never again openly interfere in the Islanders' politics; nor had it succeeded in overthrowing the Marist Mission and its Lifuan followers. The Marists were firmly established at Eacho, Nathalo, and Dueulu, with the support of the great chiefs Zeula and Ukeneso and some 750–1000 Islanders,[40] but they had been unable to expand further, nor, like the LMS missionaries, could they ignore the Noumean administration. By 1870 the French government no longer felt its sovereignty over Lifu threatened for, although it had failed to end missionary activity as Guillain wished, or effectively combat English influences, it had the obedience, if not the affection, of the missions, the great chiefs, and the people of Lifu. Perhaps the most significant contribution of the French intervention was the creation of a stability within and among the three great chiefdoms. The political arrangement of Lifu was now in many ways reminiscent of the situation during the earliest years of European contact before the LMS missionaries and teachers in conjunction with Bula and Wainya overthrew the traditional power structure in both Wet and Gaitcha.

The Protestant and Catholic Lifuans had themselves drawn closer together since June 1864, partly in opposition to the first major external threat since European contact—the French soldiers—and partly because they realised that the French would not tolerate any more tribal fighting. The Lifuans had 'a wholesome dread of the powers that be', commented Creagh.[41] Throughout the remainder of the century Europeans described the harmonious relations between former enemies: 'the hatreds between village and village, tribe and tribe have disappeared'.[42] Such harmony, however, was not to be found on the other two islands and, having subdued the Lifuans and their missionaries, the Noumean administration was forced to turn its attention to Uvea.

7
Uvea 1864–1875

Until relative peace and political stability were established by about 1875, two related issues dominated Uvean affairs—the question of the future existence of the Protestant minority in areas of the district of Fayawe, and the efforts of Bazit, Whenegay and his regent Ombalu, and Dumai to strengthen and consolidate their influence within and beyond their own chiefdoms.

The initial reaction among the Fayawe Protestants, led by the regent Ombalu, to the news of Guillain's Lifu expedition was one of fear. Ombalu immediately hoisted a French flag and changed his allegiance from the Protestant teachers to the Marist priests, Bernard and Barriol. He and forty others accepted the Catholic medal, ordered the Marean and Polynesian teachers to leave the village, and declared that the Protestant church was now a Catholic one.[1] When the permanent LMS missionary, Samuel Ella, landed on Uvea in December 1864, many others who had seriously considered turning to the priests decided to remain with the Protestant cause for it appeared that the soldiers were not going to arrive, and Ella, who moved into Burns's old house at Fayawe and 'made a display . . . of property to attract people' gave them considerable confidence. Ombalu chose to remain with the Marists, not wishing to join the Protestant minority and antagonise the French administration, and set about imposing 'fines' on the Fayawe Protestants.[2]

Ella's presence encouraged the Protestants to adopt a more aggressive outlook, and stronger pockets of support were noticeable among several clans in the villages of Wadrilla, Wakat, Lekin, and Banut. On the small island of Muli there was a split between Pumeli, who abandoned his allegiance to the priests and turned to support Ella in the hope of dominating Dumai. Dumai responded by burning down Pumeli's village and for some years afterwards the island was riven by the mutual hostilities of these two men.[3] The three great chiefs, Bazit, Ombalu, and Dumai, who were no longer fighting amongst each other, and who had found common cause in supporting the Marists, concentrated on the task of obtaining the loyalty of their clan chiefs, often by violence. In the village of Fayawe, Ella found himself surrounded by constant fighting and sadly commented: 'Religion and politics mixed up in all our meetings'.[4] The presence of both Ella and Barriol at Fayawe centred conflict on the church originally built by the Protestants. Ombalu and Barriol claimed it for the Catholics, and whichever side could raise the most powerful congregation usually took control. Ella described one incident in which one of the Marists 'marched at the head of an armed party of his adherents and first assailed our congregation'. Once inside, the priest, said Ella, performed 'mummeries' to hallow the church for his faith.[5] Brawls within the church were commonplace.[6]

Guillain, not wishing to let events once again get out of hand as at Lifu before his expedition, landed at Fayawe in June 1865. After a brief inquiry he declared that Ella was entirely responsible for tensions building up to an 'imminent' war between the Catholics and Protestants.

> His presence has more than a little contributed to revive the pretensions of the catechists and native protestants. But the severe lesson of Lifou has at least cleared the political question and I did not find at Ouvéa the resistance and spirit of rebellion which was shown on my arrival on [Lifu] . . . .[7]

Guillain divided Uvea into three administrative districts—'Ouvéa, Faiaoué, and Mouli', with Bazit, the young Whenegay and his regent Ombalu, and Dumai as great chiefs. Guillain's regulations included the following points:

> ART. 5   Each of the Great Chiefs is responsible for his own district, and answers to the Lifu commandant. He can arrest any individual causing disorder or who refuses to obey him; but he must be good and just with everybody and is to be considered their father.
>
> ART. 7   When a crime is committed, the chief of the district will send the guilty person to the Lifu commandant who will act in accordance with the Governor's instructions.

ART. 8 Any chief who does not execute the Governor's instructions will be dismissed from his chiefship and taken to Port-de-France, for he will not be worthy of command.⁸

Guillain's regulations provide an excellent example of the misconceptions many Europeans held of the Islanders' socio-political organisations. Guillain thought he was 'legalising' the existing patterns of indigenous authority, which, if maintained, would have provided a convenient administrative framework for the French. But while the three districts with the three great chiefs roughly corresponded to the three major areas of political control, Guillain's view of them was far too simple. He did not realise or perhaps would not accept that within each of the three areas other chiefs had varying degrees of autonomy, as opposed to independence, from Bazit, Whenegay, and Dumai. Furthermore, he did not take account of the many ties of allegiance, especially at the clan level, which transcended the boundaries he laid down. Unaware of the real nature of chiefly authority, with its responsibilities and obligations within the fraternity and the checks and balances to chiefly despotism, Guillain saw the great chiefs as commanders with unlimited personal control; but he hoped that they would at least be paternalistic in their despotism. Such opinions coincided with the views of the Marist priests on Uvea and the LMS missionaries on Lifu and Mare, all of whom saw that their influence depended upon the support of those they considered to hold positions of greatest authority within the indigenous society. In common with the great chiefs and some clan chiefs on Lifu and Mare, the Uvean great chiefs were only too ready to take advantage of the opportunities offered to them by the Europeans to assume an authority they might not otherwise have had.

Before leaving, Guillain made further specific regulations: the people of Onyat who had been driven south by Bazit could either remain at Wadrilla, as long as they agreed to accept Whenegay's authority, or they could return to Onyat, and Bazit was forbidden to harm them; as for the church at Fayawe, each mission had to build another, and the old one was to be pulled down.⁹ Ella was furious with Guillain's measures. Uvea, he said,

> was to be in the hands of the three popish chiefs who had worked all the mischief here. . . . Thus the rule of this island is given into the hands of the Romish priests for these chiefs are easily their tools, ready to obey their directions in any evil work.¹⁰

As soon as Guillain sailed from the lagoon the fighting was renewed. Bazit drove back those people who tried to reach Onyat, and on Muli,

Dumai and Pumeli continued their hostilities until Pumeli died in 1867 and his son opted once again for the Catholics.[11] In the village of Fayawe the Protestants and Catholics broke up each other's services and antagonised each other's missionaries. Ella described how the Catholics, led by Ombalu, held 'nightly revels' and beat a wooden church bell 'for hours in our ears, accompanied by the savage shrieks, shouts and yellings of the dancers'. Ella lived in a constant state of blustering indignation:

> As a summary I may say, that in some places, protestant villages have been burned down; in others families have been driven from their homes; and the houses and lands taken from them by the persecuting chiefs and given to papists.
>
> What a malignant inconquerably malicious spirit Popery is![12]

The letters of Barriol and Bernard are silent about most of the fighting, probably because the Catholics were often the main instigators, though the Protestants doubtless provoked and antagonised them, and probably because the priests had a vested interest in Bazit and Ombalu bringing to heel those who refused to submit to them and accept the Catholic religion.

Ella's constant barrage of protests against Catholic 'outrages' was relayed to Paris through the British Foreign Office.[13] Guillain, embarrassed by Ella's accusations, was nevertheless reluctant to intervene. He did not want to send soldiers and risk another reprimand from Paris, nor had he the resources to establish a permanent official on the island. His compromise solution was to send a three-man commission of inquiry in 1869. To the Marist Mission's dismay, the commission upheld most of Ella's accusations and ordered the mission to recall Barriol.[14] Bernard was also recalled shortly afterwards. The removal of these two allegedly 'ardent' priests had no effect whatsoever on Bazit and Ombalu, who continued to attack the Protestants.[15] With every act of violence more and more Protestants considered it expedient to submit to the chiefs. By 1873 the Protestant population numbered less than 250.[16] From Mare, Jones wrote:

> It seems Naisiline's plan was the best, take things into his own hands, & risk the consequences. 'Nothing ventured nothing gained'. Well there seems little escape for Uvea, but annihilation of the protestant party, unless they can manage to get someone as leader and pitch into the rascals and have a regular battle & see who is the strongest.[17]

The French administration held a further inquiry in 1873 and again upheld the Protestants' claims. Ombalu was imprisoned in Noumea.[18] Whenegay, by now old enough to take over the chiefship of Fayawe, attempted to stand above the factionalism within his chiefdom and refused to support either the Catholic or Protestant missionaries. But he soon found himself siding with the Protestants as Waesolot, who led the Catholic forces in Fayawe after Ombalu's departure, challenged Whenegay's right to the chiefship. Whenegay burnt Waesolot's hut and then found himself, along with all the Protestants, besieged in his fortification in the village of Fayawe by Waesolot and most of the Uvean Catholics. Whenegay held out for two months until thirst and hunger finally drove him and the Protestants to submit.[19] The priests were jubilant. Jean Nestor Pionnier wrote to a friend: 'Finally . . . I can shout—Victory!' and Jacques Roussel noted: 'St Michel has once again crushed the Devil'.[20] The French Resident on Lifu rushed to Uvea and had Waesolot and some twenty-nine supporters imprisoned in Noumea.[21]

The submission of the Protestants effectively brought to an end the worst of the violence on Uvea, and resulted in a relatively stable political arrangement in the district of Fayawe. Ella described the Protestants' miserable condition: 'Instead of our flourishing villages, all was ruin and destruction; not a house standing only charred posts and debris'.[22] To Ella's horror Whenegay went to Noumea to plead for the release of Ombalu, for without his support and influence he could not hope to have any authority over the Fayawe district. Governor Richerie agreed to his request and Ombalu returned to the acclaim of the majority of the population.[23] Having made his peace with the Catholic supporters and Ombalu, who held the effective power, Whenegay had to remain content as the nominal great chief. The Protestants were in no mood to continue their fight and settled down quietly to the task of reconstruction. Since they acknowledged their submission to both Whenegay and Ombalu, they were allowed to practise their religion provided it was divorced from any political aspirations.[24]

After the Fayawe siege the French took a more active interest in Uvea and, although they did not provide a resident during the remainder of the century, their warships visited the lagoon some four or five times a year as a warning that soldiers could be landed there as easily as they had been at Chepenehe.

The tensions among the Islanders were further eased by the departure of the abrasive missionaries. The Lifu Resident's detailed denunciations of Roussel and Pionnier caused the Marist Mission in Noumea some embarrassment—Bishop Vitte admitted: 'Unfortunately . . . our Fathers were too much involved in the affair [the siege at Fayawe], and excited their neophytes instead of seeking peace'.[25] Roussel left Uvea in 1874 and Pionnier left the year after; Ella also returned to London in 1875. Once the fighting had ended, and with their majority support, the priests who took over from Roussel and Pionnier were able to extend their mission activity and turn Uvea into the Catholic showplace of the Loyalty Islands. The Protestants were in a weak position compared with those on Mare or Lifu. James Hadfield took over Ella's station at Fayawe from 1879 until 1886 and from then on made only brief visits until 1920; after 1886 there was no permanent Protestant missionary on Uvea until the 1930s. Under Hadfield's guidance the Protestant population stabilised at about 700 and was limited to the villages of Fayawe, Banut, Wadrilla, and Wakat.[26]

In Muli, Ohwen, and Fayawe, the Dumai, Bazit, and Whenegay/Ombalu chiefships, with the aid of the Marists and their laws and with the theoretical justification provided by Guillain's 1865 regulations, had an intensive control over and beyond their particular chiefdoms. Bazit was the most successful, having brought the chiefdoms of Beka, Imwene, and Nekelo closely under his supervision, and having expelled Owa.[27] Ombalu, too, had finally imposed his will upon the reluctant clans who had clung to Protestantism as their means of independence. But when placed in perspective with Uvea's recent pre-history such developments were by no means unprecedented. Although they were influenced by European presence they were essentially a continuation of the pre-contact processes of the regrouping and rearranging of areas of political control.

The French administration was next forced to turn its attention to Mare where the turbulent nature of indigenous politics delayed until 1895 the peace and political stability achieved on Lifu by 1871 and Uvea by 1875.

8
Mare 1866–1895

The struggle between Naisiline Nidoish, who ruled the north-western half of Mare and was supported by the LMS missionaries, and the southern and eastern tribes associated with the Marist missionaries remained a dominant theme of Mare's political history.

Like Ombalu on Uvea, Naisiline Nidoish had watched in great anguish as the French soldiers closed down the LMS mission on Lifu and forced the Lifuan great chiefs to submit to their will. Although Guillain was censured by the Paris government for the conduct of his expedition, Naisiline Nidoish remained constantly fearful of French intervention on Mare. Although he squabbled with the Catholic tribes over issues of land, and supported those few individuals who wished to challenge their Catholic chiefs,[1] not until 1869 did he pluck up courage to launch an all-out attack on the tribes to the south and east, and then in a manner calculated to pander to Guillain's anti-clericalism; abandoning his earlier 'chief of Jehovah' war cry, he marched instead under a tricolour, which he had procured from the French Commandant on Lifu, and claimed that he was the 'Napoleon of Mare' out to end the 'lawlessness' fomented by the priests and put the Catholic tribes in 'their proper order'. He destroyed the principal Catholic villages including the priests' posts at Awi, Penelo, and La Roche. Both Guitta and Beaulieu together with some 600 supporters took refuge on *titi* at La Roche.[2] The LMS missionaries were jubilant, for their patron had finally conquered the whole of the island, but they had to convince the commandant on Lifu that the Protestants' actions had been justified. Naisiline Nidoish hastily paddled to Chepenehe but Beaulieu arrived before him and gave his story to the official; when Naisiline Nidoish set foot ashore he was imprisoned for several weeks.[3] Although the Guillain administration had no desire actively to protect the Marist Mission on Mare it did want to limit Naisiline Nidoish's and the LMS missionaries' influence to the north-west of the island. But it could not afford to send a sufficient number of soldiers to check any future aggressions, and the priests, fearful that the Si Gwahma chief would soon return to the attack, transported the 900 Mare Catholics to the Isle of Pines.[4] The LMS missionaries believed that Mare was truly 'won for Christ'[5] and for the next five years they and Naisiline Nidoish reigned supreme.

In 1875 most of the Mare Catholics and the priests returned. Their stay at the Isle of Pines had been an unhappy one mainly because they outnumbered the Isle of Pines' population and food resources were strained.[6] Moreover the French administration was eager to see them leave because it was preparing the island as a prison for the deportees from the Paris Commune. The LMS missionaries were outraged that the Catholics should be allowed to return to their former lands and still be considered independent from Naisiline Nidoish for, they argued, they were his subjects according to the 'etiquette' of Marean warfare.[7] These missionaries never considered their contradictory attitudes towards indigenous warfare: when it suited them to abide by 'native law', as in Naisiline Nidoish's case, they vehemently did so, but when such laws were to their disadvantage, as in the case of the defeated Uvean Protestants, they always reverted to the 'higher' laws of 'European justice'. But instead of resorting to intimidation Naisiline Nidoish opened a campaign on the diplomatic front, doubtless under the inspiration of Jones.[8] In November 1875 Naisiline Nidoish organised a 'constitutional convention' at Netche and announced the formation of a Parliament of Mare with an upper and lower house and with himself as leader. He also presented himself with a petition begging that he might assume the chiefship over all of Mare. When few of his enemies attended the meeting he forged their signatures on the petition. The documents were written in the Mare language and in English and sent to Governor Leopold de Pritzbuer in Noumea for approval; Pritzbuer repudiated them.[9]

Naisiline Nidoish immediately re-involved himself in the local squabbles over land and rights to chiefship among the southern and eastern tribes.[10] In the late 1870s the French administration sent four commissions to mark out boundaries beyond which Naisiline Nidoish was not to go, and to try to sort out the issues dividing the rest of Mare.[11] All their attempts were unsuccessful, although Naisiline Nidoish's refusal to accept the findings of one commission earned him six months working on a government farm in New Caledonia, and several of his allies from the south and east who challenged their Catholic chiefs for leadership were exiled to Tahiti.[12] Any inquiries into the problems of land ownership and rights to chiefships in the south and east of the island led immediately to evidence of the massacre of the *eletok*. Much of the unrest on Mare, the French officials realised, resulted from the political and territorial division of the island since that time. One commission noted in despair that it was impossible to adjudicate to the Islanders' satisfaction because there was not one village on the whole island that was possessed by the original owners and that chiefs had 'always made war to increase their powers and their domains'.[13] The French officials' task was made none the easier by missionaries who did their utmost to impress them with vast amounts of historical detail and genealogies echoing either true or, as was more often the case, distorted accounts given them by their informants.[14] Even the missionaries themselves became a little discouraged by the constant squabbling over these issues and began to lose patience with some of their supporters: the Islanders seemed to be making more use of the missionaries than the missionaries were of the Islanders. Jones explained that it was 'difficult to get the chiefs to distinguish between the political and ecclesiastical. They would like to rule in both departments'.[15] Lubin Gaide, who replaced Guitta, thought the Mareans were:

> ... naturally and essentially battlers, they know only to hit, they reflect after they have done something terrible. They are always quarrelling ... over the boundaries of their land. In their hearts, full of such ideas, ... christian virtues take root with difficulty, and any roots are still shallow. Our plague on Mare is the jealousy between chiefs and tribes. We have 3 chiefs of tribes, or great chiefs, and it is impossible for us to establish a union among them; when two are together, the other is enraged with jealousy, and continually tries to destroy the excellent harmony between the other two—you already know that the majority of the population of Mare is protestant; even today we have obtained few conversions.[16]

> All the Mare affairs always were, and still are caused by everyone's claims to land; and this contesting of property is not only between individuals, but between tribes.[17]

Naisiline Nidoish died in 1880 at the age of sixty-five. He was much eulogised by Jones as the grand old man of the Protestant cause on Mare;

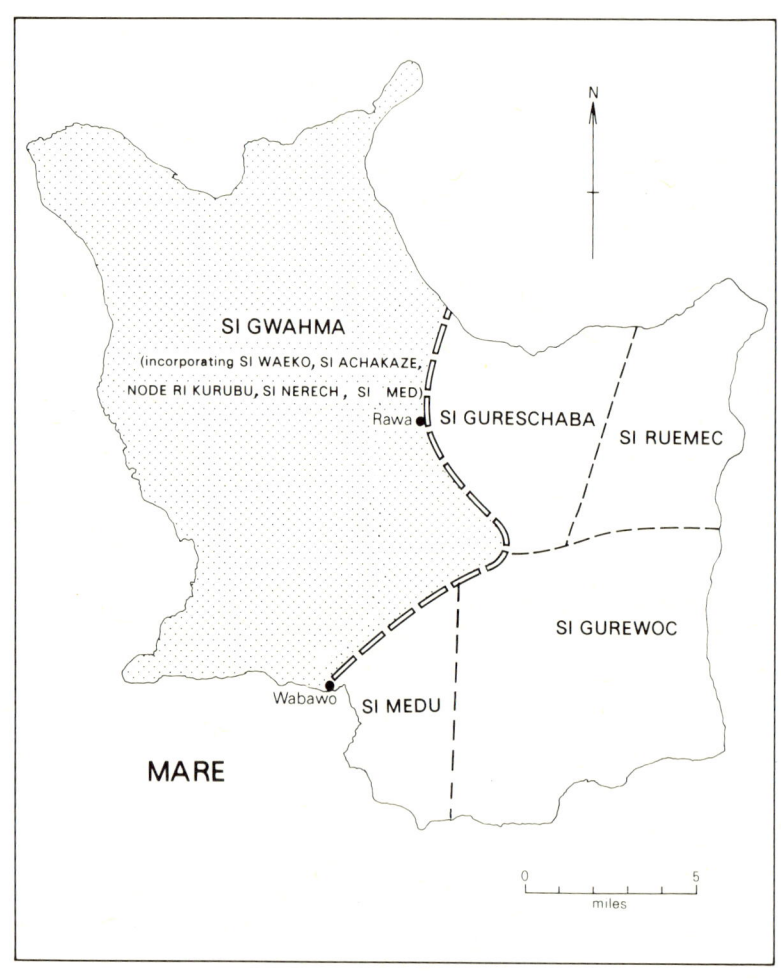

MAP 5   Mare. Si Gwahma control in the 1870s

Gaide and Beaulieu bid him good riddance.[18] Yiewene Dokucas Naisiline, Naisiline Nidoish's son, took over the Si Gwahma chiefship. Aged thirty, he had been virtually brought up in the Jones family and had received a good deal of English middle-class schooling; he had even briefly visited England with Jones in the late 1860s. Jones hoped that Yiewene's staunchness in religious matters and his devotion to the church combined with his youthful enthusiasm might well inspire his people to renew attempts to spread Protestantism throughout the rest of Mare. Jones was delighted therefore when, one month after assuming the chiefship, Yiewene threw caution to the winds and destroyed the Catholics' villages at Awi, Penelo, and La Roche; for the second time in ten years the priests and the Mare Catholics took refuge on top of the coral fortress at La Roche.[19] When they refused to submit to Yiewene he scoured the countryside for stray enemy parties and rounded up numbers of women and children who had been unable to reach safety in time and were hiding in the bush. Thirteen of the children were battered to death with coral boulders on Yiewene's orders. Jones commented that some 'of the Protestants committed cruel deeds and forgot the principles of religion they had been taught by killing some of the male children', but, he added, Yiewene at least refrained from killing their mothers:

> ... indeed they behaved most kindly to them and their children were not killed promiscuously. It was an attempt to wipe out an old score where both infants, women and chiefs were all treacherously & most barbarously massacred in the night by this same party. Who can wonder that a man, in hot blood should wish to take vengeance on the child of the man, who had disembowelled his mother great with child, as well as murdered other near relations.[20]

As for the damage to the villages and plantations, Jones dismissed it lightly: 'The destruction of native property was of course legitimate in time of war'.[21]

In contrast to its mild reaction to the 1869 attack, the Noumean administration, sick and tired of the continuing trouble on Mare, immediately dispatched a warship and exiled to Cochin-China fifteen of Yiewene's allies from amongst the southern and eastern tribes.[22] Their removal brought an end to the fighting if not the hostility between Catholics and Protestants over issues of land and chiefships and, as eleven of the exiles died by 1882 through illness and utter despondency in the harsh climate and conditions,[23] aspirants to chiefly positions dared not to antagonise the French any further. The return to peaceful conditions in the south and east was celebrated by a 'Peace Feast' held at La Roche by the priests in 1882 and was attended by Catholic and Protestant Islanders from all over Mare.[24]

The loss of his allies and influence in these regions was of little moment to Yiewene, however, for he had to face far more serious consequences within his own chiefdom. To save himself from exile he swore undying loyalty to the French administration and promised to break his ties with Jones and the LMS mission. The French officials spared him, not because they were fooled by his overnight change of heart, but because they believed that the only way to achieve a lasting peace on Mare was to secure the support of the most powerful chief.[25] They were also determined to eradicate once and for all the anti-French prejudices of Yiewene's people. In 1883 one French official drew up a report on Mare and concluded the island was 'French only in name'; the real influence, he claimed, was 'English exercised by the protestant missionaries'. He likened Mare to an English colony where everyone spoke English, dressed in English clothes, and adopted English manners and customs, and he was disgusted to see pictures and paintings of Queen Victoria in many of the Protestants' huts: 'It is a situation contrary to the national dignity, harmful to our interests and one which we must try to modify'.[26] Visitors to the island invariably commented on the Protestants' sentiments of 'continual ill-feeling, insubordination and even rebellion' towards the French.[27] The administration laid the blame squarely on Jones's shoulders, and also held him responsible for all the tribal fighting. Their charge that he had caused the war of 1880[28] was perhaps exaggerated, although Jones made it perfectly clear that he supported Yiewene's campaign, and his sermons exhorting the Si Gwahma 'Christian soldiers' to win the island for Christ doubtless helped to incite popular enthusiasm for the war. Jones always denied involvement in the Islanders' politics, although the French officials could scarcely be blamed for not believing him, since he wrote scores of letters to the administration throughout the 1870s and early 1880s declaring that the Catholics were rebels and should submit to Yiewene, and that the war of 1880 was God's way of punishing those responsible for 'continual rebellion'.[29] Since 1870 numerous Governors of New Caledonia had considered expelling Jones[30] but because of the diplomatic pressure the LMS was continually bringing to bear on the Paris government through the British Foreign Office,[31] the Noumean administration was hesitant to take such a step for fear of 'international consequences'.[32]

Late in 1883 the Noumean authorities sent a French Protestant missionary, Jean-Pierre Cru, to Mare in an attempt to combat the English influences of the LMS mission without upsetting the Protestants' religious scruples. Cru tried to take over the running of the church and joined forces with Yiewene. Jones and the Marean church officials, together with the majority of the Si Gwahma tribe, were horrified by Cru's presence and his association with their great chief. When it was discovered that Cru was not a member of an accredited missionary society Jones vilified him as a 'paid state agent'. Yiewene's popularity dropped dramatically and Jones gave the Protestant church its independence from the LMS and encouraged the Mare pastors and all their supporters to rebel against Cru and Yiewene.[33] The resulting schism between the church hierarchy and the chiefship left Yiewene powerless. In 1886 he complained to the Noumean administration, 'the religious question has become a political question and two parties that are enemies have formed in my land'—a minority following him and France, and a majority owing allegiance to Jones and England: 'This [latter] party refuses to obey me and ignores my authority. I know that this resistance is intended as a revolt against my chiefship and aspires to independence, and I come to ask you for advice and protection'.[34] Yiewene, although tempted to transfer his loyalty back to Jones and so unite his chiefdom, was well aware that the French government ultimately held the power throughout the Loyalty Islands. Relying on French backing, he and some trusted henchmen attacked and imprisoned a number of Mare pastors who were openly advocating rebellion against him.[35] The French government quickly exiled the pastors to the Isle of Pines and New Caledonia and the rift in the Si Gwahma chiefdom assumed more serious proportions. A number of individuals who had long harboured grudges against the Naisiline leadership openly displayed their feelings.[36] Gocene, the former great chief of the Si Achakaze who had been defeated by Yiewene's father in 1860, had long awaited his chance to even the score. He travelled around the north and west showing off his scarred neck where he had been speared at the time of his defeat and claimed that he would lead the people from the tyranny of Yiewene and the French. Some 2500 Mareans from amongst the Si Gwahma, Si Waeko, and Si Achakaze tribes followed him inland and settled between Menaku and La Roche; only 400 people remained loyal to Yiewene.[37]

By turning against the church organisation which had helped to make the Naisiline chiefship the most powerful on Mare, Yiewene brought the chiefship to the nadir of its fortunes: no longer could it command its own people let alone any other tribes on Mare. Ironically, however, although Yiewene lost his chiefdom, he was among the first of his people to realise and accept the political reality that Mare was a French territory: to attempt to dominate the rest of the island, to cultivate anti-French influences, and to adopt pretensions of independence were impossible for the Naisilines as long as France controlled New Caledonia. It took ten years for the majority of the Si Gwahma to adopt a similar view.

Until 1895 the 'bush party' led by Gocene and proclaiming its allegiance to Jones and England lived apart from the 'sea party' which supported Yiewene and the French. The Noumean administration made some effort to unite the two factions by removing Cru, expelling Jones in 1887,[38] and exiling Gocene to the Isle of Pines. But the French were reluctant to force the bush party to return. So strongly did the party identify with Jones, and in view of the public outcry in Britain and Australia against his expulsion, the French had no wish to aggravate matters further. But by the mid-1890s the bush party's resolve flagged. Having lost all its militant leaders, aware that the French had no intention of ever allowing another LMS missionary to set foot on the island, and realising that the administration did not want to destroy its church, the bush party rejoined Yiewene and agreed to obey the French.[39] The uniting of the two groups was symbolised in the acceptance in 1898 of a member of the Société des Missions Evangéliques de Paris, to whom the LMS officially transferred the Protestant mission on Mare.

Interlude: A Review of Political Change

The 'pacification' of Mare marked the end of the religious, national, and indigenous political conflicts which characterised much of the history of the Loyalty Islands in the nineteenth century; the major disputes between Catholicism and Protestantism, between English and French influences, and between rival indigenous interests had largely been settled. Henceforth the islands were to be of minimal concern to those European groups most involved in nineteenth-century internal affairs—the LMS and Marist Missions and the administrators in Noumea.

At this point it is appropriate to review briefly the major themes of indigenous political change largely occasioned by the presence of these three interest groups. There were two notable developments in indigenous politics—the division of each of the Loyalty Islands into areas of Protestant and Catholic support, and a strengthening of chiefly authority. The former was permanent, the latter temporary.

The religious division of the islands had two significant features. Once there was a permanent representative of each mission on an island, the inhabitants classified themselves quickly with the general lines often quite apparent some years beforehand. The division had taken place on Uvea by 1864, Lifu by 1858, and Mare by 1866. Once it was complete, so strong were the Islanders' associations with their chosen mission that in spite of all the subsequent hostilities the areas of respective mission influence remained essentially unchanged. The Protestants were dominant on Mare and Lifu, with the Catholics limited mainly to Eacho, Nathalo, and Dueulu on Lifu, and La Roche, Penelo, and Medu on Mare. By the 1880s, the Catholics numbered some 950 out of a total population of about 6500 on Lifu, and 800 out of the Mare population of about 3600. The figures were reversed on Uvea where, by the same time, the Protestants numbered 700 out of a population of just over 2000. The ratio of Catholics to Protestants on all three islands was virtually the same as at the time of the initial division. Even today the religious divisions of the islands are virtually identical, indicating that traditional kin and political affiliations still determine which church the Islanders choose to follow.

The missionaries, especially those of the LMS, conferred upon their patron chiefs considerable socio-economic status and strengthened their personal power with laws, policemen, and teachers. Chiefs like Naisiline Nidoish, Bazit, Ombalu, and Bula assumed an unprecedented control over the everyday activities of individuals within and beyond their chiefdoms. Mission presence enabled these chiefs to become the despots which many Europeans had erroneously always considered them to be. At the height of mission influence a great chief's obligations within the tribal fraternity and the built-in limits to his personal authority were seriously weakened. Government influence upon the power of the great chiefs was only minor in this respect: the regulations defining the position of a great chief certainly sanctioned an increased authority, but the rulings probably meant more on paper than they did in practice. The only time the administration worked directly through the great chiefs was on Lifu from 1864 until 1870 when it compelled them to supply men for the *corvées*.

It is important to emphasise the distinction between a great chief's personal authority as opposed to any new structural authority given him by the missionaries. Despotic chiefly powers were largely dependent upon the character of the individual chief, as well as upon the nature of his European assistance, and were not automatically inherited by his successor, as Naisiline Nidoish's son found to his distress.

The most fundamental difference between the political situation in 1840 and that in 1900 was that by the latter date there was peace, and a permanence given to boundaries of chiefdoms. Great chiefs were no longer subject to challenges by ambitious men from within their own chiefdoms, nor were they able to extend their chiefdoms into other lands. Peace and political stability coincided with a weakening of both mission and chiefly authority. The more militant missionaries had departed, would-be leaders feared exile if they caused further trouble and, less obviously, the missionary-inspired power structures in the larger chiefdoms were increasingly irrelevant in times of peace. Chiefly despotism was far more difficult to maintain without politico-religious crises and/or expansionist drives. By the late nineteenth and early twentieth centuries the pre-missionary structures of great chiefdoms slowly reasserted themselves, although all members of the hierarchy remained at least nominally Christian. In particular, councils of elders once again became effective bodies in aiding and also limiting great chiefs' authority. Both the Protestant and Catholic missions remained powerful influences on the Loyalty Islands but lost much of their old militancy and with it their ability to control individuals closely.

The reversion to more traditional forms of political control was aided by the Noumean administration's lack of interest in the economically insignificant Loyalty Islands once the troubles were over. French officials had no need to have chiefs carry out any major administrative functions, in contrast to the situation on New Caledonia where the government wanted as much land as possible to exploit its agricultural and mineral potential, was intent upon a policy of *cantonnement*, and was concerned with defining and strengthening chiefly authority which it could conceivably exploit. The government made no attempts to impose any European administrative structure upon the Loyalty Islanders' own socio-political organisations and, indeed, the residents on Lifu were strictly forbidden to do so. Although the Islanders may have disliked the French they had no cause to rebel against the administration as did many New Caledonians in the latter part of the nineteenth and early twentieth centuries. Spared from the demands of government men, the Loyalty Islanders' way of life was further protected when the islands were declared 'Native Reserves' in 1900, isolating the populations from the usual consequences of large-scale European settlement and loss of land.

In the twentieth century the French government has generally remained content to rule through the existing chiefs and their hierarchies, and present-day administrative districts coincide with the boundaries of the later nineteenth century chiefdoms. Loyalty Islands chiefships continue to have structures more akin to their pre-European organisations than to those inspired by the missionaries at the height of their influence in the mid-nineteenth century.

Adventure and Advantage

Adventure and Advantage 85

One common theme of the Islanders' responses to Europeans dominates the contact history of the Loyalty Islands as outlined so far—the Islanders' ability to grasp the opportunities provided by European presence, particularly by manipulating and attempting to turn to their own individual or collective advantage both the divergent religious and national interests of the French government, and the Marist and LMS missionaries. And in their reactions to other aspects of European presence the Islanders displayed similar initiative, enthusiasm, and aggression.

While much of the history of nineteenth-century culture contacts on the Loyalty Islands necessarily centres on religious, national, and indigenous political conflicts there are other major contemporaneous themes which deserve detailed investigation for the further light they shed on the nature of the Islanders' responses to the European world and the consequences for the islands' communities. Three of the most striking developments which began in the 1840s and continued into the twentieth century were the Islanders' enthusiasm for travelling and working overseas, their eagerness and expertise in trading with Europeans, and their devotion to the Christian religions and their responsiveness to European example and teaching.

9
Travel

Loyalty Islanders immediately took advantage of commercial shipping by sailing as crews or travelling to labour in other countries in return for payment. Almost without exception visiting Europeans considered the Islanders a 'superior race' among those in the south-west Pacific and wrote in glowing terms of their ability to excel as sailors on the trading vessels.

> Through all the South Seas . . . no men are more noted for bravery than those of this group; so that if there is any reckless expedition or voyage of discovery on hand, the promoter always endeavours to obtain a Loyalty Island crew.[1]

> The men, especially those of Maré, make good sailors and boatmen, and are in great request among traders and whalers. As swimmers and divers they stand in the foremost rank, even among South Sea Islanders.[2]

> Brave, intelligent, trustworthy, there are no natives of the South Seas whom I so much respect.[3]

As well as exploiting the fine stands of sandalwood on the Loyalty Islands, the earliest traders were quick to appreciate and utilise the Islanders' maritime skills and made innumerable calls to hire crews before continuing on to New Caledonia or the New Hebrides to cut wood there. As early as 1846 one French traveller reported that every English ship he saw in New Caledonian waters had Loyalty Islands crew members and that the masters habitually put into Mare in particular to take on 'a great number' of men as sailors and labourers, as well as women for 'wives'.[4] Although the san-

Travel

dalwood was cut out of the Loyalty Islands by the early 1850s, they continued as a focal point for sandalwood trading activities because of the reputation the Islanders had as excellent sailors and their willingness to labour for Europeans. Henry Burns's station on Uvea, which became a major entrepôt for sandalwood trading in the south-west Pacific from 1856 until 1861, was dependent upon Loyalty Islands crews and labourers. His vessels sailed to other islands to gather the wood, returned to Uvea where it was cleaned and processed, and then sailed with it to Canton where it was sold. Three-quarters of the crews on four of his ships, *Cheetah*, *Vulture*, *Coquette*, and *Adolphus Yates*, consisted of Loyalty Islanders.[5] Ross Lewin, who was employed by Burns, often enlisted up to 100 Islanders at a time to cut and prepare sandalwood. Burns commented that when these men were returned and paid off they were eager to set sail again.[6] When Burns left Uvea in 1861 because of French pressure, he set up a station on Aneityum in the New Hebrides but still continued to employ Loyalty Islanders on his vessels and in cutting and cleaning parties. Other traders, prominent men like Andrew Henry, Charles Edwards, and Hugh Mair, with stations on Eromanga and elsewhere throughout the New Hebrides, similarly hired Loyalty Islanders.[7] In the 1850s, when the Australian gold rushes made European labour in the Pacific scarce and expensive, a typical sandalwood vessel's complement was that of Captain Streeter's *New Forest* with three Englishmen, one American, four Tahitians, two Maoris, and thirty-two Lifuans.[8] The policy of intensive recruitment of Loyalty Islanders continued unabated until the sandalwood trade in the south-west Pacific petered out in the mid-1860s, but by then other trading concerns had centred their attention on the Loyalty Islands and the inhabitants found themselves in more demand than ever as sailors and labourers.

The channel between New Caledonia and the Loyalty Islands forms a migratory passage for whales and some time in July, August, or September whales were (and still are) plentiful in the bay at Tadine on Mare and more especially in Sandalwood Bay on Lifu. While little is yet known of the extent of the whaling trade in New Caledonian waters it was undoubtedly considerable during the season, for throughout the 1860s and 1870s there are numerous references to English, French, and especially American whalers operating from and around the Loyalty Islands and employing local labour.[9] Boiling-down stations were set up along the west coasts of Mare and Lifu. Present-day inhabitants at Eacho in Sandalwood Bay tell stories passed on by their forefathers about whaling vessels in the bay and the activities of the 'many' Europeans at the station. They describe how the ships had two sets of crews so that when one returned exhausted from a chase the second could leap on board and so keep the ship in constant use. Such an operation was essential, for the whales, though plentiful, might stay for only a few days.

But by far the greatest number of visitors to the Loyalty Islands were Englishmen trading in island produce who began their operations out of Sydney in the 1850s and then, by the 1860s, out of Noumea on the local New Caledonian, Isle of Pines, and Loyalty Islands run, and on a larger circuit taking in the New Hebrides. Until 1886 at least 1000 visits by licensed traders from Noumea to the Loyalty Islands were recorded.[10] Apart from collecting Loyalty Islands goods for the flourishing trade in tropical exports from New Caledonia, the traders called to discharge and sign on crews for, as one of them explained, the vessels on the circuit were 'principally manned by natives of the [Loyalty] islands, who take service on the understanding that they are to be returned to their own country at some future time'.[11] It was also not 'an uncommon practice for captains (white men) of small crafts plying up and down the east coast of Nouvelle Calédonie, to take unto themselves Mare or Lifu women for wives'. By all accounts they too were excellent sailors:

> These women are, as a rule, massive, well built, and, notwithstanding a few tattooed lines on their faces, pleasant looking. They know how to splice a rope, and to take the tiller when required; they are most useful to their mates, and behave in a more creditable manner than many of the dusky females from other Pacific Islands do . . . . South Sea Island women, even if they are ornamental, must be useful; and white men who live with them reckon their value according as they display plenty of 'savey' as well as personal attractiveness.[12]

There were many other vessels, not licensed by the French, which sought Loyalty Islands crews and labourers for other areas of the Pacific. These vessels are difficult to identify as their captains, again mostly English, were anxious to avoid the Noumean officials who were becoming increasingly alarmed at the number of English ships which they felt were monopolising trade and, in by-passing Noumea, hindering the commercial development of the colony. Perhaps more importantly the French administration thought that such traders were influencing the Islanders with their 'Englishness', and were 'illegally' employing French subjects. As early as 1855 it was forbidden for European traders to land on French territories where there were no resident officials, as was the case on the Loyalty Islands until one went to Lifu in 1864, and all who wished to go ashore had first to sail to Noumea for permission and to declare any firearms. But French naval patrols were few and far between and there were numerous clandestine visits by English traders throughout the 1860s. Captains recruited Loyalty Islanders for bêche-de-mer fishing in the Admiralty Islands and Torres Strait. Merriman had three ships, *Telegraph*, *Metaris*, and *Blue Bell*, working full-time on the Sydney, Loyalty Islands, Torres Strait circuit. Burns and other captains took Loyalty Islanders on pearl diving expeditions to the Belep Islands.[13] As on the local trading circuit, strong bonds of friendship were often built up between English captains and their Loyalty Islands crews. Merriman had a Lifuan as his personal servant and Captain Banner married a Lifu woman and sent their children to school in Sydney.[14]

When labour recruiting for Queensland plantations began in the New Hebrides in the mid-1860s and the Solomon Islands in the 1870s, Loyalty Islanders were sought after as crews and 'boat bosses' for the recruiting vessels. Lewin always used, he said, a 'black crew' when he went ashore to sign on labourers. He, and other recruiters, made a point of calling at the Loyalty Islands on their way northwards from Australia, picking up a crew, sailing on to the New Hebrides to gather labourers, and then discharging the crew at the Loyalty Islands on his return voyage.[15] French officials were incensed that 'nearly all' English recruiting vessels they came across in New Caledonian and New Hebridean waters had some Loyalty Islanders among their crews.[16]

The policy of recruiting Loyalty Islanders to serve on English commercial ships was a long-standing one by the 1860s, for there were few English vessels working regularly in the south-west Pacific from the 1840s onwards without some Loyalty Islanders on board. It is difficult to give any accurate indication of the numbers who did sail. For tasks involving a high labour content, such as cutting and cleaning sandalwood, and pearl and bêche-de-mer diving, it was not uncommon for forty or fifty, or even up to 100 islanders at a time to sign on.[17] Smaller numbers were needed as sailors for the local coastal shipping or for labour recruiting, but given the extent of such contacts over long periods of time, the overall total would have been very considerable. Without doubt those Loyalty Islanders who sailed about the Pacific would have formed a significant proportion of the population of about 12,500 in the mid-1860s. The missionaries frequently remarked on the Islanders' overseas experience. In 1857 the LMS missionaries reported: 'Many of the young men . . . have been away in ships to California, Sydney, and other places', and the Marists noted in 1861: 'The passion for travel, to see other countries, to become like *Whitemen*, to be admired, often takes possession of the young men; and many, leaving their islands, are happy to cross the seas'.[18]

In addition to being keen sailors, Loyalty Islanders were eager to labour in Australia. As early as 1847 Captains Kirsopp and Lancaster were ordered by Benjamin Boyd to the Loyalty Islands in the *Portenia* and *Velocity* where they recruited over seventy young men from Lifu and Uvea. Boyd intended to employ them as farm labourers in New South Wales but for some reason most of them jumped ship at Rotuma and were later returned to their islands by other vessels.[19] After Boyd's ill-fated labour experiment in the 1840s there was no large-scale organised recruitment of Pacific Islanders to labour in Australia until the 1860s. But during this time many Loyalty Islanders made their way independently to Australia as crews on ships and it was common for them to work on the Sydney waterfront. The capitalist Robert Towns employed them on his wharves from the early 1840s and Burns was in the habit of bringing them to Sydney.[20]

The first Queensland recruiting ships reached the Loyalty Islands in 1865 and until 1874 thirty-nine visits can be documented.[21] The real number was undoubtedly greater because of the clandestine nature of recruiting necessary to escape hostile French attention. Recruiting activities at the Loyalty Islands tailed off in the early 1870s not only as a result of French protests to the British and Australian governments, but also because most of those Loyalty Islands men willing and able to go had already done so, and the Solomon Islands by then provided a far greater source of labour for the recruiters. Those Loyalty Islanders who wanted to leave still had ample opportunity to do so as crews for recruiting vessels and local coastal shipping, and as labourers for the newly developing mines in New Caledonia. Loyalty Islanders were never recruited for Fiji.

There is limited information on the number of Loyalty Islanders who worked in Queensland. When the Polynesian Labourers Act was passed in March 1868 there were reported to be 438 Loyalty Islanders already there.[22] From this date until the end of recruiting on the Loyalty Islands in the early 1870s another 560 officially went to Queensland.[23] The correct figure is probably higher as a Royal Commission in 1869 was told that 567 Loyalty Islanders had been recruited in 1868–1869.[24] But even to accept the official total of 998 would mean that at least 8 per cent of all Loyalty Islanders (and at least 16 per cent of all males) at some time during an eight-year period worked in Queensland. Taking into account the possibilities of a larger figure, as well as the number who worked on sandalwood,

Travel

whaling, and other trading vessels, some idea can be gained of the very considerable number of Loyalty Islanders who travelled and worked with Englishmen around the Pacific. 'The young men from the ships', said Jones, 'on board vessels going to Australia and the other parts of the world, pick up English, and they come back; and *almost all* have gone at one time or another'.[25]

Probably no other episode in the history of European activities in the Pacific has received more condemnation from historians and others than the labour recruitment for the Queensland and Fijian plantations from the mid-1860s onwards. Until recently most writers have unquestioningly accepted the anti-labour trade propaganda conducted by missionaries and other humanitarians in the later nineteenth century. The trade was branded as kidnapping and slavery which, it was claimed, rivalled the worst excesses of the earlier African slave trade. A recent study of the trade in the Solomon Islands using primary material has effectively demonstrated that such emotive opinions generally bore little relation to the reality of recruiting,[26] and the same appears to be the case for the Loyalty Islands.

Accusations of 'slave trading' were common long before the Queensland trade began. The New South Wales authorities inquired into the activities of Lancaster and Kirsopp at the Loyalty Islands in the 1840s. Both men hotly denied charges of kidnapping and described how the Islanders flocked about their ships and how some even swam 10 miles out to sea to board them. Kirsopp stressed that those who signed on were 'in the habit of trading with Europeans', which was certainly true, and Lancaster explained how he instructed the Islanders in the principles of contract labour and their duties in Australia.

> ... they would have to work minding Cattle and Sheep for 60 moons. They have no Cattle and Sheep of their own—but three of the Natives were up at Sydney and went back and from them they learnt what cattle and sheep were—I could not explain anything about money to them but I told them they would have muskets and powder, Shirts and Trousers and plenty to eat.[27]

Captain Oliver in HMS *Fly* made further investigations into rumours of kidnapping in New Caledonian waters in the early 1850s. Though he did not visit Mare or Lifu he did talk to chiefs on Uvea and in his report made no mention of kidnapping there.[28] By the 1860s the French administration was becoming increasingly hostile to English ships 'illegally' taking away Loyalty Islanders as crews and labourers, and their anger was increased by their frustration at being powerless to do anything about it. The commandants stationed on Lifu from 1864 to 1870 spent many weary days marching soldiers to those places where they had heard a ship was taking on young men. Invariably the soldiers arrived exhausted and far too late to do anything beyond fire in the direction of disappearing sails.[29] By 1868 Governor Guillain was writing frequently to his minister in Paris begging him to take some action against the Queensland labour vessels which, he claimed, were 'tending to depopulate' the Loyalty Islands.[30] At the same time as these protests were being relayed to Sydney via diplomatic channels in Paris and London, some mission societies in Sydney and the Presbyterian missionaries in the New Hebrides were becoming vocal about what they felt was 'kidnapping' for Queensland and the treatment of the islanders as 'unwilling and helpless slaves'.[31] In March 1869 Commander Palmer was dispatched to Noumea with instructions to 'make inquiries into the kidnapping of natives at New Caledonia and its Dependencies'. He interviewed Guillain, who presented him with a list of ships alleged to have taken on Loyalty Islanders and made two complaints: that these Islanders had been taken against their will, and that he believed the 'missionaries themselves connive at the traffic'.[32]

Later the same year the New South Wales authorities established a Royal Commission to investigate 'certain alleged cases of kidnapping of natives of the Loyalty Islands'. All the traders and recruiters who gave evidence were adamant that force and deception were completely unnecessary to remove the Islanders. Burns testified that they were only too willing to work on his ships and that if he wished he could 'take the whole of the people away. There is no kidnapping about the matter; I never heard the word before in reference to the taking away of these people from their islands'. Henry and Merriman both expressed similar opinions. 'I do not think there is any necessity for kidnapping, or using any kind of force, to obtain these people. They always appeared to be willing to come on board when I was at the islands; and were ready enough to engage with anyone who would treat them well, and return them home at the proper time', said Merriman. Captain Lancelot Dawson declared that he could go to the Loyalty Islands 'and get a shipload of them without kidnapping one, because they know me and have confidence in me'; 'It seemed to be a voluntary emigration of these people. They were anxious to go'. The difficulty of deceiving the Loyalty Islanders was explained by James Row who argued that these people had 'superior knowledge' to other Islanders and could understand agreements because of missionary instruction and would argue

Travel

over and have changes made in unsatisfactory clauses of the contract before signing on. The necessity to be fair and develop friendly personal relationships with the Islanders was emphasised by all the traders and recruiters who gave evidence. And it is true that those masters who had bad reputations among the Islanders always had difficulty in getting them to sign on. One or two ships are known to have sailed from the islands without having recruited a single person while the next day the Islanders would flock on board another. As Burns very reasonably commented: 'You cannot trade with these people and fight them too'.[33]

Cynics might still argue that these men lied to the Commission to protect their vested interests, but such a charge could scarcely be levelled at the Loyalty Islands missionaries on this issue. They too were unanimous that the Islanders voluntarily sailed away. Creagh on Mare wrote: 'There is a great rage, almost a mania, for emigration to Queensland. We have scarcely any yg. men and lads left in the district'. He also said that all those who had gone to Australia from Mare and Lifu had 'left of their own free choice'.[34] On seeing his converts rush the recruiting vessels, Jones noted with resignation that the 'Captains of vessels are glad to engage them and they are glad to go'.[35] Similar statements were made by the Catholic missionaries: 'There is always a frenzy to leave for Sidni', said Lubin Gaide, and added that by the time boys reached the age of twelve to fifteen they felt they simply had to leave if the opportunity arose. Jean-Nestor Pionnier explained how the young men appeared happy and contented with their life on Uvea but as soon as an English ship arrived the urge to travel was so strong that they left without hesitation.[36] Claudius Joly, who acted as the Sydney agent for the Marists on the Loyalty Islands, told the Commission that 'the natives left willingly—that no compulsion, violence, nor unlawful means were used'.[37] And those Loyalty Islanders interviewed by the Commission all said that their countrymen were 'glad to go in an English ship, and to go to Queensland'.[38]

There were suggestions that, although the Islanders may have left for Queensland of their own free will, they did not understand that they were required to work for three years. Yet missionaries on the spot said that the people left with 'their eyes open' and were well aware of the terms of service,[39] and the general opinion among the traders and missionaries was that the Islanders knew they would be away for a long time—three yam seasons. Missionaries often explained the contracts to the Islanders and stressed the time they were required to work.[40] Also when the first people to go for three years returned, the enthusiasm among their families and friends to go to Queensland themselves was greater than ever—perhaps one of the most effective counters to the suggestion that the Islanders were taken by force and treated as slaves on the plantations. Another accusation was that chiefs were 'bribed' with goods by unscrupulous recruiters to send off their young men. There is no documentary evidence to support the claim, and present-day informants unanimously agree that chiefs never sent young men to Australia against their will. On the contrary it was hardly in a chief's interest to have his fittest young men away for so long, and there are instances of chiefs complaining that men had disobeyed their instructions and run off to Australia.[41] Chiefs were prepared to allow their men to go on short working cruises around New Caledonia and the New Hebrides, for they knew they would not be away for long and were well paid.

The Royal Commission concluded that the Loyalty Islanders had a 'migratory disposition' and that although there may have been isolated cases of unfair recruiting, Guillain's accusation that force and deception were used could not be upheld:

> ... the strongest desire is manifested by the natives ... of the Loyalty [Islands] ... to leave their homes, either to serve on board English ships, or to labour on the plantations of Queensland; and that any attempt to kidnap them would be not only unnecessary, but most impolitic, and even dangerous.[42]

There is no reason to doubt this conclusion, and even the French officials made similar statements some years later.[43] It is worth emphasising that, for more than twenty years before the Queensland labour trade began, Loyalty Islanders had been in the habit of signing contracts, travelling and working on European ships, and labouring in Australia. They were by no means the poor, ignorant savages intimidated or duped into slavery by unscrupulous whitemen as portrayed in much of the anti-labour trade propaganda.

Guillain's second complaint, that both Catholic and Protestant missionaries tolerated and even assisted the labour recruiters, needs some explanation. The Catholic missionaries were very much opposed to the young men leaving the islands and did what they could to persuade them to stay, not because they believed labour recruiting was in itself an evil, but because the church was suffering numerically by the departure of so many young men. In 1872 Gaide suggested that he may as well leave Lifu because so many Catholics had emigrated to Australia, and Pionnier in 1874 angrily complained that at his services there were only women and old men where previously the churches had always been full to overflowing with people of all ages.[44] The Marists' opposition to emigration was further heightened because their converts were going to an English country where Protestantism prevailed. Yet there was little point in their protesting to the French administration because the priests knew well that the Islanders left voluntarily.

Palmer was particularly puzzled by Guillain's accusation that the LMS missionaries were party to the 'traffic', for Palmer was aware of the complaints about 'kidnapping' by the Presbyterian missionaries in the New Hebrides and it seemed to him 'inconceivable that their brethren in the Loyalty Group should entertain opposite opinions'.[45] The protests against recruiting for Queensland in the New Hebrides by the Protestant missionaries do contrast with the attitudes of the Protestant missionaries on the Loyalty Islands for, like the Marists, not once did they make official complaints to anyone. Nevertheless they were opposed to the emigration and noted with dismay their diminishing numbers. In 1868 Creagh felt that unless something was done to stop the 'mania' for emigration the population of Mare would 'be destroyed'.[46] Women whose husbands had sailed away often took other men and the 'disputes and quarrels' when the men returned sorely troubled the LMS missionaries. They did what they could to persuade their converts to stay and in some cases they advised a chief to appoint 'policemen' in an attempt to hold the young men back, but to little avail. The missionaries had to accept the hard fact that the people wanted to go and there was nothing they could do about it. Instead they tried to make the best of the situation by explaining written contracts to would-be recruits and attempting to make sure the terms were fair.[47] Also the LMS missionaries consoled themselves with the knowledge that their converts were sailing to an English Christian country where they would not lose touch with the church and where it was indeed possible, the missionaries thought, for them to profit morally and socially from contact with 'civilisation'. Isolated themselves from 'civilisation' the missionaries tended to idealise Australia and were either ignorant of, or overlooked, the realities of colonial life. Jones praised the 'liberty enjoyed under English rule' that his converts would find in Australia.[48]

Underlying such rationalisations was the LMS missionaries' attitude to Guillain and his administration. No matter what reservations the missionaries might have had about the labour trade at the Loyalty Islands, it would have been inconceivable for them to have complained about the activities of fellow Englishmen, given Guillain's intense dislike of English influences close to New Caledonia. The missionaries had no intention of giving him the slightest justification for taking any action to inhibit the expansion of English religious and commercial interests. The French attitude therefore had a unifying effect upon most Englishmen of disparate occupations on or around New Caledonia, and consolidated the already friendly economic ties between the LMS missionaries on the Loyalty Islands and English traders of all kinds. Not only were the missionaries dependent upon these men for their own supplies and mail, but the prosperity of the mission depended upon the extent of trade with the Islanders. Ella on Uvea frequently dined with masters of recruiting vessels for, contrary to opinions expressed by missionaries elsewhere in the Pacific, they were not all drunken, godless scoundrels. On the Loyalty Islands their company as Englishmen was much appreciated by a missionary and his family.[49] The friendship between missionaries and traders worked two ways. Good relations with the missionaries eased the traders' task in dealing with the Islanders. Also traders sometimes took young men, often sons of chiefs, to Sydney, where they were shown theatres, railways, factories and other wonders so that on their return they were 'regarded as great men' by the other Islanders. Such a policy was said to promote 'a friendly feeling towards the traders'.[50]

The LMS missionaries, therefore, made no complaints about 'kidnapping' because they did not consider labour recruiting as practised at the Loyalty Islands to be so, and because any complaints to the French or English authorities would have been directed against Englishmen upon whom the missionaries depended and who were, as Englishmen, considered eminently superior to the French on New Caledonia. The success of Protestant missionary propaganda against the labour trade has not only been responsible for the commonly accepted sweeping and emotional generalisations as to the nature of the trade, but has also encouraged the notion that all Protestant missionaries were vehemently and unanimously opposed to recruiting which they labelled 'slave trading'. But on the Loyalty Islands LMS missionaries' opinions about the trade derived not from preconceived or popular ideas but from the circumstances of their island existence and the nature of the trade as they saw it.

One of the most common reasons for Loyalty Islanders working on English ships or in Australia was their love of travel and new experiences. When Erskine visited the Loyalty Islands in 1849 he was struck by the Islanders' 'love of wandering, for which they seem to be distinguished', and surrounded by people imploring him to take them to Sydney 'which word generally implies with all these islanders the country of the English strangers'.[51] The 'great disposition on the part of these men to travel' impressed Dawson, and Burns spoke of the 'great spirit of enterprise and adventure among them'. They are, he said, 'full of adventure, and like to be able to go about where they please—they do not like to be kept at home'.[52] Travellers, missionaries, and French administrators all emphasised the Islanders' enthusiasm for travel—'to nourish an inborn taste for sailing and the spirit of curiosity to see, to understand new things that they find in other people's countries'.[53]

Associated with the excitement of voyages were the opportunities for material gain. According to Captain Rees the Islanders wanted to go to 'Queensland, or anywhere,—that they did not wish to stop longer at the Loyalty Islands, but to go and get clothes and money'.[54] And there is no doubt that overseas trips were profitable, for the Islanders proudly returned with large quantities of the goods they most wanted—tools, cloth, and tobacco. One English captain who returned two Lifu women after they had been working for Europeans for two years was amazed at all their goods which half filled his boat and which 'in variety as well as quantity would have enabled these coloured ladies to set up a small store if so inclined'.[55] Friends of those returning with such riches were inspired to travel themselves, for there was excitement, experience, profit and prestige to be gained from working for Englishmen. Young boys whose imaginations were fired by the stories they heard of other countries had to be forcibly restrained from rushing onto vessels recruiting sailors or labourers.[56] It was common practice for many people to sail again and again on the local ships, and some spent most of their lives doing so, and there were individuals who went to Queensland more than once.[57] Although many labourers in Queensland were only too eager to return to their island homes, it was common for others to work on in the plantations as 'time-expired boys', receiving higher wages than when initially under contract, or to make their way to Sydney where they worked on the wharves or were hired as crews for recruiting vessels travelling to the New Hebrides and the Solomon Islands.[58] Numbers of Loyalty Islanders remained permanently in Australia to take advantage of the material and other opportunities. Of the 998 labourers who officially worked in Queensland 541 had been returned to their islands by 1878,[59] and while there are no figures for the period after this, it was commonly acknowledged on the Loyalty Islands that many of the remaining 457 did not wish to return.

Another motive for travel was noticeable when the French commandant on Lifu imposed a series of *corvées* from 1864 to 1870. So much did some Lifuans dislike labouring for the French soldiers, building quarters and supplying food, that they made a rush for any English vessels looking for men. Some Lifuans begged captains to sign them on. 'The poor creatures', said one LMS missionary, 'were only too glad to get away'.[60] Albert Hovell, a trader who had 'been often' to the Loyalty Islands, told the Royal Commission:

> The natives go away of their own accord, to Queensland . . . I think, partly to avoid being employed by the French. They do not like the French—they prefer the English, or the whites, as they call us. I have heard the traders say that the French have sentries around the island, and that the natives make fires at night as signals to the vessels, when they send their boats on shore and bring off the natives.[61]

Although the *corvées* applied only to Lifu, Mare and Uvea had their domestic upheavals in the form of warfare which caused some people to leave. When a ship returned an Uvean crew in 1872, many of them immediately signed on again when they heard about recent fighting.[62] Later, after the defeat of the Uvean Protestants by the Catholic tribes in 1874, Ella was told that Whenegay and 'all his young men were going off in an *American!* vessel'. Although only ten finally did so, Ella reported that the others were itching for another chance to sail away.[63] But it should also be mentioned that fighting could prevent men from leaving. Charles Bridget, a beachcomber on Lifu, told Lancaster in 1847 that owing to an outbreak of war he would get no more Islanders because the chiefs needed every available man to fight.[64]

At various times during the contact period Europeans believed that the Islanders were eager to leave because they were starving. When he was collecting labourers in 1847, Kirsopp said that 'The scarcity of provisions at Lee Foo [Lifu] is such that half the People of the Island would come if I would take them';[65] Whenegay was always 'bothering' Burns to remove him and his people to another country 'because their island was a poor one', and, according to Burns, Whenegay offered him 100 tons of coconut oil if he would do so. 'The people', said Burns, 'are at times greatly distressed for food', and together with James Paddon he was toying with the idea of shifting the entire Uvean population to Queensland.[66] On the other hand, both Palmer and Hovell stated categorically that in their opinion the Islanders did not leave for Australia because of any scarcity of food.[67] The available evidence seems to suggest that hunger may have been a reason

Travel 99

why some men went overseas but it is most unlikely that it was ever a general motive. Food shortages were infrequent and usually of short duration, and there is no indication of periods of actual starvation. Furthermore, Islanders flocked on board ships at all times, even the most prosperous, and one must be wary of European judgments as to the wretchedness of the Islanders' diet: yams and coconuts were usually considered by visiting Europeans to be more suitable for pigs than humans.

Island conditions, while driving away some men at certain times, were not a major reason for the majority of Islanders leaving their homes. They began to travel in the 1840s and were to do so well into the twentieth century, and domestic troubles were not of sufficient and continuous intensity to force people away over such a length of time. Most Islanders viewed the prospect of overseas travel as a possible enrichment of their lives, not as a refuge from any island tensions.[68]

French opposition to the English labour recruiting was understandable enough; they felt that French subjects were being taken away illegally and with impunity. Nor, as Palmer explained, was their opposition attributable to 'motives of humanity'.[69] They were eager to recruit labour themselves and had an active policy of supplying Island workers to New Caledonian capitalists. In the 1850s Henry worked for the French administration bringing labourers from the New Hebrides to New Caledonia in return for free sandalwood. He did not recruit Loyalty Islanders, although Hovell tried to recruit them for the French, without much success, in the late 1850s.[70] They were loth to work on any French vessels and to labour in New Caledonia. 'They prefer going in English ships to any other employment', said Henry.[71] Joly explained: 'The reason they give for the preference is, there is nothing new to attract them in New Caledonia—that the island is like their own; and that they will have to work very hard, and receive very little pay and very little food'.[72] Whenever a French vessel called to collect labourers or sailors it usually left empty, much to the fury of the French who knew that the same people were eager to sail with Englishmen.

But by the end of the 1870s the Loyalty Islanders became more willing to work for the French, even at times enthusiastic. Their change in attitude can be explained by the tailing off of labour recruiting for Queensland and by the development of chrome, gold, and nickel mining in New Caledonia in the late 1870s and 1880s. The European population in New Caledonia increased from 420 in 1862 to 8000 in 1886, and to 10,000 by 1896. Along with the attraction of labouring for wages in the mines, the Islanders enjoyed Noumea, which was transformed from a deadend outpost to a thriving colonial town with the usual entertainments, or as the LMS missionaries would have it, a 'cesspool of vice and debauchery'.[73] Money, goods, and all kinds of European novelties were now readily available close to the Loyalty Islands. French officials sent to recruit labour in the 1880s were delighted with the Islanders' eagerness to work on the mines.[74] Missionaries began to use phrases that echoed their comments about emigration to Australia years beforehand. Once again they spoke of a 'craze for migration'.[75] In 1906 there were officially 386 Loyalty Islanders in New Caledonia and by 1911, 405 (343 men, 42 women, 20 children).[76] It was estimated that in the same year 600 Lifuans were away—working in New Caledonia and on coastal vessels.[77] The population remaining on the Loyalty Islands at this time was approximately 11,500.

By 1900 the pattern for twentieth-century labour movements by Loyalty Islanders was already well established. Today these people, along with Hebrideans, form the bulk of the mining labour force in New Caledonia, one of the world's biggest known deposits of nickel. At any one time up to half the current population of about 12,500 might be in temporary residence on the mainland.

10
Trade

The Loyalty Islanders' pre-European patterns of trade among the three islands, the Isle of Pines, and New Caledonia[1] came to an end in the 1840s, for the influx of European shipping into New Caledonian waters instantly created opportunities for new items and systems of trade. Even the most sleazy sandalwood ship was an argosy laden with new and exciting riches for the Islanders. Initially, they responded most enthusiastically to those items which were more efficient, novel, and convenient substitutes for their own material culture. Glass beads, especially large blue ones, quickly became their chief ornaments, complementing and often replacing their shell and jade necklaces imported from the Isle of Pines and southern New Caledonia.[2] Similarly, abandoning their tortoise and sea-shell fish-hooks, they crowded around the first missionaries 'like bees; a yam in one hand, holding on by the boat with the other, and clamorous for fish-hooks'.[3] The thousands of fish-hooks sold and given away by sandalwood traders and missionaries very quickly made the Islanders' own hooks obsolete, not because metal hooks were necessarily better for catching fish but because the Islanders no longer had to spend hours constructing them out of obdurate materials.[4] The Islanders also prized glass bottles but did not use them as containers: instead, they broke them and used the pieces as cutting instruments. Shaving was at once revolutionised when the comfort of a sharp edge replaced the painful plucking of whiskers with shells.[5] Any metal, and especially hoop-iron and nails, was eagerly sought, and most metal items were beaten and sharpened into a tool edge. Within a year or two, more sophisticated European tools like knives, scissors, saws, files and tomahawks were in demand. The sandalwood tree, which had hitherto been of no value to the Islanders, was the main item of exchange. And they quickly realised that they also had unexpected wealth in coconuts, yams, and other local produce.

> Our decks [wrote Cheyne] swarming with Natives during the day, and no possibility of keeping them out of the ship. they bring us daily a plentiful supply of cocoa nuts and yams, which they dispose of for mere trifles, our prices are as follows. One fowl for 1 glass bottle, or one piece of Iron Hoop—or one large fish hook—one cocoanut for 2 very small glass beads—1 yam for one large blue glass bead—or one small fishhook—one bunch of sweet potatoes for 1 large bead. one bunch of Bananas for one empty bottle, Sugar cane for small beads.[6]

From the beginning, trading between Europeans and Loyalty Islanders was never a one-sided, European-dominated arrangement; in fact the Islanders usually held the advantage. They had the superiority of numbers and strength during the early years of trading. Even when they had no intention of capturing a ship, they stole from, abused and threatened the traders in the expectation of getting more than was offered. Cheyne's harrowing dealings in the early 1840s, trading with a gun in one hand and a piece of hoop-iron in the other, and keeping all-night watches in case of attack,[7] were common enough experiences for traders and others in the first years of contact. On their earliest voyages the missionaries feared putting themselves and their boats into the 'power' of the Islanders.[8] Masters of ships visiting the Loyalty Islands were warned 'to be continually guarded against treachery and not allow *any* of the natives on deck, as they are by no means to be trusted'.[9] But by the later 1840s, and especially after mission settlement, bartering was usually peaceful and efficient, although some captains occasionally found it necessary to give the more troublesome Islanders 'a few inches of the point of a sword in the glutens maximus'.[10]

Yet another disadvantage the Europeans faced throughout the nineteenth century was the Loyalty Islanders' negotiating skills: if allowed they bartered and haggled all day. Erskine found 'conversation on serious subjects impossible' once the Islanders started to barter for 'the most trifling articles of European manufacture'.[11] MacFarlane quickly discovered on his first day the difficulties of trading with the Lifuans.

Bartering was a new thing to me: I would rather have had to do with the £.s.d., than with fish-hooks and cottons, hatchets and knives, shirts and calicoes. In my day dreams of missionary life, this sort of work had no place: however, I went at it: I knew that we must have some pork to eat, and something to feed the pigs with. We must have mats for the floor; we must also have servants, and food for them: and over all, and most expensive of all, the natives knew that I was a 'new hand', and inexperienced, and took the advantage. I bought, and bought, and bought, but finding that some of the things were moving in a circle, and having no inclination to pay half-a-dozen times for the same article, I was obliged to close the market, at the expense of my popularity.[12]

The Islanders never lost their enthusiasm for trading with passing vessels, and even after a generation of contact still flocked around traders as eagerly as they did in the 1840s. In 1870 one European wrote:

... from every little passage in the reef, canoes had put off, bringing coral, fowls, eggs, and yams, and the deck was covered with natives asking eager questions about everybody and everything.... On going down to our boat we found the beach literally covered with natives of all ages and sexes, each with a pile of yams, gesticulating and talking at the pitch of his or her voice.....[13]

Loyalty Islanders were widely known for their 'particular aptitude for commerce', considered 'greater than among any other islanders'. Europeans thought them shrewd salesmen 'conversant with many of the tricks of trade . . . [who could] drive a hard bargain'.[14]

But the Islanders' greatest advantage in their commercial dealings was that for traders to get the produce they wanted they had to satisfy the Islanders' changing demands. Beads and trinkets, bottles and hoop-iron soon glutted the market. By the late 1840s the Islanders had instead discovered the pleasures of tobacco and European fabrics. MacFarlane explained that 'Traders calling, found that they could not any longer obtain pigs and sandal-wood for beads and pieces of hoop-iron; clothing and other useful articles were called for, and in this case the demand created the supply'.[15] In 1849 Erskine found the Uveans begging 'for "tapa", and were delighted with pieces of printed calico, which some applied as head-dresses and others as petticoats.... any article of clothing ... I believe in every respect would be the best means for an European to traffic with'.[16] By the early 1850s most Loyalty Islanders had some piece of European clothing or cloth attached to some part of their bodies, often to the amusement of Europeans: 'it was laughable to see the variety of dress, native and European, the most ludicrous of which was a fellow strutting along with an old hat and dress coat without any trousers', said one missionary.[17] Within a few years, however, missionaries noted that 'good and appropriate clothing' was worn; European visitors too commented on the 'most civilized' appearance of the people: 'The men were all decently dressed in shirts and waist-cloths, the women in large loose gowns of blue calico'.[18]

The craving for tobacco also began in the late 1840s and continued unabated throughout the century. When Selwyn was at Uvea in 1849 the Islanders dived for pieces of tobacco that the sailors threw overboard. Men and women stretched out their arms in 'supplication' and Selwyn thought that their faces:

> . . . expressive of earnestness and desire, would have been beautiful and striking but for the drawback, that all this picturesque earnestness of entreaty, which might have served for a lesson for a painter or a sculptor, was wasted upon broken pipes and bits of tobacco.[19]

The Islanders became compulsive, obsessive smokers. 'Everyone, without exception, is incessantly smoking. Tobacco is the article of commerce which of all others is the most sought for. A little piece of tobacco will obtain a man's day's work', commented one European visitor.[20] Another described them as 'most expert thieves stealing things out of your pocket and then returning it to you for a piece of tobacco which is the great article of trade'.[21]

Two items of trade which featured in commercial dealings between Islanders and Europeans elsewhere in the Pacific—sex and muskets—were of no economic significance on the Loyalty Islands. Sailors were never mobbed by women as they were at Tahiti or New Zealand. Uvean women were noted for their sexual reticence. 'At this island [wrote Cheyne] strict chastity is observed among both sexes before marriage and promiscuo[u]s intercourse expressly forbidden'.[22] Even the Marists thought that the people had little or no interest in sex, and spoke of them as 'loveless' characters.[23] Sexual relationships between the Uveans and Europeans were unheard of.[24] The women of Mare and Lifu had fewer inhibitions and sometimes swam out to ships and posed erotically in the water for the sailors. The married women were willing enough to go with sailors to their cabins. Henry Swainson, who prided himself as a connoisseur of female pleasures, was delighted and 'quite satisfied' with the 'syrens' he took to the doctor's cabin on the *Havannah*. Tobacco and cloth was the usual payment for these dalliances. Unmarried girls, said Swainson, although 'they would allow you to take any kind of liberties with them without the slightest objection they would not allow you to go any further the reason is that chiefs keep them to broach themselves'.[25] Women were never sent on board by chiefs to offer themselves to sailors in return for trade. Sexual activities between visiting Europeans and Loyalty Islanders remained a limited pastime, and never became an organised business enterprise or political strategy.

The impact of European firearms will be considered in a later chapter; here it is sufficient to say that muskets were never an important item of trade, nor was there ever a general demand for them at any time in the contact period.

Fortunately for the Islanders the depletion of their sandalwood did not mean that they were cut off from European shipping and supplies of European goods at a time when they were becoming dependent upon them, for even greater numbers of vessels arrived to take on crews and barter for other island produce. Coconuts, taro, yams, bananas, sugar cane, and especially pigs and fowls, which since their introduction in the 1840s had thrived on coconuts, were the main exports of the 1850s. The LMS missionaries specialised in exporting coconut fibre to Sydney. In 1863 they collected 14,731 lb valued at £350.[26] The French prohibited this trade in 1864, just before the Sydney fibre market collapsed. The poverty-stricken Catholic missionaries on Uvea took advantage of the abundance of coconuts and had their followers make coconut oil which they then 'donated' to the priests, or the 'oily fathers' as they were known. Until the market declined in the 1870s, oil manufacturing on the Loyalty Islands and especially on Uvea was a flourishing industry. In the early 1860s annual exports amounted to about 22,000 lb, and by the 1870s the figure had more than trebled.[27] On Mare and Lifu the priests experimented with cotton and by 1863 they had discovered a species which grew well. So successful was the crop by the 1870s that 'cotton growing was . . . all the rage' among the Islanders: annual exports increased from about 25,000 lb in the later 1860s to 57,000 lb in 1872.[28] The trade was dominated by the Catholics on Lifu, though Jones and his Protestants had some success on Mare. Both LMS missionaries and supporters usually sold their cotton to the Catholic priests as they gave them the highest price.[29] The type of cotton that grew best was never of top quality, nor was it ever tended with the necessary care. As the cotton exports declined in quality the Islanders received less payment and quickly lost interest in the crop in the later 1870s.[30] They turned instead to producing copra for the newly flourishing market. In

1872 they sold 100,000 lb, and by 1877 the annual amount had risen to almost two million pounds.[31] Copra has remained the principal export to the present day. From the 1870s small quantities of sugar cane, bananas, coffee, bêche-de-mer, sandalwood (which had had time to regenerate), a fungus that was sold to the Chinese, and maize, along with the usual pigs, fowls and yams, also found a ready market in Noumea.[32]

Despite changes in the major exports from sandalwood to yams, pigs, fowls, to fibre, to oil and cotton, and finally to copra, the payment the Islanders demanded remained unchanged from the early 1850s until the 1870s—consisting of tobacco, cloth, and a variety of European tools and utensils.[33] Even those Islanders working on English ships, or in Australia, where they earned £6 a year and had ready access to a galaxy of European goods, were content to bring back blankets, shirts, trousers, tobacco, pipes, and axes and knives.[34] Those returning from Australia were described as being 'particularly fond of little boxes, cedar or painted red, . . . about two feet long, eighteen inches broad, and eighteen inches high. They must have locks and keys. These boxes they fill with anything they can collect'.[35] One labour recruiter, organising the return of some Loyalty Islanders and New Hebrideans, commented:

> I had for many days . . . good reason for cursing those . . . chests, as the owners kept up a constant state of disturbance, never being able to decide, when their money was running short, what desirable article they would purchase next, and, when at sea, always fetching their whole property on deck every morning and bartering among themselves, both sides being always dissatisfied with the results, and insisting on bringing me into the squabble as arbitrator.[36]

In the 1870s there was a change in the Islanders' demands. Traders reported that Islanders had developed a 'pretty good idea of the value of money, and in many cases prefer it to any other article of exchange'.[37] By the 1880s both missionaries and traders noted that they had 'an exact idea of the value of money; in all cases they prefer it to articles of exchange'.[38]

Once the Loyalty Islanders moved into the vortex of commercial interchange with Europeans they quickly abandoned their previous patterns of trade. The change was not disruptive for the Loyalty Islanders—steel replaced imported stone, whaleboats and cutters replaced their canoes built of imported timber,[39] and chiefs' daughters were married to European settlers who could confer a prestige and wealth as great, if not greater, than many New Caledonian chiefs. Strong social and family ties with New Caledonia and the Isle of Pines were retained, but, from the 1860s, travel to

Trade

these places was severely restricted by the French because they feared Loyalty Islanders would spread their dangerous Protestant and English ideas. But though the Loyalty Islanders discarded one pattern of trade for another there was one element of similarity between the old and the new: pre-European trading had been peaceful and based on the mutual requirements of all those involved. In commercial exchanges with Europeans the changing patterns of imports and exports indicates, too, that both Europeans and Loyalty Islanders displayed an ability to understand and accommodate to mutual advantage the commercial needs of the other.

Marketing techniques, like the patterns of imports and exports, also changed periodically to suit requirements and conditions. The Islanders traded directly with ships' masters in the earliest years of contact. Once permanent missionaries landed they encouraged, organised, and directed the export of local produce. As vessels arrived in ever-increasing numbers the Islanders used the missionaries as middle-men to draw up contracts and negotiate prices on the understanding that payment belonged to the Islanders and not to the missions. Mission commercial agents in Sydney and later Noumea were particularly useful for such dealings.[40] Marketing systems were based on a broad network in which Islanders, missionaries, and European shippers were dependent upon each other, and for the most part relations were harmonious.[41] There was apparently tacit agreement between Marist and LMS missionaries not to become too economically competitive for fear that both missions might suffer from diminishing profits. The success of the traders depended upon missionary encouragement and organisation of labour and production. Without friendship with the missionaries, traders were unable to do business on a profitable scale.[42] In turn the missionaries were dependent upon the coastal shipping for their supplies and the well-being of their missions. A bad season resulted in fewer shipping contacts which meant less wealth for the Islanders, a lowering of church contributions, and a subsequent cut back in mission activities.[43]

The participation of the missionaries in most of the commercial activity on the Loyalty Islands angered the French administration. Guillain complained to Commander Palmer:

> ... the chiefs are entirely under their control, owing to the traffic in provisions and stores which goes on between them ... the Protestant and Roman Catholic missionaries were all alike engaged in trade ... their excuse for trafficking with the natives being, that by doing so they prevent the latter being robbed by the traders... this traffic is not altogether for the benefit of the Mission, but also for their own.[44]

MacFarlane and Jones were especially singled out as men who were amassing personal fortunes, and not without justification, for when they were made to leave, both abandoned acres of property and houses and workshops which would have been the delight of many an English squire.

As the volume of commerce increased, resident traders were enticed to the Islands, particularly Lifu, and some chiefs were eager enough to do business with them for they felt that the missionaries had too much control over their commercial affairs. Such opinions became widely accepted by the Islanders when they found that they often received better prices from these traders than they did from the missionaries, and consequently they took their business directly to these wealthier, or more generous, Europeans. But competition between the traders diminished their profits drastically and they were finally forced to agree amongst themselves to 'give no more than mutually understood fair prices'.[45] Unfortunately for the Islanders these controlled prices were usually much lower than before, and the missionaries, too, suffered because contributions were correspondingly lowered. Some chiefs once again worked through the missionaries, while others saw the necessity to become more independent and traded directly with ships' masters or, more commonly, with agents in Noumea.[46] The wealthier LMS villages of Ro, Netche, Chepenehe, Luengoni, and Mu, and the Catholic villages of St Joseph and Nathalo chartered and even bought schooners to transport their produce to Noumea.[47] By the end of the century, there were very few temporary European traders left on the islands: the French residents' liberal trade licensing policies (one issued seventy licences in one year) meant that competition among these traders for what little section of the market remained open to them was so keen that most were unable to make a living.[48] The departure of all but one LMS missionary towards the end of the century also had little effect on the islands' economy. Many of the people, partly as a result of LMS teaching and example, had developed considerable expertise in marketing their produce, and they no longer had to contribute hundreds of pounds to support these same missionaries. By the 1890s the Loyalty Islanders had a considerable independence and control over their commerce with non-resident Europeans and although this commerce had reached new levels of sophistication it was perhaps more reminiscent of the days of direct trading of the 1840s than of the height of missionary trading influence in the 1860s and 1870s.

The monetary value of the Loyalty Islanders' exports can never be fully assessed but it was undoubtedly considerable. Some idea of this value emerges from an analysis of the shipping reports in the *Moniteur*, which

Trade

listed the cargoes and their value landed in Noumea by the licensed vessels on the local trading routes for the years 1863 to 1876. The figures which follow are considerably less than the real amounts exported because the value of a cargo was not always published, some vessels known to have arrived were omitted altogether, and there were many other vessels which took cargoes from the Loyalty Islands to the New Hebrides or Australia without passing through Noumea. The following figures, incomplete as they may be, are given simply as a guide to the value of visible exports brought to Noumea from the Loyalty Islands by the licensed traders, and to indicate the rapid expansion of the Islanders' production of their local resources.[49]

1863	£300	1870	£1450
1864	525	1871	1900
1865	925	1872	3935
1866	500	1873	5212
1867	1125	1874	5825
1868	2012	1875	6525
1869	1610	1876	9950

These European values had little relation to the payments the Islanders received: if an Uvean sold fungus worth £20 on the Noumean market, it was unlikely he would have received £20 worth of tobacco, cloth, or cash; and there is little point in speculating on his estimation of the worth of whatever he was paid. Nevertheless, there are indications that many people collectively, if not individually, had considerable purchasing power on the European market especially as a result of cash payments for their exports after 1870. The contributions given to the LMS were large. From 1879 to 1886, for example, by which time all contributions were in cash, the Lifuan Protestants donated over £2700.[50] These same people paid hundreds of pounds for books from the mission presses, and between 1870 and 1880 spent £375 on horses and £2595 for a schooner and whaleboats. Throughout the islands most Protestant villages and the wealthier Catholic ones had whaleboats worth £50 each.[51]

While the overall picture is one of material prosperity there were some serious weaknesses in the Islanders' economy. The decline of the cotton and oil markets forced the immediate development of new export crops. Drought periodically affected crops. Hurricanes also damaged plantations; a severe cyclone in 1880 destroyed almost every hut on the islands, 'ravaged' the crops, and led to a drop in trading activities. Nor was prosperity evenly distributed. Uvea and Mare suffered because of the destruction of plantations during the tribal wars. Mare was particularly hard hit in the early 1880s by a plague of locusts which prevented coconuts from growing for over a decade afterwards. A species of bird on Uvea and Lifu protected the coconut trees from the locusts, but attempts to introduce these birds on Mare were unsuccessful. Missing out on the benefits of the copra trade the Mareans turned instead to growing maize, but it required far more labour and was much less profitable than copra.[52] The Mare Catholics were the poorest of all the Loyalty Islanders. Apart from the wars, droughts, storms, and locusts they were unable to find markets for their cotton and had great difficulty in exporting their maize because of poor internal communications and lack of harbours or safe landing places. Gaide mournfully wrote: 'Mare is excessively poor, it is the poorest of our New Caledonian missions; nothing is produced'.[53] The Protestants on Mare had the advantage of anchorages and could readily export maize, and Creagh thought they had 'a considerable amount of material comfort'.[54] The Lifu Protestants were the wealthiest of all the Loyalty Islanders and, by the late 1880s, admitted that the Catholics too had done much to improve their material wealth. Hadfield described Nathalo as 'quite a flourishing settlement' with its sheep and goats, houses, and trading schooner.[55] The Uveans, though not as rich as the Lifuans, were also thought to be 'relatively affluent'.[56] A French official reported in 1883:

> The Loyalty Islanders are enterprising, they make very good sailors, they have a very developed sense of personal property, and finally they are rich, thanks to the commerce in copra which they undertake because of the numerous coconut trees.[57]

Visitors to the Loyalty Islands were amazed at the Islanders' settlements with whitewashed, concrete houses, churches with towering spires, and the well-clothed, civil, industrious inhabitants who were accustomed to receiving Europeans. These visitors were shown wells sunk up to 150 feet through solid coral to fresh water, roads cut through coral and bush, horses and carts carrying produce for export, and schooners and whaleboats owned and manned by the Islanders. Time and time again visitors recorded their amazement at such developments which they interpreted as pleasing signs of the Islanders' progress towards 'civilisation'—their 'rapid and wonderful' rise from barbarism to 'material and mercantile prosperity': it was generally agreed amongst Europeans that they were 'entitled to be ranked as the foremost tribes of Western Polynesia'.[58]

> In the three islands, they are very intelligent . . . and they have a degree of civilization which one is astonished to find so close to New Caledonia.[59]
>
> [Loyalty Islanders] are the most advanced of any natives in Western Polynesia. This remark applies especially to the inhabitants of Mare.[60]
>
> [The Loyalty Islands are] occupied by really the highest type of coloured men I have seen.[61]

Such opinions were largely a product of an educated European's belief that aspects of his technology, when adopted by a non-European society, could bring about desirable social change. But many of the apparently more spectacular changes in the Islanders' material culture were not as significant or as extensive as many Europeans thought.

The large, sparkling white concrete houses with glass windows, venetian blinds, European furniture and decorations were certainly impressive. Naisiline Nidoish's house has already been described. Wainya's house at Chepenehe was considered 'vastly superior' to MacFarlane's own grand home. Wainya had his fitted out with glass folding doors, a large English bed, tables, chairs, a sofa, and pictures which, said MacFarlane, 'gives it quite a European appearance'.[62] But such houses were only for the privileged few—the wealthiest chiefs, the Rarotongan and Samoan teachers, the Loyalty Islands teachers, missionaries, and a few of the permanent resident traders. And those Loyalty Islanders who owned such buildings kept them mainly for a display of prestige and wealth and seldom used them, except to receive European guests. The Islanders never slept in the houses, preferring to spend the night in the communal huts. The overwhelming majority of the population, including most of the chiefs of the smaller clans, had only their huts made from pandanus, grass, and coconut tree fronds. The missionaries constantly regretted that the people preferred to live in their 'low dirty smoky huts' and 'wretched hovels' scattered about the villages 'without the slightest efforts at order'.[63] In 1880 Creagh complained that their huts were 'for the most part little better than those their grandfathers occupied'.[64] The Islanders had neither inclination nor reason to change their dwellings, which were comfortable and, with fires perpetually smouldering on the floors, warm and free from mosquitoes. Furthermore, their huts were easily and cheaply built out of readily available materials. Almost every year, severe cyclones blew down many buildings and it was far simpler to re-erect a grass hut than a concrete structure. And the Islanders certainly had enough building to do for their chiefs and missionaries. Some of the mission churches involved years of continual work: the church Jones built at Ro had concrete walls 3 feet thick set on foundations 12 feet below the surface of the coral, and 30 feet high; it could hold over 800 people and took more than nine years to construct.[65] Creagh decided to pay the Islanders to cut wood he supplied if they used it to build themselves European styled houses but his plan failed miserably. They were more interested in the pay than in cutting wood:

> Eight or ten will be connected with one saw; the other six will be sitting & lying down while two of their number work half-an-hour & then perhaps two more will take the saw. Now they think or seem to think that those who are merely looking on aut to be paid as well as those who work. They have to learn by experience the proper rate of wages.[66]

While the missionaries admitted their failure to persuade their supporters to build 'decent' houses, they claimed to have changed settlement patterns by grouping people in villages near the sea instead of their living inland as in pre-European times.[67] It is difficult to understand where the missionaries got this idea from, for although such population movements were common elsewhere in the Pacific as a result of European contact, they did not occur on the Loyalty Islands. By the 1840s the coastal villages of Netche, Mebuet, Eoche, Ro, Tadine, Medu, Mu, Dueulu, Peng, Chepenehe, Eacho, Inangod, We, and Luengoni were already well established, and all the villages on Uvea had to be near the sea because of the island's shape. Furthermore, the inland villages of Rawa, Menaku, La Roche, Penelo, Tawained, Wiwatul, Meleck, Nathalo, and Kumo, to name the major ones, were neither abandoned nor moved closer to some part of the coast even though it was obviously economically advantageous to do so after European contact. Political and territorial arrangements precluded any such moves. Minor changes undoubtedly took place: some people may have moved from one village where there was no missionary to one where there was, providing that they did not resettle in enemy lands. Also during the planting and harvesting seasons in pre-European times the people normally remained at their inland plantations in temporary huts until the work was completed. After mission contact they still lived in these huts but returned to their villages every weekend for church activities.

Communications and transport were only marginally improved. The sections of road capable of taking horses and carts were very rough, limited to the outskirts of the largest villages, and could be measured in yards rather than miles. No new major routes were opened up, though some of the more important tracks were widened to enable horses to get by. By the 1880s most areas on Lifu and Mare could be reached on horseback and the Islanders considered this sufficient.[68] They lacked the resources, manpower, and inclination to crush, burn, and smooth out the twisted coral into a network of highways as the missionaries urged. Horses and donkeys helped to transport some produce from the plantations to the sea, but even in the 1880s most of the produce was still carried by the women.[69]

> It is [wrote Creagh's daughter] quite usual to see a family returning home after a day in their garden, walking single file, the man first carrying nothing but a club to defend his family from possible enemies, then the woman, bowed down with a huge bundle of garden produce on her back, the baby in a sling in front and the rest of the family trailing behind.[70]

Whaleboats had largely replaced canoes by the 1880s,[71] but they did not necessarily improve inter-island travel; the Islanders' largest double canoes could travel just as fast and hold as many people as a whaleboat. The advantage of a European craft was that the Islanders were saved the task of importing wood and then building their canoes. Whaleboats were also easier to sail and appear to have been a good deal safer.[72]

The new export crops did not involve changes in cultivation techniques. Cotton and maize grew virtually wild. The Islanders cut down areas of bush, left it to dry, and then burnt it, just as they did when preparing their yam and taro gardens. Seeds or shoots were then planted in the exposed pockets of soil. The missionaries were amazed that cotton 'grew with but little or no trouble'[73] and, as with their yam crops, the Islanders gave little attention to their new plants, apart from the occasional weeding, between planting and harvesting times. The Islanders were not interested in using certain agricultural methods Europeans took for granted. The idea of ever manuring their soil, for example, filled them with disgust.[74] It was 'not in accordance with native ideas' to constantly tend to their growing crops,[75] and it was through such neglect that the quality of the cotton declined. The most profitable crops for the Islanders—sandalwood and coconuts—needed virtually no attention at all.

European axes and knives lightened the task of cutting down the dense bush but no European tools were used for tilling the soil, for it is extremely light and a pointed stick was sufficient. European agricultural implements were unnecessary and unsuitable. Ploughs, for example, could not be used for the soil is in small pockets, thin, and usually dotted with coral rocks and outcrops.

The herds of cattle owned by some villages were very small because of lack of water and grazing land and were a source of prestige rather than a viable commercial asset. Pigs and fowls, which were major export goods, thrived on coconuts and looked after themselves. In general terms the Loyalty Islanders' export trade was limited by both the environment and certain cultural traits: the bulk of their profits, apart from those earned by the sale of their labour, came from those animal and indigenous crops which required the minimum of attention.

Visiting Europeans, who highlighted the more obvious manifestations of European material culture in the Loyalty Islands as evidence of rapid and desirable social change, underestimated the patterns of continuity in the Islanders' daily existence. The commonly reiterated interpretation of these changes as the Europeanisation of the 'native' way of life, could perhaps have been more accurately described as the 'nativisation' of the European way of life.[76] However, underlying the continuity, European technology and commerce were producing socio-economic changes which were not so readily apparent to European observers who were too busy looking for more concrete signs of 'civilisation'. The introduction of steel tools and the stimulus of trade resulted in a rearrangement of patterns and priorities of work. European tools and substitute items reduced the time and effort required for the traditional tasks of clearing bush for plantations, building huts, and trading for materials and then making canoes, fish-hooks, stone and shell implements and decorations. This work was normally performed by the men; the women benefited less, for European technology could not assist them much in looking after the household, the children, and in their many other duties. Steel tools and other items of European technology resulted in a degree of surplus labour which provided opportunities for young men to travel overseas, as well as enabling a rapid change from subsistence to surplus production of island produce. Although European tools and techniques lightened some of the burdens of everyday living and stimulated the new surplus agriculture, this export production still demanded a great deal of time and energy. The collection of sandalwood and the making of coconut fibre, oil, and copra, for example, were year-round tasks which broke the former clearly defined seasonal agricultural work patterns of planting and harvesting. In addition to these new tasks and to their own food growing requirements the Islanders engaged in other labour intensive activities such as widening tracks, digging wells, and building and rebuilding churches, houses, and workshops which were periodically destroyed by cyclones, as well as devoting a great deal of time to church affairs. Overall there was a significant increase in the variety of everyday activities and the efforts these required. Overseas travel by the fittest young men may have placed a strain on some of the clans, but it seems that the pattern of randomly staggered arrivals and departures would have ensured that there was always a residual labour force. And exports continued to increase even during times of extensive migration.

European technology brought its pleasures, its labour saving devices, and increased the variety of life and the material prosperity of the Loyalty Islanders; the price they paid was an increase in time and labour spent on surplus production and on new activities. It is worth emphasising that such industry resulted from the Islanders' enthusiasm: if the inspiration for a particular project was European in origin, its undertaking and successful completion was dependent upon the Islanders' voluntary efforts. Not without good reason did Europeans speak of them as persevering and hardworking people in contrast to 'lazy' Islanders elsewhere in the Pacific.[77]

In many parts of Melanesia such new ventures for the Islanders as overseas travel and trading with Europeans had radical consequences, especially in those societies where possession of material wealth largely determined social standing and authority. In such societies changes in traditional values and priorities in the economic sphere as a result of the introduction of European goods necessarily affected the socio-political sphere as well. For example, young men returning from labouring in Fiji or Queensland with 'instant' supplies of new wealth sometimes challenged their chiefs or Big-men whose power had been achieved through long and painstaking accumulation and manipulation of traditional items of wealth. In some regions new entrepreneurial élites developed, resulting in unprecedented socio-political and economic changes. But in the Loyalty Islands rigid social stratification, where positions were ascribed and not achieved through manipulation of riches, precluded the rise of such élites. Material wealth came as a consequence and was not a determinant of political authority. No single individual, except for a chief, was able to hoard a large private supply of wealth. The need to express political obligations, as well as the deeply ingrained customs of communal redistribution and sharing, meant that any supply of goods was fragmented amongst the clans and generally ended up at the top of the socio-political structure. Even cash was subject to the same restrictions. Most people spent their money on the same goods they formerly bartered for, and the bulk of their imports into the twentieth century remained firmly based on cloth, tobacco, tools, and utensils. More expensive items, such as whaleboats, horses, cattle and schooners, were far beyond the reach of individuals and were bought on a corporate basis. Money left over after the Islanders had satisfied their personal needs was given to the missions and to their chiefs, who hoarded it until they could afford to purchase these items for their village. Those ambitious men who challenged clan and great chiefs for their positions usually did so on the basis of disputed ancestry, and not solely on the basis of any newly acquired wealth; the aspirants to leadership were always men of some social standing in their local communities rather than 'commoners'.

Missionaries fought hard to root out the system of redistribution of wealth, claiming that it removed incentives for 'personal betterment'. They accused chiefs of shamefully appropriating their followers' wealth, and they were horrified when people 'stole' goods from friends returning from overseas trips with their boxes. Anyone who managed to 'improve his position', complained the missionaries, was the target for the 'cupidity and indolence of all about him'.[78]

> It was quite impossible for a native to keep any of his own belongings, if a friend cast a longing eye upon anything he possessed, it must change hands. When a young couple married, a great feast was prepared—the friends on both sides were all expected to bring contributions, which were piled in two great heaps. When the feast was over what was left was divided amongst the friends and relations, those from the bride's friends being distributed among the bridegroom's friends and vice versa, the young couple being left with nothing to begin housekeeping with,—but as communistic ideas prevail amongst them, they share and share alike and no one goes hungry.[79]

The socio-economic developments and changes that took place as a result of overseas travel and trading with Europeans were largely determined by and remained within the framework of indigenous self-determination and, while not without their tensions, were profitable, creative, and welcomed. Loyalty Islands society, largely because of the nature and strength of its socio-political organisation, proved remarkably resilient and able to accommodate and control many of the developments stimulated by commercial dealings with Europeans. Cargo cults, so common elsewhere in Melanesia, have never appeared on the Loyalty Islands. It is perhaps important to mention again, in this context of economic impact, that although Loyalty Islanders traded extensively with Europeans, their islands never supported a large resident European population; the Islanders were able to live their lives much as they wished, spared the almost inevitable implications of a frontier society in their midst.

11
Teaching

Loyalty Islanders were renowned for their devotion to their respective missions and their enthusiasm for all activities connected with the church. Europeans thought that the congregations would have set a fine example in many a European parish. Throughout the century there was no slackening of enthusiasm. In 1890, for example, there was not one regular absentee from church events among the 8000 or more Protestants throughout the three islands.[1] Nor did the Loyalty Islanders abandon their Christian ceremonies when they went overseas. Those who worked on plantations in Queensland were rigorous and exacting in their own religious services and were a constant source of amazement to European overseers and missionaries who considered them to be 'an example to the white men among whom they lived'.[2]

There is no simple explanation as to why Loyalty Islanders were such ardent supporters of the Christian churches. The Islanders accepted the missionaries largely within the framework of their own political aspirations. As has been suggested earlier, the decision to follow one or other of the missions was made for most individuals by their great chiefs or clan chiefs and the exact moment when the Islanders throughout all regions began to behave as, and call themselves, Catholics or Protestants can readily be documented. They continued to associate themselves with the missionaries throughout the remainder of the nineteenth century largely because it was politically and, to a lesser extent, economically expedient to do so. But this reason is not sufficient on its own to explain the popular enthusiasm for

Christianity, once a decision had been made to follow its tenets, and neither does it fully explain the nature of the Islanders' Christianity.

It is necessary, first of all, to emphasise that Christian practices and doctrines, as the Islanders interpreted them and as they were often explained by the LMS teachers and both LMS and Marist missionaries, were not in essence incompatible with their former beliefs and rituals. The Islanders' own 'religion' was essentially pragmatic, designed to influence numerous spirit-beings who were believed responsible for all cause and effect.[3] The apparent ease and speed with which the Islanders accepted aspects of the Christian doctrine and ritual once they associated themselves with a mission can be explained partly by the way in which the missionaries' god was introduced to them: he was another spirit-being, but one who could carry out alone the multiplicity of activities of their own spirit-beings, and one who was apparently very powerful. Given their preoccupation with spirit-beings, Loyalty Islanders found it perfectly acceptable that the first Europeans and LMS Polynesian teachers they met had their own supernatural champion with whom they communicated ritualistically. Although the Islanders initially felt that the European deity may have been irrelevant to their way of life they never denied his presence or that he had some power. When the epidemics swept through the islands in the early 1840s the new god was quickly implicated. The Rarotongan teacher Ta'unga described how the Mare people 'searched and searched for the reasons for that sickness'. Some initially blamed and killed several of their priests. Then they turned and accused the teachers and their god. When cursing the Christian deity failed to appease the disease-making forces, several Mareans attempted to solicit his aid instead, but only, as Ta'unga explained, 'because they feared death from the disease'.[4] Rumours that this new spirit-being either was responsible for the sickness or could cure it spread through the islands as fast as the epidemics themselves.

Hence from the earliest years of European contact, the Islanders' conception of the Christian god was explicable in their own terms, and they experimented accordingly. Sometimes the powers of their own and the European deities were put directly to the test. The LMS mission reported the following incident on their voyage to Mare in 1848:

> An old chief, hearing the teachers tracing diseases to divine and not human agency, sent for a noted priest, and engaged him to exert his power and bring disease upon some of the teachers, to see whether Jehovah or the priests of Maré were true. The priest went to the bush behind the teachers' house, with his basket of relics, viz., the hair, fingernails, bones, etc., of his forefathers; and, striking the air with his club, looked to see whether there was blood on

his basket—a sign that vengeance had gone forth on the teachers. He beat the air and looked at his basket until he was tired. No blood appeared; and the chief and priest concluded that 'Jehovah, the God of the teachers, must be a true God and a mighty one'.[5]

Missionaries and teachers were keen to encourage such experimentation, and emphasised that their one god could do all that the Islanders' spirits could do, and a great deal more. Often explicit in such arguments was the threat that those who refused to believe in the new deity faced certain death.[6] Teachers and missionaries always made the most of epidemics, telling the Islanders that the illnesses were Jehovah's curse upon them for not believing in him.[7] Other strange and dangerous phenomena, such as earthquakes, were attributed to the Christian god's wrath at the people's failure to 'accept the Gospel'.[8] Jehovah was also portrayed as being invincible in war. Missionaries told defeated warriors that their fallen comrades would still have been alive had they believed.[9] Such claims gained credence, especially when the first 'Christian soldiers' were victorious over 'heathens'.

The Christian god's affinity with the Islanders' own spirit-beings was further emphasised not only by the range of his capabilities but by the indigenous names given to him by teachers and missionaries. On Lifu, Marists adopted the word *haze*, a term usually given to stones thought to contain great supernatural power, and LMS missionaries at first called him Cahaze—the *ca* meaning one. LMS missionaries later adopted the term Akotesi, the Miny equivalent. In the Iai language LMS teachers used Kong, meaning an evil spirit-being capable of great wrath. Ella tried to change it to Atua for he felt that Kong reinforced the notion that religion was 'merely a conciliation of an Evil Spirit', but even by the 1870s most Protestant Uveans still retained the word Kong.[10]

Even the adaptation of the external trappings of Christianity indicates continuity rather than radical change. Although the Islanders abandoned many of their sacred artefacts, these were replaced with novel and, they considered, more impressive ones, especially from the Marists—statues of Christ and the Virgin, rosary beads, religious paintings in churches, and their own individual medallions bearing Christ's image. Although the LMS missionaries frequently accused the Marists of indulging in idolatry, they too provided their supporters with similar visual manifestations of their religion—crosses, bibles, altars, stained glass windows in churches, and the coconut juice and yams for communion—all of which were imbued with supernatural presence. Similarly missionary prayers, sermons, their devotions for the sick, and their blessing of newly planted crops and new churches all had their pre-European counterparts.[11] Words such as amen and Jehovah were widely used as incantations by the Islanders for they 'thought . . . [them] of far more importance than the prayer itself'.[12] Christian burial techniques and the notion of a spiritual afterlife were not incompatible with the Islanders' own beliefs and customs. Most were buried underground in 'coffins' of canoes or specially hollowed out tree trunks (great chiefs, however, often had their canoes hoisted up to caves overlooking the sea). The Islanders believed dead people lived on in spirit form although they did not go to any one place, and there was no concept of reward or punishment after death. Spirits normally remained about the islands and were in frequent contact with the living.[13]

Marist missionaries were instructed that 'the fear of superstition does not exclude faith' and were, in fact, encouraged to take advantage of many of the Islanders' beliefs: 'considering that our natives have a superstitious veneration for their ancestors, we believe it is necessary to direct, use, Christianize this traditional tendency'.[14] The priests were urged to place crosses and statues in all those places where the Islanders claimed evil spirits lived, and to conduct impressive masses for the dead, and to pay particular attention to holding memorial services each year for deceased great chiefs and other prominent persons. They were also instructed to build fine cemeteries where 'faith and art' combined.[15] The LMS missionaries were just as aware of the necessity to accommodate aspects of the Islanders' 'superstition'. MacFarlane explained:

> . . . feeling the tendency of the natives to regard the sacrament with superstitious feelings, and the desirability of keeping it as simple and primitive as possible, and also of using elements that might be easily procured by the natives themselves, we determined to use the *bread and wine of the country*, viz., the beautiful white yams for which the Loyalty group is celebrated, and cocoanut milk . . . .[16]

In many respects, Christianity provided the Islanders with new forms of animism and ritual such that their pre- and post-contact beliefs differed in degree rather than kind. And the missionaries were only too well aware that Christianity had been mingled with their former beliefs. In 1848 Turner explained: 'the people generally still amalgamate with their Christianity their former rites of heathenism',[17] and in 1880 Creagh echoed similar sentiments:

> . . . there is a vast amount of superstition, error, & ignorance still pervading the minds of great numbers of our church members. Their religion is more a thing to be seen than to be felt & enjoyed in the soul.[18]

Teaching

The Islanders' conception of Christianity was reflected in what the missionaries thought was a lack of spiritual understanding and feeling. Time and time again the LMS missionaries returned to the theme that there was no 'deep heart-felt repentance on account of Sin. They never appear sorry for what they did before the Gospel was brought to them'.[19] The Marist missionaries were less concerned than the LMS missionaries to see a show of repentance, but they complained that the Islanders' approach to life was too light-hearted, so precluding the acceptance of 'serious ideas' of religion: 'there is not yet a well developed Christian spirit, but however, [they] observe with great fidelity the main tenets of Christian life'.[20]

The missionaries naturally made much of the theological differences between their respective Catholic and Protestant converts, and the Islanders also were well aware of some of the more noticeable divisive issues. Public debating between Catholic and Protestant Islanders was common: the Catholics taunted the Protestants for their ignorance of the Holy Spirit, the Virgin, and Purgatory, and the Protestants retaliated by criticising the Pope, the Catholic 'idols', and their 'compromising' in matters of faith and social behaviour—pointing to the priests who smoked and drank wine. But for the Islanders, such differences were not based on theological grounds. Rather they were utilised to highlight their conflicting political positions. In the handful of cases where individuals changed their religion they were motivated by temporal aspirations. It was a constant source of regret for both missions that, once the lines of demarcation between Catholic and Protestant supporters were established, neither mission made further gains. As Fabvre sadly commented: 'since the beginning of the mission, I do not believe that there has been one true conversion from Protestantism to Catholicism, not one real defection from Catholicism to Protestantism'.[21]

Christianity, as the Islanders accepted and understood it, was not the intellectual and spiritual bombshell the missionaries intended. The Islanders' own beliefs did not pose any philosophical or metaphysical obstacle to the following of the new God. If the Christian deity was all-powerful there was every reason to accept his protection and invoke his aid. The selection and adaptation of various Christian notions and customs did not, therefore, involve any fundamental or disturbing changes in their view of existence, and heightened the pleasure of other attractions the missions offered.

Most islanders were exceptionally fond of their missionaries, and as many of the missionaries remained on the islands for long periods of time they built up very strong personal ties with their followers. Beaulieu spent over fifty years there, Jones and Creagh over thirty, Sleigh and Fabvre over twenty, and Bernard sixteen. Whenever a missionary departed permanently the people in his area were known as 'the deserted ones' and 'winced under the taunt', for their missionary was their 'pride and joy'.[22] The Islanders were also fiercely proud of the mission stations and their chiefs' stately homes—particularly at the LMS villages at Ro, Netche, Chepenehe, and Mu, and the Marist villages at St Joseph, Nathalo, and La Roche. Whenever a church or some other building was completed, several thousand people from all over the islands came to gaze in wonder and admiration.

The missionaries, particularly those of the LMS, were closely identified by the Islanders with the technological apparatus of the European world. Tools and utensils which they introduced in large quantities were a constant source of admiration and eagerly sought after. People crowded around LMS stations in the earlier years muttering 'how rich these foreigners are!'[23] As a Marist missionary commented: 'It is not only with religion you must impress the natives, but . . . with things of material interest'.[24] Axes, saws, and other tools together with such techniques as digging wells were of great benefit to the Islanders, relieving some of the burdens of their everyday living. And in addition to its usefulness, the missionaries' technology sometimes had considerable novelty value. One priest who owned a camera had would-be models flock to him in the hundreds, and Hadfield drew crowds with his magic lantern shows.[25] But the material attractions of the mission stations should not be over-estimated: LMS missionaries never managed to seduce the Marists' followers with their wealth; political considerations determined that people did not change their allegiance to their chosen missions, even if it was economically advantageous to do so.

Christian ritual and doctrine also gave great pleasure. Missionaries were commonly kept up until dawn answering questions and relating Biblical tales. The efforts and energy Islanders put into the attainment of literacy,[26] singing hymns, memorising catechisms, and organising church affairs, were ever a source of comment by European visitors. The church also provided opportunities for social advancement and prestige. Baptism and church membership added to an individual's dignity. As MacFarlane explained:

> I have found natives so anxious to be admitted to the church, that in order to accomplish their object, they would profess faith in Christ, or in anybody, or anything else; although there was evidently no change of heart . . . . They will make any sacrifice to be admitted to the church; would, no doubt, go round the island on 'all fours' if required . . . .[27]

Young children were encouraged by their parents to sit for examinations the missionaries held periodically—a child might win some prize or be picked as a bell ringer or a minor church official if successful. Adults who had no chance of ever becoming teachers had the opportunity to work in the local church administration as organisers and overseers of the various church activities. The LMS missionaries appointed large numbers of 'chapel keepers' whose job was to watch over young people to make sure they did not read, talk, or fall asleep when they should be listening or worshipping. The Marists had a system of 'censors' who were responsible for reporting any 'misdemeanours' on church occasions to the priests. Some individuals who might not otherwise have gone to church and taken part in the religious activities were forced to do so by the Marist censors and the LMS police. In 1869 MacFarlane wrote of some members of his congregations: 'Tis all fear, fear, fear; they are afraid of God, and afraid of the missionaries . . . . They fear of hell, expulsion from churches . . .'.[28] But such moods were not characteristic of the majority of people, who certainly showed their enthusiasm for the church every weekend and on special religious occasions. Each Saturday they returned from their inland plantations and prepared food and practised their lessons for the following day. On Sunday everyone dressed in his finest European clothes and participated in long church services, vast outdoor question-and-answer meetings, and feasting. The special collection days for both missions, the celebrations on the anniversaries of the founding of the respective missions, mass baptisms, and meetings to welcome visiting mission personalities were the most impressive occasions, where a thousand or more Islanders displayed their wealth in produce and their oratorical capabilities. So successful were the LMS collection meetings that the missionaries soon abandoned the practice of holding them at the mission stations twice a year and organised numerous separate village collections. The people thought the idea was a good one for there were far more opportunities for feasting and, said Creagh, 'it gives a greater number of orators an opportunity of displaying their powers'.[29] Such meetings were also occasions for running and spear throwing competitions and other 'innocent games'. Always there were flags, processions, and people dancing madly about. Fireworks sometimes climaxed the proceedings.[30]

Christianity was generally eagerly accepted by Loyalty Islanders and rapidly became one of the most dominant popular forces in their society. But although the people acted and identified themselves as either Catholics or Protestants, the evangelists looked in vain for spiritual conversion which betokened ultimate success for their mission. In spite of the obvious changes to their way of life and impressive external manifestations of Christianity, the reasons why the Islanders accepted and the way in which they interpreted the new doctrines lay within the patterns of their own political, economic, and social aspirations, and their own beliefs.

Both LMS and Marist missionaries attempted formally to educate young Islanders in the hope of creating a future adult generation in the image of 'civilised' and 'enlightened' Europeans. Immediately on their arrival the LMS missionaries on Mare and Lifu organised day schools at their stations. By the 1860s nominal rolls at each school were as high as 400 but absenteeism tempered the missionaries' success. Parents were reluctant to leave their children behind when they went to their inland gardens during the week, and in planting and harvesting seasons the children were usually required to help with the work.[31] To keep the pupils under the 'yoke of instruction' the LMS missionaries organised boarding schools, and MacFarlane also established a seminary at Chepenehe, where he trained teachers to run the church on the Loyalty Islands and prepared them for their planned future penetration into New Caledonia, the New Hebrides, and beyond. The Noumean administration ordered the closure of all LMS schools in 1864 although, because there was no French presence on Mare, Jones continued his programs untroubled, and MacFarlane secretly taught his pupils in his seminary. Lack of numbers together with the politico-religious trouble on Uvea prevented the LMS missionary there from conducting schools until 1879. Once the LMS was given permission to recommence its schools in 1865, the day schools were moved out to the villages and were conducted by the Islanders themselves. The new system fared little better than the old. The problem of absenteeism remained, and parents lost their earlier enthusiasm for sending their children to school because those held in their villages did not confer the same degree of prestige upon their sons and daughters as those conducted by the missionaries at their station. Also the parents were expected to finance the local schools, as the parent LMS organisation did not provide for them in its annual budgets.[32] The missionaries thought that the greatest weakness of such schools was the inefficiency of the teachers:

> Some of our best preachers or pastors (who are the teachers of the schools) are our worst scholars . . . . Our pastors seem to have the idea that their main or only business is to stand up and preach, notwithstanding our repeatedly telling them to look well after the children & to insist on the parents cooperating with them in their efforts . . . . Many were chosen merely because they could speak; but there were no better to be had.[33]

The LMS missionaries remaining on the islands were not unduly disturbed when the French finally closed all such schools in 1884. After 1865 the LMS missionaries concentrated their efforts on boarding schools on Lifu and Mare, but after several years boarding schools too proved virtually unworkable. They absorbed too much of the missionaries' time and, when the LMS cut down on funds available for them, were a heavy burden on local LMS resources.[34]

For all their considerable efforts, the LMS missionaries' achievement in the field of schooling fell far below their expectations. In 1883 Creagh summed up the situation by saying that though the people had not so much gone back in their educational progress, they had not reached 'to that high standard which we aim at'.[35] The missionaries were inclined to blame the Islanders' low 'intellectual capacity'. Creagh complained that his pupils could manage 'compound add. sub. mult. & div of money, and a few simple questions in calculating money, English & French; but they are puzzled & fail in most cases at all complicated which require any independent thought'.[36] The most successful Protestant school was the seminary at Chepenehe. Apart from educating scores of young men to preach on their own islands, fourteen were trained and sent to New Caledonia between 1871, when the French finally allowed them in, and 1900; another twelve pioneered Protestant missionary work in New Guinea between 1871 and 1882.[37]

Because of the Marist Mission's lack of resources, most formal education on the Loyalty Islands in the nineteenth century was under LMS auspices. The Marists never bothered with day schools and concentrated on boarding schools, where they hoped to isolate the children from their 'corrupting' village environment. But lacking finance, and support on Mare and Lifu, it was not until the 1870s that small schools were commenced on Lifu and Uvea, and the 1880s on Mare.

Although their educational programs failed to produce students in the image of English middle-class school children, the LMS missionaries' greatest achievement was in providing the basic tools which enabled the Islanders to become literate in their own languages. With Ta'unga's assistance the LMS prepared a few pages in Nengone which they distributed to the teachers on Mare in 1848. The pamphlets were instantly popular and by 1852 the Si Gwahma people were 'vigorously applying themselves to read'; eighty read well and 'hundreds' more were learning.[38] Nihill set up a small press at Netche in the early 1850s and trained Mareans to operate it. He translated 'simple' portions of scripture and liturgy which were widely distributed. When the permanent LMS missionaries arrived in 1854 some 250 Islanders could read and forty could write.[39] The LMS missionaries set up a much larger press and with Nihill's aid and his knowledge of the language began to translate and print chapters of the Bible. The slim books were seized eagerly and the Islanders throughout the northern and western areas of Mare formed themselves into small groups to practise reading and writing. Those who were given slates avidly copied parts of the sermons they heard and afterwards were surrounded by crowds of people eager to discuss what they had written.[40] By the mid-1850s portions of scripture were printed in Dehu and sent to Lifu where there was tremendous enthusiasm for them. Anything printed, said Jones 'is prized as the nugget would be by the Australian scrivner and is sought after with equal . . . [?] and the house of the missionary being the receptacle for all such publications, is crowded continually'.[41] Printed material was scrupulously cared for and a piece of paper for a cover was a valuable extra. Jones was forced to set aside one morning a week to distribute old newspapers and advertising pages of evangelical magazines just for this purpose. The Islanders also wove special bags to carry their books about.[42]

Until Jones was expelled in 1887, books poured from the LMS presses on Mare. By the mid-1860s the missionaries had printed 1500 copies of much of the New Testament in Nengone; 5000 copies of a 120 page Lifuan hymn book; 6000 copies of the Gospel of John, and 5000 catechisms in Dehu.[43] By 1871 most of the Bible had been translated and printed in Dehu, Nengone, and Iai.[44] The Islanders' enthusiasm for books never died out; even as late as 1877 an edition of 4000 Lifuan hymn books virtually sold out in a few hours. 'This', said the missionaries, 'pleasantly shows that neither tobacco nor clothing presented stronger attractions'.[45] The desire to read was also sustained throughout the latter half of the nineteenth century. In the 1870s the Islanders were still in the habit of copying down missionary sermons, checking them later against the missionary's own notes, and then forming groups where the sermons were again copied out and discussed.[46]

Most of the Uvean Protestants could read by the mid-1860s and many took great delight in writing with sticks in the sand.[47] In 1871 Creagh reported that on Mare 'nearly every young man & woman can read and write',[48] and the French administration was disturbed when Salinis explained in 1884 that the entire Protestant population under the age of twenty-seven was literate.[49] Creagh wrote in the 1880s that most of the Lifuans had 'attained the art of reading, & many are able to write, after a fashion'.[50] Hadfield took a census of literacy on Uvea and Lifu in 1894:

2453 out of 5659 Lifuan Protestants could read and by 1901 the figure had risen to 3193; 510 out of 712 Uvean Protestants were able to read.[51]

One of the most remarkable features of the rapid change from a pre-literate to a literate society on the Loyalty Islands was that it resulted largely from the Islanders' mutual instruction. The LMS missionaries provided them with an alphabet and printed material and taught pupils in the day schools before 1864 and in the boarding schools and the seminaries how to read and write, and from there the movement snowballed. The missionaries themselves were amazed that every night 'in almost every hut . . . a group of most earnest learners . . . [could] be seen'.[52]

In the earlier contact years printed material was often seen as 'a kind of talisman which gave as magic the knowledge of thoughts'.[53] Books and pamphlets were also prestige possessions and provided opportunities for people to show off their skill in reading, so emulating Europeans. Montrouzier was most sceptical of the Protestants he saw ostensibly reading at Chepenehe in 1858 and described how they could keep on reading out loud when the books were taken away for they had learnt the words off by heart.[54] MacFarlane gave the example of one Islander who 'had on a pair of spectacles; he was looking intently, with the most hypocritical face, upon a small hymn book which was turned upside down'.[55] However, from the 1860s onwards, there is every indication that books were desired for pleasure and information and that an extremely high proportion of Loyalty Islanders could read their own language.

The Marists did little in the field of translating and printing, mainly because they had not the resources to set up a press, and they were forced to use the scriptures printed by the LMS missionaries in Nengone and Dehu. They were in difficulties on Uvea because the LMS missionaries printed in Iai, whereas a large proportion of the Catholics spoke Uvea. The Marists were particularly at a disadvantage with regard to printed catechisms, for they could obviously not use those the LMS circulated, and throughout the remainder of the century they were much disheartened by their inability to emulate the LMS mission printing program.[56]

The French administration accused the LMS mission of having taught the Loyalty Islanders English and English customs, but such learning resulted from their association with Englishmen generally and not from formal mission training. In the LMS boarding schools and the seminaries some attempt was made to teach the brightest pupils how to read and write English but with very little success. When the directors of the LMS suggested in 1882 that more effort should be made by the missionaries on the Loyalty Islands to teach the people to read English, Jones answered that such a task was impossible: since 1857, he pointed out, only two Mareans had managed to use 'with intelligence' books in English.[57]

An ability to communicate in English came quickly to the Loyalty Islanders. Nihill reported in 1850 that the Lifuans had adopted 'every low and degraded habit and expression to be found among the worst of our countrymen';[58] the LMS missionaries on their first voyage to Uvea, in 1857, commented that many of the young men had travelled around the Pacific on English trading vessels 'and, consequently, speak a little English. Some of them, indeed, spoke English so well, that we had no difficulty in conversing with them';[59] and the 'greater part' of the Mareans were reported to speak 'imperfect English, as many of them have been in vessels for bêche-de-mer'.[60] French administrators and other European travellers frequently commented upon the Islanders' knowledge of the English language and their ability to emulate the example set by the Englishmen with whom they lived and worked. One Frenchman who called into Uvea showed an Islander a watch and waited for the man's expected reaction of great excitement and bewilderment at such a wondrous object. Instead the Uvean glanced at it and said, correctly, 'It's half-past eleven'.[61]

The French administration and the Marists made little headway in teaching the Islanders French until well into the twentieth century, and most of the middle-aged and older Islanders today had parents and certainly grandparents whom they remember spoke English. Although most of the present-day Islanders speak French, in addition to their own languages, they count and tell the time in English, and virtually every European item that was originally introduced in the nineteenth century still retains its English name.

The Islanders' social habits were not noticeably affected by the religious, formal, or informal secular instruction they received from Europeans. Patteson, in 1858, was one of the first missionaries to strongly criticise those Islanders who were ostensibly practising Christians:

> The same dirt, the same houses, the same idle vicious habits in most cases—no sense of decency or but very little—Where is the expression of the Scriptual life . . . ? A man reads a chapter in his filthy hut, men, women & children, pigs & fowls all huddled together—The Chap. contains warnings agst. immorality. This over, *instantly* they all lie down together & with minute accuracy discuss some case of adultery that has taken place in the village—children & all alive, eagerly alive, to the interest of all the conversation, and as the filthy poison sinks into their minds they congratulate themselves that they are spiritual & so forth.[62]

Throughout the century such complaints were common enough from the missionaries. In 1880 Creagh wrote:

> We have not that amount of social elevation we could desire; the people for the most part cling to their old habits—herd promiscuously together; sleep in dirt and squalor in houses with but one room & no window; wear but scant clothing except on service days & holidays, & use language offensive to civilized ears . . . refinement does not exist amongst them, and their moral feelings are not at all elevated.[63]

The LMS missionaries initially had hopes that 'moral improvement' would result from the Islanders' visits to 'civilised' countries as well as through mission activities on their own islands. In 1848 the missionaries were pleased to find that so many Mareans had already been to Sydney and related their adventures to spellbound audiences. They described 'great houses for the worship of God, crowds attending, schools for the children etc.; and are thus testifying to their countrymen that what the teachers have told them of Christianity must be true'.[64] The Melanesian Mission policy was based on similar assumptions—it was hoped that those returning from school in Auckland would become models of 'decency' to their own people. Unfortunately for the missionaries very little 'respectability' rubbed off onto the Islanders overseas. Nihill noted with dismay the reaction of the Melanesian Mission pupils as they neared their islands after their sojourn in Auckland: 'they seem to get wilder again; tie on handkerchiefs in room of native head-dresses; talk more of their own tongue, and in louder tones'.[65] The LMS missionaries explained that all those Islanders who travelled on English ships 'seem to have profited little from what they have seen; for they have all returned to their former savage life'.[66]

Such comments were naturally a reflection of the missionaries' own narrow moral outlook and were based on their assumption that the consequence of accepting Christianity should have been 'social elevation'—the substitution of the values of European respectability for the Islanders' own habits. The comments, nevertheless, are significant for they indicate that the Islanders selected and adapted only aspects of Christianity and all it was supposed to involve, and they did so for their own reasons and in their own way.

The Question of Impact

The Question of Impact

Loyalty Islanders displayed a remarkable self-determination characterised by confidence, enthusiasm, and creativeness in their responses to rival mission societies, to the doctrines and customs of Christianity and other European notions, as well as in their travelling and trading with Europeans. It was a reaction of an island people intent on taking the initiative and turning to their advantage rather than passively accepting, or simply rejecting, the presence of Europeans and their ways.

Charges that the activities of missionaries, traders, and administrators upset the general well-being of Pacific societies cannot be substantiated on the Loyalty Islands. There is every indication that the communities were not in any state of cultural depression, disruption, or dislocation as a result of these Europeans in their midst. Advocates of 'fatal impact' theories, however, ultimately base their case on the assertion that Europeans unavoidably brought with them certain pernicious influences—namely firearms, diseases and alcohol—which led to serious depopulation of island communities throughout the Pacific.

12
Firearms

Most studies of culture contacts in the Pacific assert that the introduction of firearms into existing indigenous hostilities resulted in unprecedented mortality. Such statements as firearms enabled 'the islanders to decimate themselves much more efficiently than was possible when they had to depend upon mere clubs and spears'[1] are legion. Similar assumptions have been made about the fighting on the Loyalty Islands where, it has been argued, firearms turned the Islanders' feuds into 'bloody wars' and gave them 'a desperate character' unknown in 'traditional' warfare.[2] Comments by Europeans in the nineteenth century lend weight to such an opinion: in 1860 the Governor of New Caledonia reported that fighting on Uvea had turned 'very deadly' since firearms had been introduced by English traders,[3] and both LMS and Marist missionaries sometimes spoke of 'wars of extermination' and 'decimation'. Closer investigation, however, suggests that such statements are misleading.

Europeans and other visitors calling at the Loyalty Islands in the 1840s all thought that tribal wars were virtually continuous and formed the Islanders' 'principal employment'. Even in times of 'peace' there was always great hostility and mutual suspicion between enemies. Early travellers described three methods of warfare. Unique to Lifu was a formalised combat where, as a result of some insult, one party issued a declaration of war against another and both sides arranged a time and place for 'a fair open fight'. No matter how serious the issue, the formalities of consultation and the 'etiquette of war' were always strictly followed. For several days the warriors prepared their weapons, sang and danced, and practised for the battle. Then they performed rituals to make themselves invincible, blackened their chests and faces, and arranged *tapa* and feathers in their hair before marching off to fight.[4] The sandalwood trader Andrew Cheyne has left an excellent description of a typical battle:

> ... on the day appointed both parties meet on a clear spot of Ground between the two tribes—and form in line abreast of each other about 100 yards (or more) distant. The fight is then commenced by throwing Spears from both Armies and which they generally catch and throw back again. The two lines then make a charge, meet, exchange blows with their clubs in passing—and again halt, at about the same distance, having changed positions. they continue these manoeuvres, until some of either party is killed. The victorious army then carry off the bodies of their Slain enemies, and return home with them.[5]

These contests seldom lasted more than a few hours and were usually between the two principal chiefdoms, Wet and Losi, on the beach at We, one of the few large open areas on the island and conveniently situated on a common boundary.

Apart from these formal battles, a common form of warfare on all three islands was ambushing. Small groups prowled through the bush by day or night and waylaid stragglers from fishing or planting parties. Cheyne explained that the attackers did 'not scruple to Murder defenceless Men, Women or children ... & carry their bodies home and feast on them'.[6] The third method of warfare can be loosely categorised as organised raids upon an enemy. As many warriors as possible were gathered for these expeditions and they usually tried to take their intended victims by surprise. Once the attack began they 'gave vent to their feelings by wild, hideous gestures, yells, and shoutings .... No order or discipline was observed, but each man was allowed to follow his own inclinations'.[7] Even in the largest raids very little fighting was ever in the open and there were few pitched battles. 'Their Wars are sometimes carried on in open fight, but stratagem is more generally resorted to', said Cheyne, and Ta'unga noted: 'Relatively few people are taken in open warfare. A much greater number are obtained in fighting by stealth, like kidnapping'.[8] If the surprise assaults did not destroy or immediately put the enemy to flight, there could be brief hand to hand combat, but as soon as one side began losing men it fled through the bush. The villages and plantations of the defeated party were then burnt if the issue was considered a serious one. When faced with aggression by a larger force, a smaller group quickly retreated to the top of high coral outcrops or into man-made fortifications such as the large stone fort on the plain at Hnaened on Mare and wooden barricades at Heo, Weneki, and Fayawe on Uvea. The attackers then roamed about, pillaging and destroying villages and plantations, scouring the countryside and killing any refugees who had been unable to reach safety in time, and attempting to starve or intimidate those in the strongholds into submission. The larger and more aggressive wars were usually undertaken in attempts to extend the authority and territory of a particular chief.

The methods of warfare were related to the political and territorial arrangements on each island as they existed in the 1840s. Formalised combat was possible only on Lifu because the chiefdoms of Wet and Losi were of equal strength and neither side felt able to conquer the other by armed aggression. The fighting instead evolved into a method which still provided opportunities for displays of bravery and outlets for vengeance and anger, though without the difficulties and uncertainties of a long war of attrition. Tensions in and between these chiefdoms could, however, still result in ambushes and small skirmishes. On Uvea, and particularly on Mare, where chiefdoms were numerous, small, and often politically unstable, ambitious leaders saw opportunities for engaging frequently in wars of conquest. According to Europeans both islands were in states of constant 'anarchy'[9] where the niceties of any formalised combat were irrelevant.

Pre-European weapons were clubs, spears, and slings and stones. The clubs were either crudely shaped out of knotty roots of hardwood trees, or highly polished and painstakingly carved with a variety of rounded heads, or with very sharp beak-like points. The spears were made from thin pieces of hardwood 8 to 10 feet long. They were usually without barbs or poison, and were launched with a *sip*, a short cord made of coconut fibre.[10]

The Loyalty Islanders quickly discovered the power of some European firearms. At Uvea, Cheyne said they:

> ... expressed great astonishment at the [ship's] Big Guns, and it was amusing to see the curiosity excited among them all, when they were told the large guns were to be fired; when the firing took place they expressed great surprise and astonishment at the Ball flying along tearing the water up; and on the firing of the second gun, [chief Whenegay] begged that no more should be fired as the noise had almost distracted him.[11]

The people of Mare and Lifu had much more unpleasant introductions to firearms in their skirmishes with sandalwood traders. Cheyne once felt it necessary to open fire on Lifu warriors who were threatening to board his

Firearms

vessel from their canoes: 'I gave them the contents of one of the Nine pounder Carronades, which by the crash it made when it struck the Canoe, I have no doubt sickened them pretty well'.[12] Mareans learned of the power of European munitions when Yiewene's son was killed in the explosion of a stolen powder barrel. But Loyalty Islanders seemed little interested in adding European arms and munitions to their own collection of weapons. Tomahawks, however, were a different matter and they quickly became 'preferred to any other weapon'. Cheyne believed that with one tomahawk he could 'purchase the head of any native on the Island [of Lifu]'.[13] They were not so much a new addition to the Islanders' arsenal as more efficient substitutes for clubs. Europeans were usually hesitant to give muskets as presents or payment, although some had no qualms about doing so, but it was thought safe enough to give away or trade with tomahawks. The Islanders quickly became discerning in their choice and both traders and missionaries had to supply particular types.[14] Missionaries, as well as traders, introduced large numbers of tomahawks, and orders for four dozen at a time for one mission station were common.[15] By the 1850s tomahawks were widespread throughout the Loyalty Islands and were used universally in battles, but they never completely replaced the wooden clubs. And while tomahawks made very good weapons, they had a great many other peaceful purposes which helps to explain the demand. Not only were they more efficient than stone cutting tools but they came ready-made, so sparing the Islanders from journeying to New Caledonia in search of suitable obdurate materials. Throughout the nineteenth century tomahawks remained valuable items of trade but were never as keenly sought after as cloth and tobacco.

The first Islanders to own muskets were chiefs who were given them as gifts by traders and missionaries.[16] Muskets were always regarded as valuable possessions but they were never in the same demand as tomahawks. Traders and missionaries were never forced to sell muskets to the local communities in order to buy protection and food as happened elsewhere in the Pacific,[17] nor were these weapons ever a significant item in the trade in labour and island produce.[18] Some Islanders did bring back muskets as payment for working in Queensland plantations or on commercial vessels in New Caledonian waters but eagle-eyed missionaries counted out in ones and twos, seldom more, the muskets being unloaded from ships and carried to the villages. Many of the imported firearms were fowling pieces which fired shot instead of bullets and which enabled the Islanders to hunt birds and flying foxes and even despatch their own fowls more effectively.

The French banned the importation of firearms into New Caledonia and dependencies in 1855 but, because they had neither the men nor the ships to police the coasts properly and because of the volume of commercial shipping around New Caledonia, the Islanders had little trouble in smuggling arms ashore if they wished.

By the 1860s only a 'small number' of Uveans were said to possess firearms and they usually belonged to those who had worked on European vessels.[19] Saisset, Governor of New Caledonia, told his minister in 1860 that Bazit, the leader of the Catholic tribes in the north of Uvea, had 3000 warriors armed with muskets sold by English traders.[20] Such an estimate was quite unrealistic and can safely be ignored. The total population of Uvea was scarcely 3000 and Bazit ruled over approximately 1000 people altogether. Saisset guessed wildly and was less concerned with giving accurate figures than stressing how dangerous he thought it was to allow so much English shipping around French territories. The administration's paranoia was summed up by the resident official on Lifu when he scathingly reported that firearms were 'fraudulently introduced by small sea traders of that race which notably infects the south seas'.[21] One traveller more realistically estimated that Bazit's warriors may have had 100 muskets.[22]

By the late 1860s, however, Ella, the sole LMS missionary stationed on Uvea, estimated that the Uvean Catholics had forty firearms and most of these were confiscated by the French in 1869. Ella reported that in 1872 the Catholics had again amassed fifty muskets.[23] These figures are not likely to have been under-estimated by the Catholic-hating Ella and, as the Catholics outnumbered the Protestants by about three to one at that time, it is unlikely the Protestants had as many muskets themselves. On his expedition to Lifu in 1864, Guillain confiscated fifty-nine 'guns and pistols', but not fowling pieces, and although the French were well aware that not all the firearms had been surrendered they were satisfied that the Islanders had destroyed them rather than give the French the pleasure.[24] In the first serious 'religious war' on Mare in 1869 the Catholic tribes of the southern and eastern areas had only four muskets while the Protestants in the north and west were reported to have 'many guns'.[25] The French confiscated these weapons in 1870, and in 1876 again took away 'arms', but there is no indication of the types of weapons confiscated this second time. After the last serious war in 1880 the French once more collected weapons which consisted solely of spears and clubs.[26]

It is impossible to give accurate figures for the number of firearms introduced into the Loyalty Islands, but there is no indication that the number was large, and there was never a 'saturation' level of one gun to every fighting man.[27] The extent of shipping contacts and overseas travel gave the Islanders every opportunity to obtain muskets if they so desired, but at no stage was there a significant demand for them. There were, however, some firearms present and they could have had some impact in warfare.

From 1841 until 1880 there are twenty-four documented violent incidents among the Islanders which resulted in loss of life. They were variously referred to as battles, wars, skirmishes, armed campaigns, massacres, murders, butcherings, and assassinations. The majority of these incidents date from the time of permanent mission settlement in the 1850s and there are other references to fighting on all three islands in the 1840s. But because most of the reports of these earlier fights are based on hearsay and usually collected years after the event, they cannot be corroborated and are considered too unreliable for analysis. For example, Erskine was told that 300 people died in a war in Losi which lasted from 1847 until 1849. But MacFarlane, who later settled on Lifu, wrote that the same war had been 'more protracted than sanguinary'.[28] Once there was permanent mission settlement on the islands every violent incident was noted by both Marist and LMS missionaries, who wrote very long and detailed accounts of any fighting and listed the number of their converts wounded and killed and, although their respective accounts almost always presented conflicting interpretations as to who first provoked hostilities, the details of the events themselves are virtually identical. The French administration also carefully investigated the fighting, and commissions of inquiry presented lengthy reports including testimonies of the protagonists.

In all the documented incidents the methods of warfare remained unchanged until the fighting ended altogether. The formal combats at We were the first to finish, some time in the late 1840s or early 1850s. The acceptance of LMS Polynesian teachers in the mid-1840s by Bula, great chief of Losi, may have made such contests irrelevant, for the LMS techniques of organising teachers and policemen gave him unprecedented opportunities to extend his influence into the rival chiefdom of Wet. Furthermore, the Polynesian teacher Fao was known to have accompanied Bula's warriors to the battlefield at We, and it is possible that he may have instructed them to abandon the usual rules of combat and fight more ruthlessly: Ukeneso, great chief of Wet, told MacFarlane that Fao was 'the chief cause of his defeat in their late wars'.[29] Ambushing remained the common method for settling scores on all three islands and, in spite of mission influence, women and children were often victims. On Mare and Uvea the organised raids followed their pre-European patterns without changes in strategies of attack or defensive arrangements. 'It is rare', explained de Rochas, 'for two enemy parties to make frontal assaults on each other . . . because the tactics of war lie in surprise and ambushes'.[30] Firearms played only a minor role. One missionary claimed that the surprise tactics could hardly be called 'fighting—rather butchering & murdering with tomahawks'.[31]

Fighting on Lifu from the time of first mission settlement until peace in 1864 was on a very small scale and the numbers killed were minimal. MacFarlane explained:

> I remember the first [war] that took place after my arrival on Lifu. From the report and from a letter hastily written by the French priest I thought that, before I could get to the spot (ten miles off), the combatants would be in the condition of the Kilkenny cats. I soon found, however, that, whatever they might have suffered or lost in the struggle, they had not lost their legs, nor yet the ability to use them. Both armies had decamped, each claiming the victory, four men being left behind severely wounded by tomahawks, two from each side. This is a fair specimen of wars among the natives.[32]

On Mare and Uvea fighting tended to be more violent but even the most serious incidents hardly resulted in high mortality. There were two major battles on Uvea. The first involved the assassination of Whenegay by Bazit's warriors in 1856. Forty-five men were killed in the ensuing hostilities. Bazit's men were armed with about 100 muskets and fired upon Whenegay's party who managed to dodge the first volley by hiding behind trees and coral boulders. And while their assailants were furiously trying to reload their weapons, Whenegay's warriors rushed upon them with clubs and tomahawks, killing about forty.

> It is the bloodiest incident [wrote de Rochas] which has ever taken place in the Caledonian archipelago . . . . It is explained by the imprudence of the attackers who, having too much confidence in their guns, had neglected to arm themselves with tomahawks and clubs.[33]

The Catholics' three-month siege of the Protestants at Fayawe in 1873 was more spectacular than deadly. The warriors spent each day taunting, threatening, and screaming obscenities at each other, throwing spears, catching them, and hurling them back with further abuse. The French official who investigated the fighting said that it was never 'pursued with vigour'. Altogether fifteen people lost their lives. Only seven were killed in the fighting around the palisade, and at least one of them was shot. The re-

Firearms 141

maining victims were Protestant women who, in a party of sixteen, crept through enemy lines one night in search of food and water. They were captured and had their hands placed on coconut tree stumps and pulverised with the backs of tomahawks—only eight survived the mutilation.[34]

The most publicised and said to be the most ruthless fighting throughout the Loyalty Islands took place when the Mare Protestants attacked the Si Achakaze tribe in 1860 and the Catholic tribes in 1869 and 1880. In 1860 Naisiline Nidoish's warriors, who were known to possess some muskets, killed forty of the Si Achakaze. Both Marist and LMS missionaries reported that all were 'hacked to pieces' with tomahawks.[35] In 1869 Naisiline Nidoish's men killed eighteen Catholics, of whom thirteen were shot, and lost one man themselves.[36] In 1880 the Catholics lost twenty-three people. At least eight were clubbed to death and another thirteen were children who were battered to death with coral boulders by the Protestants. No Protestants were killed.[37]

From 1858 until 1880, 174 people died in battles on Mare; and from 1856 until 1873, 92 people were killed on Uvea. Apart from those killed in the incidents mentioned here, most victims died in numerous small skirmishes. And of the total mortality figure of 266 there is reliable documentary evidence that over 200 were killed by weapons other than firearms.[38]

European technology appears to have had a minimal influence on fighting in the Loyalty Islands. Gunpowder helped to destroy plantations and villages in several instances, but it was used as an incendiary, not an explosive, device. Tomahawks were universal weapons but did not completely replace wooden clubs, which were just as effective for splitting skulls.

> The clubs [wrote Emma Hadfield] . . . although they were very heavy, and appeared somewhat unwieldy, they were handled with great skill and force. The father of one of our old schoolboys was struck in the back with a club of the bird's beak shape; the weapon completely penetrated his body from back to front.[39]

Several reasons can be suggested for the minor role of firearms. The types available to the Loyalty Islanders were smooth-bore, muzzle-loading muskets which were cumbersome and complicated to use, inefficient, inaccurate,[40] and very often in a dilapidated condition. De Rochas thought that most of the muskets he saw on Uvea in the late 1850s were 'useless',[41] and there had been little improvement by the 1870s. At the siege of Fayawe in 1873, Pionnier explained: 'the few firearms that are to found there often in very bad condition manufactured I do not know when misfire everytime for some [warriors] or else produce nothing but a useless detonation'.[42] In the heat of battle, warriors were known to forget essential steps of the loading procedure. Two Si Gwahma men who hurriedly fired at some Catholics found, said MacFarlane, that the 'shots were perfectly harmless, the men having forgotten to put in the balls'![43] Some Islanders had little faith in muskets. One Catholic, about to lead his men into the bush after some Protestants, shook with fear and asked Bernard to bless a medal he was wearing. Bernard commented that the terrified man 'had more confidence in that than in his inferior musket someone had given him'.[44] Apart from muskets, the Uveans had at least one blunderbuss, and the Lifuans had a small number of pistols which, like the muskets, were smooth-bored and muzzle-loading. The efficient breech-loading Snider rifles and Boxer all-metal cartridges developed in the later 1860s[45] never made an appearance in the fighting. By the time such weapons could have been imported in any number, the fighting on Lifu and Uvea had finished and firearms were not seen in battles on Mare after 1870.

Yet the unreliability of firearms cannot be the only reason for the unimportant part they played in tribal hostilities; other Pacific Islanders may well have used muskets effectively. A more important explanation can be found in the nature of fighting on the Loyalty Islands. Single-shot fire-arms which took time to load were unsuited to the 'strategem' and 'stealth', or what would now be called guerrilla tactics, which characterised much of the Loyalty Islanders' warfare. Bazit's resounding defeat when well armed with muskets in 1856 was a stern lesson in the superiority of clubs and spears at close quarters in heavy bush. The Islanders had no reason to adopt new tactics or new weapons of doubtful efficiency, especially since they never had to face European soldiers in battle. Even if muskets had been reliable, they would still have been unsuited to the rough, over-grown landscape, and to the Islanders' style of fighting.

But perhaps the most important reason was that the killing of large numbers of the enemy was apparently not a feature of the Islanders' raids, at least in the form they took in the early contact period. The aim was not to annihilate enemies, enslave them, or take away their lands. A defeated party remained on its own clan land but was expected to acknowledge its inferiority and pay tribute in produce to its conquerors instead of to its former chief.[46] There was no slave class. The Islanders, therefore, probably did not see firearms in European terms—as a potential means for mass killing, enslavement, and destruction. The missionaries were often extremely annoyed with the Islanders' apparent satisfaction with their own way of fighting and their failure to adopt European military philosophy and tac-

Firearms   143

tics. Frequently their supporters decided to retreat when the enemy was clearly losing. 'An army of natives knows neither discipline, nor duty, nor a leader, nor an obligation to espouse a public cause' wrote one disgusted priest when his men stopped chasing a group of defeated Protestants through the bush.[47] Pionnier described with some resignation the time wasted by his warriors and their, to him, ineffective tactics:

> ... our poor natives, in military tactics, as in a thousand other things, are still infants.... The two parties meet each other with ear-splitting screams, or provoke each other, brandishing tomahawks over their heads and leaping like demons, then comes a shower of spears, you turn away for fear of seeing blood run, the two camps are so close and the spears are thrown so fiercely that there must be many victims, but be assured ... no one is ever scratched. The adroitness of these islanders in dodging missiles is extraordinary, standing still to examine the direction of the spears aimed at them, then turning to the right or left bending double, throwing themselves on the ground on their backs or stomachs with the suppleness of a snake .... Then after further insults and shameful language each one chases his adversary, provokes him and the struggle begins again always with the number of dead and wounded equal to zero.[48]

MacFarlane commented:

> ... their wars are by no means so serious and fatal as those amongst civilised nations. They are not sufficiently advanced in civilisation yet to understand the art of killing by thousands; with them there is great preparation, great skirmishing, great noise, but few lives are lost.[49]

De Rochas also noted that there could not be found 'in the savages' military tactics, the skillful manoeuvres which make us so honoured in the art of war'.[50]

Such ethnocentric interpretations indicate a failure on the part of some Europeans to understand the nature and seriousness of the fighting for the Islanders. On the other hand, comments by missionaries and others about 'wars of extermination' can invariably be attributed to guesswork, heat of the moment outrage, propaganda, or combinations of all three. Of the statements about the serious effects of wars on the Loyalty Islands mentioned earlier, Saisset's was pure speculation and reflected his paranoia about nearby English influences. As for the missionaries' comments, it is necessary to make a distinction between the dramatic, emotional terminology they adopted, especially when describing wars whose outcome could either extend or diminish their influence, and the actual details they presented of the events. Both missions were likely to talk about 'massacres' and 'exterminations' and then in the very same reports list some small number of Islanders who were killed. A careful investigation and cross-check of mortality figures given by the French administration and the LMS and Marist missionaries demonstrates that relatively few people died in the battles.

The assumption that firearms had a devastating effect when introduced into hostilities in the Pacific is not supported by events on the Loyalty Islands. There, Europeans and their technology did not change the tactics and techniques of warfare as long as it lasted, and firearms in particular were responsible for killing only a small proportion of those who died in the fighting.

13
Disease

Writers on the Pacific have usually agreed that the introduction of European diseases was one of the worst legacies for the island populations of contact with the West: 'The history of disease in the Pacific in the century after Wallis landed at Tahiti in 1767 is a depressing and tragic one'.[1] While such a general view is justified it has perhaps been too readily assumed that one of the most important consequences of European diseases was rapid depopulation of the island communities—a notion that has recently been questioned by demographic studies.[2] Furthermore, little distinction has been made by historians and others between pre- and post-contact diseases, and between endemic and epidemic diseases and their respective effects.

During the nineteenth century contact period, the most prevalent endemic diseases on the Loyalty Islands were yaws, filariasis (notably elephantiasis of the lower limbs and male genitalia), and diseases under the general name of, and associated with tuberculosis—such as *tabes mesenterica*, pleurisy, pulmonary tuberculosis (consumption), and a wide variety of scrofulous sores and abscesses. Of these diseases both yaws and filariasis were widespread in the Pacific long before Europeans arrived,[3] and were present in New Caledonia and the Loyalty Islands. In 1774 Cook saw cases of elephantiasis and hydrocele on the east coast of New Caledonia: 'Swelled and ulcerated legs and feet are very common amongst the Men; swelled Testicles are likewise very common'. Cheyne reported in

1842 that some Uveans also suffered from elephantiasis and hydrocele.⁴ Tubercular diseases were most probably introduced into the Pacific by Europeans and can be traced back to the 1780s in eastern Polynesia.⁵ There is little point in speculating whether tuberculosis was endemic on the Loyalty Islands before 1841; certainly by the 1850s European visitors recorded that tuberculosis, along with filariasis and yaws, was one of the most significant endemic diseases.

There is little quantitative evidence to document any possible increases in the incidence of such diseases from the 1840s through to the 1860s; and it could be argued that these diseases are mentioned more in the 1860s simply because there are more extant records for this time. However, it seems most likely that these diseases had worsened since the time of European contact. In the 1840s Europeans believed most Loyalty Islanders were 'in general' healthy and 'tolerably free from disease'.⁶ In contrast, Patteson remarked in 1858 that there was a 'tendency to consumptive diseases' which existed 'in the constitution of nearly all' the Islanders. 'Nearly all the diseases' on Lifu, he commented, could be 'referred to the scrofulous disposition of the race'.⁷ Missionaries and travellers described the prevalence of 'scrofulous' and 'pulmonary' diseases. De Rochas estimated that a third of the Uvean people had some scrofulous affliction.⁸ Yaws was seldom referred to as such by people with little or no knowledge of medicine and was usually put in the category of tuberculous sores or abscesses. All these diseases were widespread throughout all three islands.

Filariasis was especially prevalent on Uvea, where by 1860 it was said to be rare to see anyone without some stage of infection.⁹ Recent research has discovered that filariasis abounds on Uvea because the local vector, the *Aedes vigilax* mosquito, thrives in the large swampy areas. Lifu and Mare have few mosquitos because they are higher and drier islands with very few swamp regions.¹⁰

There are several reasons why these diseases could have become more widespread from the time of the first European visits. Heavy and obsessive smoking of low quality tobacco with a high nicotine content, combined with the stuffy atmosphere of the huts, was likely to have aggravated any pulmonary conditions. Jouan saw some people in their twenties die of 'asthma' and he thought smoking may have been the major cause.¹¹ Futhermore, any tubercular condition can make yaws much more serious than it might normally be.¹² Also lack of hygiene would have helped to increase and spread skin abscesses and sores, and it is highly probable that the large numbers of pigs and fowls which were allowed to roam freely

Disease 147

about villages and inside huts would have increased unhealthy conditions. According to Sleigh, 'natives often neglected personal cleanliness, and thought washing would induce illness'.[13] The first Lifu primer lesson was: 'Don't go out during public worship to pick out and eat fleas'.[14]

> Few things were unclean to the natives of these islands. Running sores were left exposed, and ulcerous matter was allowed to accumulate and overflow on to adjacent parts of the body; or, if wiped off with the fingers, it was either left to dry on the hands, or transferred to the nearest mat or tree.
>
> Mucus from the children's noses was treated in the same way, or drawn off by the mother's mouth.
>
> Lice were searched for in each other's heads, and cracked between the teeth with apparent relish.[15]

Changes in clothing and diet as a result of European presence have often been cited as contributing to ill-health among Pacific Islanders, but there is no evidence that these factors had any significance in the Loyalty Islands. The Islanders' diet remained virtually unchanged throughout the nineteenth century and was based on the foods the earliest Europeans saw there—yams, taro, coconuts, bananas, sugar cane and fish. It was uncommon for them to eat pigs and fowls after they had been introduced and the Islanders raised them almost solely for the export market.[16] By the 1880s a few Islanders sometimes added small quantities of flour, rice, tea, and sugar to their diets. (A high sugar intake in the twentieth century has led to widespread tooth decay.) Methods of cooking remained unchanged—food was either boiled, in metal rather than the traditional clay pots, roasted over an open fire, or, as was most common, wrapped in leaves, placed on glowing hot coral stones, and covered with earth and leaves.

The Islanders wore only light, loose fitting European clothing and were fully dressed up only on Sundays. During the week the men normally wore a skirt of cloth and perhaps a light shirt. The women wore loose fitting neck to ankle 'Mother Hubbard' dresses designed by the LMS missionaries' wives. If the women worked hard these dresses were often rolled to the waist, and when inland at their gardens, safely out of sight of the missionaries, both men and women went about naked. Because the Loyalty Islands do not have the high rainfall and humidity of the higher and more northerly islands, the people did not walk about in wet clothes for long periods. Nor did the Loyalty Islanders adopt heavy clothing as did the New Zealand Maoris, who consequently contracted a variety of illnesses from being constantly wrapped up in blankets all year round.[17]

Two French doctors, Mialaret and Noc, who investigated the Islanders' health towards the end of the century, found that tuberculosis, yaws, and filariasis were still the principal endemic diseases.[18] Yaws, in particular, seems to have increased markedly, and was thought to be 'universal' among the population. In some villages on Lifu half the children were covered in severe eruptions. So widespread had it become that it was accepted as part of the way of life; parents whose children did not have it thought that it was a sign of something amiss. Emma Hadfield explained that yaws

> ... generally attacked children of two or three years of age, that is, soon after they were weaned, and sometimes covered the little body from head to foot with scab-like sores, upon which greedy flies feasted from sunrise to sunset. Tonas [yaws] usually disappeared after about twelve months; but occasionally they formed large ulcerated sores which were most obstinate in healing.[19]

In the 1880s some new types of sores were noticed and sixty or seventy people were suspected of having leprosy. In 1890 Mialaret confirmed forty-nine cases on Mare, fewer on Lifu, and found none on Uvea. Leprosy was thought to have been introduced by Protestant teachers returning from duty in New Guinea, or from China via New Caledonia where there were confirmed cases of leprosy in 1878. The French administration immediately built lepers' camps and isolated suspect cases. In 1909 there were 107 cases on Mare, 75 on Lifu, and 39 on Uvea.[20] Why there was the highest incidence of leprosy on Mare, even in the twentieth century, has yet to be explained.

There were no epidemics of sexual diseases and therefore none became endemic. There are some references to 'syphilitic disease' but these were most likely a mistaken diagnosis of yaws or scrofulous sores.[21] In 1904 Noc found no primary or secondary symptoms of venereal syphilis, and said that those sores most resembling syphilis were scrofulous, for they responded to treatment with potassium iodide.[22] One of the main reasons why venereal syphilis was a rare disease, throughout the Pacific in fact, was because yaws built up an immunity to it. It is now considered that 'The major effect of yaws ... was to protect ... island populations from the potential devastations of its relative—venereal syphilis'.[23] In those places where yaws was not endemic, notably New Zealand, venereal syphilis had rapid and severe effects upon the people.

Gonorrhoea was never recorded on the Loyalty Islands. Even if there were undetected cases there was little likelihood of the disease being a major one. Gonorrhoea is 'dependent upon promiscuity for its survival'.

For most Melanesian cultures, with a few spectacular exceptions, gonorrhoea seems to have been a minor cause of lowered fertility or even morbidity. This would correlate with the usual Melanesian attitude towards sex, which is often diffident and circumscribed when compared to that of other Island peoples.[24]

Attention has already been drawn to the sexual reticence of the Loyalty Islanders, and especially the Uveans. With the possible exception of pulmonary tuberculosis, the endemic diseases discussed so far did not noticeably increase mortality rates. Yaws is seldom fatal and is considered to have 'no direct effect upon fertility'.[25] Filariasis and scrofulous diseases are similarly not normally fatal. Nor did filariasis have any bearing on the fecundity of the population, for it is most commonly found in mature and older men.[26] However painful and unpleasant these diseases might have been for the Loyalty Islanders they were not directly responsible for any depopulation. But they most certainly helped lower the Islanders' resistance to epidemics of European diseases which were often fatal.

Pre-European diseases present on the Loyalty Islands were long-lasting chronic infections. The spirochaete (*Treponema pertenue*) responsible for yaws and the filarial worm can survive indefinitely in isolated communities, with children being infected by their parents. Epidemic diseases, however, such as measles and smallpox cannot exist in small, isolated communities, and it seems likely that the Pacific Islanders were naturally protected from such epidemics in pre-European days.

Epidemics periodically occurred on the Loyalty Islands throughout the nineteenth century. Mareans claimed that an epidemic resembling measles or smallpox swept through their island wiping out whole villages soon after the massacre of the *eletok*.[27] Epidemics certainly were common once the islands were visited by sandalwood and LMS mission vessels. Influenza and dysentery were recorded on Mare and Lifu in the 1840s, and dysentery made regular appearances on Mare in the 1850s.[28] Unfortunately there are no mortality figures. The most serious epidemic to hit the islands was scarlet fever in 1860. Out of a local population of 1000 at Netche on Mare, Creagh recorded for that year 63 deaths and 43 births. On Lifu several hundred people died, and the Marist missionaries lost 240 of their Uvean converts.[29] Dysentery recurred on Lifu and Uvea in the early 1860s although recorded deaths were less than 100. By the mid-1860s it seems that Islanders were building up immunity to epidemics, for there are many more references to people recovering from illnesses which had formerly proved fatal.[30] Influenza, dysentery, and whooping cough all reappeared occasionally in the 1870s yet recorded deaths amounted to fewer than twenty. Ella, who had some medical training, observed in 1875 that the Islanders were healthy, confident and remained free from any epidemics.[31] The 1880s too were a healthy decade. Mialaret recorded influenza on Mare in 1890 and he thought it had come from Fiji where he had recently seen it. But he said that the Mare influenza was 'very mild' compared to its Fijian counterpart.[32]

Loyalty Islanders usually attributed sickness and death to some wrong doing on the part of the sufferer or the deceased, to some enemy's imprecation, or to Kolemije—a demon seen in dreams. They had a variety of remedies for their diseases in pre-European times, and they continued to use many of them during the contact period. Patients were treated by either a *tene haze*, a man who possessed a haze and 'worked by the instrumentality of spirits or demons', or a *tene dosinoe*, a man who could make and administer herbal remedies. 'Sometimes', said Emma Hadfield, 'the two arts seemed to merge into each other, and the magical element was introduced into the ordinary practice of medicine'.[33] De Rochas, a medical doctor, thought some of the herbal remedies he saw used in the 1860s were quite effective for treating some of the minor illnesses, but useless for anything serious.[34]

Their common remedy for head and stomach pains and bilious attacks was to purge themselves by drinking large quantities of salt water.

> In order to make them vomit [wrote MacFarlane] . . . they use the bark of a certain tree. Covering it over with leaves, they tie it up, and with this they lave the water into their mouths until they have swallowed nearly a bucketful (they declare that they can take two bucketsful!). Then like distended leeches they lie or roll on the grass or sand until they vomit, after which they say they are well and feel strong, although it sometimes proves fatal.[35]

Lancing was a common treatment for most external sores and swellings, and after European contact splinters of broken glass replaced lancets of wood, shell, or stone. Sores such as boils may have been cured in this way but, when the Islanders cut out their yaws, leprous, and scrofulous abscesses, they doubtless helped to spread the infection. Nevertheless, it gave 'the sufferer real pleasure to be able to say after an operation that the blood is black (*wetewet*), *very* black, showing that the ailment merited the operation'.[36] Some Islanders even attempted to burn away their leprosy.[37] All aches, bruises, and pains, were also lanced.

On Uvea skull operations, or trepanning, had reached a level of some sophistication in pre-European times. If someone suffered from headaches his scalp was cut with sharp shells or stones and the skull exposed. The 'surgeon' then scraped away a section of the skull nearest to the centre of the pain and replaced the bone with smooth, shaped pieces of coconut shell. Throughout the operation an assistant trickled water over the patient's exposed skull. The scalp was then carefully stitched back with a needle made from the wing bone of a flying fox and fine twine. After contact with Europeans the Islanders copied techniques they presumably picked up from watching European ships' surgeons at work. One Uvean 'surgeon' wore a pair of dirty, white calico trousers and, in addition to his glass scalpels, his instruments included a butcher's knife and a pair of rusty scissors.[38] In 1864 Ella said that half the adult population on Uvea had undergone the operation.[39] Some people endured it several times, and it was Emma Hadfield's opinion that 'the whole top of their heads must be a kind of mosaic work of coconut shell'.[40] Most patients walked away after the operation and apparently suffered no lasting ill-effects, though not surprisingly a few died in the coconut grove theatres.

Visible sores, stomach upsets, swellings, and aches and pains were all familiar afflictions to the Islanders and they attempted to use their traditional remedies even though these may have been unsuccessful in curing the new ailments. But epidemics of dysentery, influenza, and scarlet fever were beyond their experience and comprehension. Unable to appease whatever supernatural force had sent such a curse upon them, and unable to cure themselves, the most common reaction during subsequent epidemics was one of helplessness and despair until the disease passed away.

Throughout the nineteenth century the LMS missionaries provided most of the medical attention the Islanders received from Europeans. Apart from Ella these missionaries had only the most superficial knowledge of medicine, and their medical stores were limited and usually in short supply. Stomach upsets and most internal disorders were treated with olive oil and 'Turners cerate'. External sores were treated with calamine powder, sulphur, red precipitate ointment (which killed worms and visible organisms in abscesses), tincture of Arnica (to mollify wounds, burns, and putrifying sores), oxide of zinc, and potassium iodide (for scrofula). The Marist missionaries made little attempt to cure their sick for they had few or no medical supplies, and Catholic islanders frequently went to the LMS missionaries seeking medical aid. During epidemics the LMS missionaries could do nothing for their people for they had neither the numbers nor resources to attend to the hundreds of sick all over the islands, and usually they had to devote themselves to looking after their own sick families. The

Marists, however, became particularly active during epidemics and ran from village to village in a desperate attempt to baptise their dying supporters. They had no way to ease the suffering of these people but spent all their efforts trying to achieve salvation in the next world for them.[41] The French administration did little beyond sending some doctors for brief visits towards the end of the century. These men also lacked equipment. They managed to vaccinate some Islanders and instructed the missionaries how to vaccinate. They also isolated people suffering from leprosy. Apart from these measures they did little but record what they saw. The Europeans were unable to do very much to improve the Islanders' health because of lack of resources and knowledge. Nor were they able to bring about changes in the Islanders' living conditions which might have helped to prevent disease.

Once the Loyalty Islanders overcame their initial fears that missionaries caused their illnesses, and then passed the brief stage when they thought the missionaries had the power to cure everything instantly, they developed a more realistic approach towards missionary medical capabilities and European medicine. For minor internal disorders and external sores they had no objection to using missionary powders, pastes, and potions. These items were not new to the Islanders in that they had their own similar medicaments, but they realised the effectiveness of some European treatments. Vaccinations too were not a revolutionary treatment for the Islanders as they were well used to lancing, which was the technique for vaccinations at that time. They were never reluctant to come forward in large numbers to be vaccinated.[42]

With their own medical techniques and those the Europeans could supply, the Islanders were usually enthusiastic and confident, if frequently unsuccessful, in attempting to cure most of their endemic illnesses and sores.

A popularly accepted notion, conceived in nineteenth-century missionary propaganda, is that alcohol had a devastating effect upon Pacific island societies. Maurice Leenhardt, the missionary-anthropologist who spent a lifetime crusading against the evils of liquor, spoke of the people of New Caledonia being 'submerged in a flood of alcohol'.[43] Loyalty Islanders, however, had no known stimulants before the Europeans arrived, and throughout the nineteenth century most of them demanded nothing stronger than tobacco. There is no indication that the Islanders had or wanted supplies of alcohol until the 1880s. After this time there are a few references to 'drunkenness' which was blamed, probably correctly, on their experiences working in the New Caledonian mines. But up to and

Disease

well beyond the turn of the century, mention of alcohol is notably absent from government, and LMS and Marist missionary reports. Hadfield did organise temperance societies in the 1880s and 1890s but his aim was preventative and not curative with regard to alcohol. And the societies were part of a general crusade against 'indolence' and other vices, and were designed to promote interest and involve more people in church activities.[44] Hadfield's wife, after forty-one years on the Loyalty Islands, wrote that very few Lifuans drank alcohol, 'perhaps not one-half per cent, of the population of 6000 or 7000'.[45]

Those Europeans who did complain about alcohol in the Loyalty Islands were speaking more from their conviction that alcohol had the potential to kill 'directly through poisoning and indirectly through sickness and quarrelling'[46] than from the reality of the island situation. There is no evidence to suggest that drunkenness was common or that alcohol created health or social problems for Loyalty Islanders in the nineteenth century.

From the time of first European contact Loyalty Islanders were exposed to new endemic and epidemic diseases which aggravated those diseases already present and resulted in a worsening of their health. Though by today's standards such diseases are abhorrent it must not be forgotten that many European societies suffered from similar diseases at that time. And it should be emphasised that Europeans believed the Loyalty Islanders to be a healthy race. In 1890 Mialaret reported: 'I was particularly struck by the vigorous nature and health of nearly everybody' on Mare, and he thought that those diseases which were present were much milder and less widespread than on New Caledonia and certainly in Fiji. In 1904 Noc expressed his confidence in the health of the Loyalty Islanders. Both doctors emphasised the physical strength of the people and their intelligence, their willingness to be vaccinated and to seek European medical attention, and their accessibility. The doctors also stressed the importance of the salubrious climate, away from the humid malarial zone. Noc drew particular attention to the dry surface of the islands, especially on Mare and Lifu, which he thought was 'virtually free from any infection'.[47]

Though the Islanders' health was adversely affected by European presence the results were not drastic enough to destroy their general wellbeing, or, as will now be described, to have caused any significant depopulation.

14
Depopulation?

Population figures for the Loyalty Islands in the nineteenth century must be approached with some caution. Many of the earlier estimates were little more than guesses based on observations made from the deck of a ship or on information gathered from visits to one or two coastal villages. Even the first missionary estimates were liable to owe more to guesswork than to careful counting. But by the 1860s, after the missionaries had made thorough tours of the islands, their estimates can be credited with a considerable degree of accuracy if only because the islands are small, the villages were readily accessible, and the populations were only a few thousand. The first figures known to be reasonably accurate came from the censuses of the 1860s and 1870s, undertaken by the missionaries on instructions from the French administration. Then, from the turn of the century, censuses were taken every five years with the aid of missionaries and with increasing participation by both resident and visiting French officials. Until the twentieth century, census-taking usually involved a head count only with very few attempts made to ascertain carefully the age and sex structure or the fertility rate of the populations. LMS missionaries counted 4300 Mareans in 1860.[1] Another count was made just before the Catholic tribes left for the Isle of Pines in 1870 and the total came to 4500.[2] The first organised census was undertaken in 1875 when the population was put at 4020. The difference between the counts for 1870 and 1875, assuming the 1870 figure was accurate, can largely be accounted for by migration to

Depopulation

Australia and to the Isle of Pines: of the 900 who went to the latter island only 750 had returned by 1875.³ A second census was taken in 1880 with the total amounting to 3584, a decline of 436.⁴ Another government count five years later raised the figure to 3725. Subsequent censuses in 1901, 1906, and 1910 put the population at 3575, 3332, and 3764 respectively.⁵

Under instructions from the French the LMS calculated the Lifuan population in 1866 at 5748.⁶ The census of 1875 involved the missionaries in the writing down of each Lifuan's name; the total was 6249.⁷ The 1880 census raised the figure to 6576, which dropped to 5488 in 1901. By 1906 the population was 5859, and 6220 in 1910.⁸

In 1869 missionary counts put the population of Uvea at 2426.⁹ Hadfield's estimate of 3000 in 1882 was perhaps over-optimistic, for an administration calculation in 1885 came to 2050.¹⁰ Censuses of 1901, 1906, and 1911 gave 1884, 2002, and 2028 respectively.¹¹

It is impossible to do more than guess, as did the early Europeans, at the total population at the time of first European contact: possibly it was somewhere in the range of 12,000–15,000.¹² From the 1850s the missionaries, who knew more about Loyalty Islanders than any other Europeans, had few doubts that the populations were numerically in a satisfactory state. The LMS reported in 1861 that in 'the Loyalty Group, where missionaries and teachers are at work, there is no great or marked diminution' of the people as a result of European contact.¹³ Throughout the 1860s the few extant mission reports of births and deaths suggest that, although numbers died in epidemics, the number of births was still sometimes higher than the number of deaths.¹⁴ Even on Uvea, which seems to have suffered most from the epidemics of the early 1860s, the Marist missionaries expressed confidence that there would be no serious long-term depopulation.¹⁵ In spite of the overall decline in the three populations in the latter part of the nineteenth century, most contemporary observers stressed the relative stability of the population figures and claimed that the declines were largely attributable to the absence of hundreds of Islanders who were sailing on commercial vessels in the south-west Pacific and labouring in Australia and then New Caledonia.¹⁶

Graphs of population figures from the 1860s through to the present day¹⁷ show populations that were basically stable, providing the census figures are accepted as reasonably accurate. Because of the age structure of a population, demographic trends must necessarily be long term and seen over several generations. To suggest that there was 'depopulation' in the Loyalty Islands is misleading if depopulation is defined as a situation

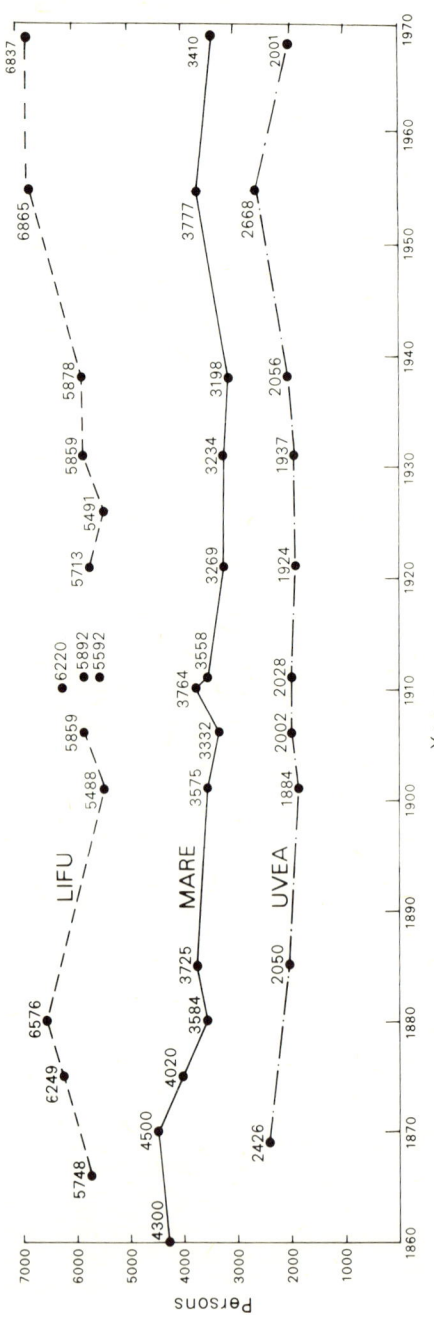

FIGURE 1 Population of the Loyalty Islands

where death rates consistently exceed birth rates. The low points in the graphs may well be recording periods when either the death rate increased and was higher than the birth rate, or when the birth rate declined relative to a stable death rate. The latter possibility may well have been the case; that is, periods of apparent numerical decline, such as 1870 to 1880 on Mare, or 1880 to 1900 on Lifu, may have been partly the result of depleted cohorts of women reaching child-bearing age. For example, the scarlet fever epidemic of the early 1860s may well have killed off significant numbers of young females, so that when these females would normally have reached child-bearing age, from about fifteen years onwards, the birth rate would have been lowered until the next cohort of women, unaffected by that epidemic, started reproducing. The apparently sharp increases in the populations after low points in the graphs are reached in the 1860s, and about 1901 and 1921, probably indicate that cohorts born after an age-selective epidemic were moving through their child-bearing age.

The fluctuations in the graphs suggest that the death rate did not constantly exceed the birth rate. Furthermore, the very considerable mobility of the populations outside the islands must also be taken into consideration; apparent numerical declines in population for particular periods may well have been largely due to emigration, as contemporary observers suggested. Fluctuations for the ninety-year period are probably indicative of migration and of several depleted or weakened cohorts of women working their way through the age structures of the populations.

No models of the nineteenth-century populations of the three islands can be constructed because of lack of information in the census returns. There is, however, nothing to suggest that age and sex structures were permanently distorted by continuous age-selective mortality or anything else. In those counts where Europeans did distinguish between males and females, there was virtually no overall numerical difference. And, in any case, it is now thought that populations can still increase even if there is a 'statistically significant excess of males amongst all children born'.[18] Furthermore, in the following report, dated 1897,[19] children of fourteen years and under formed some 40 per cent of the total population of the Loyalty Islands, a figure which indicates a healthy balance of age groupings:

Men	Women	Boys	Girls	Total
3335	3541	2300	2197	11,413

The nineteenth-century populations of the Loyalty Islands were not drastically upset by European contact and it is very doubtful if the term 'depopulation' has any relevance here. Current techniques being developed to study food resources and settlement patterns among pre-European populations have yet to be applied to the Loyalty Islands though, given the scarcity of water and the limited areas suitable for agricultural development, large increases in population were unlikely to have been tolerated. The populations may well have been controlled by abortion and infanticide, and to a lesser extent by migration to New Caledonia and the Isle of Pines. What effect the missionary insistence on monogamy may have had on population growth rates is unknown, though well into the twentieth century, the women still practised abortion,[20] indicating that some self-determined form of population control was considered necessary.

It is significant that Europeans often remarked on the striking contrast between the populations of the Loyalty Islands and those on other southwest Pacific islands, and especially neighbouring New Caledonia. 'Except for the Kanakas of the Loyalty Islands, the natives are disappearing', wrote Augustin Bernard in 1894. In analysing the results of the 1911 census, Jacques Feillet argued that the overall population of New Caledonia was decreasing but that 'In the Loyalty Islands where there lives an elite race ... the population is stationary'.[21] The situation in New Caledonia fully justified such comments. From a population of 27,000–30,000 in 1887, there were only 16,290 New Caledonians in 1906. The causes for such a catastrophic decline were allegedly epidemics, alcoholism, brutal suppression of revolts by French soldiers and, perhaps more importantly, loss of land, fragmentation and isolation of tribal remnants on reserves with consequent socio-economic and psychological disruption. The result was a high death rate and an extremely low birth rate because of abortions and sterility.[22]

The effects of European contact on Pacific island societies cannot be measured simply in terms of the increases or decreases in their populations, though there is often some causal relationship, no matter how indirect, between European influences and demographic developments. The fact that the populations of the Loyalty Islands remained almost stable while those of New Caledonia such a short distance away fell dramatically is consistent with one of the underlying contentions of this study: that, although European contact with Loyalty Islanders was extensive and constant, the Islanders were spared any drastic socio-economic upheavals.

Conclusion

Loyalty Islanders' responses to European presence in the nineteenth century are noteworthy in several respects. Most of their attitudes and policies towards these newcomers were defined very early in the contact period and, significantly, remained consistent during the rest of the century. There was no time when there was a major rethinking of their relationships with Europeans generally, and no periods of rejection of Europeans or their ways. Rather there was a constant process of selective acceptance, adaptation, and exploitation of the new ideas, activities, and material culture. Religious and national differences among the Europeans, for example, were immediately and continuously applied by the more astute chiefs to their own local politics. Various social and economic opportunities offered by Europeans were also exploited eagerly. Islanders immediately began to travel on European vessels and work in various parts of the Pacific; they were constant visitors to Australia from the 1840s to the 1870s when they turned from working on Queensland sugar cane plantations to New Caledonian mines. And they provided crews for every kind of trading vessel operating in the south-west Pacific throughout the entire period. Trading relations with Europeans were defined early and, although commodities and marketing techniques varied throughout the century, the consistent feature of commercial dealings was the understanding of the requirements of all concerned, to their mutual advantage. The same response is also seen in the Islanders' attitudes towards and participation in the external requirements of Christianity. The populations were 'Christianised' with remarkable rapidity. Missionaries were urged to settle on the islands by the people (albeit for a variety of reasons) rather than having to struggle for years to gain footholds and win converts as in most other areas of Melanesia. And the enthusiasm for Christianity and its material and intellectual trappings remained strong after more than fifty years; there was no 'backsliding' as was common among second- and third-generation Christians elsewhere in the Pacific.

The Islanders' self-determination looms large in their responses to Europeans. Rather than remaining passive or simply reacting defensively to European undertakings they generally took their own initiatives in an enthusiastic and creative way; theirs was very much an active role in relationships with these newcomers.

The turn of the century is a convenient point to terminate this study. The major religious, national, and indigenous political conflicts were at an end, and the patterns of response to European influences were well established. The history of the Loyalty Islands in the twentieth century is relatively uneventful with few new developments: trends set by the late nineteenth century continue to the present. Christianity remains a major aspect of life, with the populations still divided into Catholic and Protestant faiths, and on almost the exact numerical and geographical lines established by the mid-1860s. There are now few lingering antagonisms between the two churches and their respective tribes. The traditional socio-political organisations which more closely resembled their pre-missionary structures by 1900 remain largely unchanged with chiefs, councils of elders and other nobles and dignitaries retaining many of their former practical and ceremonial duties. Direct French government presence is minimal and any administrative requirements are usually conducted through chiefs and their hierarchies. The economy has similarly remained relatively unchanged in this century, the principal exports being copra and labour for the New Caledonian nickel mines. Overall, the social structure and way of life have changed little from the late nineteenth century, and the populations have been relatively isolated from the mainstream of social, economic, and political developments elsewhere in the Pacific. Such isolation has recently resulted in some tension. There is, for example, growing dissatisfaction with limited educational opportunities and with the French government's refusal to accommodate increasing demands for moves towards effective political and economic autonomy for New Caledonia and its dependencies.

Conclusion

Any attempt to draw up a balance sheet of nineteenth-century contact developments for the Loyalty Islands must necessarily involve many questionable assumptions. Nevertheless, there is no evidence to suggest that the indigenous society experienced any social, political and economic upheaval, leading to bewilderment and demoralisation, as a consequence of European presence. Furthermore, those changes that took place in the Islanders' way of life after 1840, though they might have been inspired by European activities and technology, were frequently the result of the Islanders' own actions. The notion of a 'fatal impact' cannot be substantiated for the Loyalty Islands. Without implying any moral or value judgment, Loyalty Islanders, while maintaining much of their own culture, were also able to adapt and come to terms with European influences much more readily than many other societies in Melanesia.

The principal reasons are environmental, historical, and cultural. Because the islands are unsuitable for large-scale European settlement and agricultural and/or mineral exploitation, the Islanders were left in undisturbed possession of their lands. Although trading contacts were constant and extensive, commercial dealings were generally fair and the Islanders were not exploited to their social and economic detriment. They had wealth in produce and labour to buy those goods they most wanted, and they had every opportunity to travel overseas. Largely because the islands are economically insignificant, the Noumean administration was content to declare them 'Native Reserves'. The existing social structure and way of life, therefore, was not threatened as on the New Caledonian mainland, where large numbers of inhabitants lost their land to Europeans, were resettled in areas not traditionally their own, and had their tribal groupings fragmented by the French administration. Whatever resentments many Loyalty Islanders may have felt towards the French government these were never expressed in open rebellion as in New Caledonia. Furthermore, and perhaps most importantly, the organisation, strength, and flexibility of the Islanders' chiefly, hierarchical communities generally facilitated accommodation of outsiders and new ideas. Loyalty Islands history and prehistory is characterised by a balance between continuity and change. At the time of first European contact, island affairs were shaped by immigration and the consequent introduction of innovative ideas and techniques, and by warfare and the rise, fall, and realignment of chiefdoms. Many aspects of the European arrival and its consequences for the local communities had striking pre-contact precedents—Europeans were not the first people to inspire socio-political and economic changes which Loyalty Islanders could exploit.

Notes

Preface
1   E.g., G.H.L. Pitt-Rivers, *The Clash of Culture and the Contact of Races*, London, 1927; W.H.R. Rivers, ed., *Essays on the Depopulation of Melanesia*, Cambridge, 1922.
2   Alan Moorehead, *The Fatal Impact*, Harmondsworth, 1968, 14, 19.
3   Norma McArthur, *Island Populations of the Pacific*, Canberra, 1967.
4   J.W. Davidson, 'Lauaki Namulau'ulu Mamoe', *Pacific Islands Portraits*, eds. J.W. Davidson and Deryck Scarr, Canberra, 1970, 267.
5   R.H. Leenhardt's *Au vent de la Grande Terre. Histoire des Iles Loyalty de 1840 à 1895*, Paris [1957], a revised version of a thesis presented to the Faculté libre de théologie protestante de Paris in 1930, is concerned solely with an outline of the Protestant missions, and the author's treatment of Loyalty Islands history is, therefore, narrow. Also the work is often factually unreliable, and not without prejudice against the Marists and especially the French administration.

Chapter 1
1   For recent developments in archaeology in New Caledonia see the works by Brou, Golson, and Shutler listed in the bibliography.
2   Victor de Rochas, 'Iles Loyalty', *Bulletin de la Société de Géographie*, 20(1860), 27.
3   Samuel MacFarlane, *The Story of the Lifu Mission*, London, 1873, 27; *enehmu* is Dehu, the Lifu language.
4   Jones, 23 August 1856, Journal, JP, A399, ML.
5   E.g., John Elphinstone Erskine, *Journal of a Cruise among the Islands of the Western Pacific*, London, 1853, 373; Murray to LMS, 3 May 1841, 'Tutuila to Sydney in the "Camden" ', SSJ; George Turner, *Nineteen Years in Polynesia*, London, 1861, 398.
6   See below, chapter 5.

7 Erskine, *Journal of a Cruise*, 18, 340; Jean Guiart, 'Nouvelle-Calédonie et Iles Loyalty. Carte du dynamisme de la société indigène à l'arrivé des Européens', *JSO*, 9(December 1953), 93–7; Gustave Glaumont, 'Ethnogénie des Insulaires de Kunié, Ile des Pins', *Revue d'Ethnographie*, 6(1887), 336–42; K.J. Hollyman, 'Polynesian Influence in New Caledonia. The Linguistic Aspect', *JPS*, 68(December 1959), 361–3; Victor de Rochas, *La Nouvelle-Calédonie et ses Habitants*, Paris, 1862, 115.

8 Murray to LMS, 3 May 1841, SSJ.

9 Andrew Cheyne, *The Trading Voyages of Andrew Cheyne 1841–1844*, ed. Dorothy Shineberg, Canberra, 1971, 104.

10 E.g., Augustin Bernard, *L'Archipel de la Nouvelle-Calédonie*, Paris, 1894, 256–73; J. Deniker, 'Les indigènes des Lifou (Iles Loyauté)', *Bulletins de la Société d'Anthropologie de Paris*, 4(1893), 791–803; de Rochas, 'Iles Loyalty', 19–20, 26–7.

11 Julian Thomas, *Cannibals and Convicts*, London, 1886, 165.

12 See below, chapter 11.

13 Henri Jouan, 'Les Iles Loyalty', reprinted from *Review Maritime et Coloniale*, 1(April 1861), 10; Le Baron L. de Vaux, 'Les Iles Loyalty, Les Nouvelles-Hébrides et Les Viti', *Revue d'Ethnographie*, 3(1884), 490.

14 G.A. Selwyn quoted in [Church of England], *The Island Mission*, London, 1869, 148. See also Jones to LMS, 20 June 1855, SSL.

15 Jouan, 'Les Iles Loyalty', 10.

16 Gaide to Mulsant, 9 March 1877, IV ONC; Goujon, 'La Mission de Maré 1860–1866', n.d., MS., N.C. La Loyalty, III ONC.

17 Erskine, *Journal of a Cruise*, 347n; Xavier Montrouzier, 'Nouvelle-Calédonie. Fragments Historiques', *Mon.*, Noumea, 7 October 1860; Philip Vigors, 'Private Journal of a Four Months Cruise', 1850, TS., Auckland Institute and Museum.

18 Descriptions of the Loyalty Islanders' religion are given in Beaulieu, MS. notes for the Marist theological conference in Noumea 1890, AAN; Bernard, 'Des superstitions' in 'Notices historiques sur l'île Ouvéa et les îles Beauprés', n.d., MS., AAN; Emma Hadfield, *Among the Natives of the Loyalty Group*, London, 1920, chapter IX; [Marist Mission], *Rapport sur les Superstitions Calédoniennes*, Noumea, 1891; S.H. Ray, 'The People and Language of Lifu, Loyalty Islands', *Journal of the Royal Anthropological Institute of Great Britain and Ireland*, 47(1917), 295–8.

19 MacFarlane, *Story of the Lifu Mission*, 16.

20 Ibid.

21 E.g., see P. Lawrence and M.J. Meggit, eds., *Gods Ghosts and Men in Melanesia*, Melbourne, 1965, 6–22. The Loyalty Islanders' religion was very similar to that of the New Caledonians; see Matthieu Gagnière, *Etude ethnologique sur la Religion des Néo-Calédoniens*, Saint Louis, 1905.

22 A.G. Haudricourt, 'New Caledonia and the Loyalty Islands', *Current Trends in Linguistics*, 8, *Linguistics in Oceania*, ed. Thomas A. Seboek, Paris, 1971, 359–96; D.T. Tryon, 'The Languages of the Loyalty Islands', Ph.D. thesis, ANU, 1967. Dictionaries of the Loyalty Islands languages by Tryon are listed in the bibliography.

23 For a general, though greatly oversimplified, comparison of Polynesian and Melanesian political systems see Marshall D. Sahlins, 'Poor Man, Rich Man, Big-Man, Chief: Political types in Melanesia and Polynesia', *Cultures of the Pacific*, ed. Thomas G. Harding and Ben J. Wallace, New York, 1970, 203–15. For an account of pre- or early contact society in New Caledonia see Bronwen Douglas, 'A History of Culture Contact in North-eastern New Caledonia 1774–1870', Ph.D. thesis, ANU, 1972, chapter 1.

24 The following description owes much to M.J. Dubois, 'La Société, le Clan, la Tribu' in 'Ethnologie de Maré', n.d., TS. microfilm in my possession; Jean Guiart, *Struc-*

ture de la Chefferie en Mélanésie du Sud, Paris, 1963, chapters VII, VIII, IX. See also Fagot, 'Relations Familiales et Coutumières entre les trois îles Loyauté', *JSO*, 5(December 1949), 87-96; Maurice Leenhardt, 'L'Archipel des Loyalty', *L'Anthropologie*, 49(1940), 833-4, and 'Les Chefferies Océaniennes', *Académie des Sciences Coloniales*, (December 1941), 359-76; Henri Naisiline, 'Notes sur l'organisation sociale du district de Nece', *Etudes Mélanésiennes*, 6(September 1952), 36-44. My 'Culture Contacts on the Loyalty Islands 1841-1895', chapter 1, contains a much fuller description than that given here.

25 Evidence of Burns, *RC*, 22; Jones to Resident, 13 June 1876, JP, A399, ML; Ray, 'The People and Language of Lifu', 290.

26 Dubois,'La Propriété Foncière Maréenne au Temps du Paganisme', *Etudes Mélanésiennes*, 5(January 1951), 69-78.

27 Dubois, 'La Société, le Clan, la Tribu'.

28 Ray, 'The People and Language of Lifu', 290.

29 Guitta to Poupinel, 26 November 1873, IV ONC.

30 Guiart, *Structure de la Chefferie*, 390. The infrequent practice of offering a chiefship to a newcomer was one of the more remarkable features of both Loyalty Islands and New Caledonian political systems. There is as yet no adequate explanation for this phenomenon. Guiart suggests that it might form part of an elaborate system to integrate strangers into the tribe: as a chief an immigrant would have status yet limited personal authority, he would not have to be accorded land and would therefore be dependent upon his followers, and he would have obligations to the chiefdom. Those inhabitants already in privileged positions might thus protect themselves from possible overthrow by migrants. See Guiart, *Structure de la Chefferie*, 641.

31 Guiart, *Structure de la Chefferie*, chapters VII, VIII, IX; Leenhardt, 'L'Archipel de Loyalty', 834, and 'Les Chefferies Océaniennes', 372-4.

32 Dubois, 'La Société, le Clan, la Tribu'; Leenhardt, 'Les Chefferies Océaniennes', 373. In contrast, New Caledonian chiefs were quasi-divine men whose essential task was to orate and exalt tribal history—they were, in essence, the personification of their tribe. See Douglas, 'A History of Culture Contact', chapter 1; Leenhardt, 'L'Archipel des Loyalty', 834.

33 Guiart, *Structure de la Chefferie*, 271-2, and chapters VII, VIII, IX.

34 Such rigidity of stratification and central importance of the nobility was less characteristic on New Caledonia, and there were no respectful languages. See Guiart, *Structure de la Chefferie*, 639-40, 653.

Chapter 2

1 Logbook of the *Britannia*, 1792-6 (Robert Murray logkeeper), Peabody Museum, Salem: PMB 214, 215.

2 Logbook of the *Providence*, 1796 (Robert Murray logkeeper), Peabody Museum: PMB 215.

3 Dumont d'Urville's charts were poor and the Loyalty Islands remained badly charted until the 1850s with much confusion over their names. Even now it is not known why they came to be called 'Loyalty'. That name first appears in the logbook of the *Providence* in 1796. Whether they were named by Captain Raven of the *Britannia* in 1793 cannot be documented, although David Collins in his *An Account of the English Colony in New South Wales*, London, 1798, notes that the 'Loyalty Islands' were discovered by Raven of the *Britannia*, and A. Arrowsmith's 1798 *Chart of the Pacific Ocean* (no. S.T.P. British Museum Map Room) has marked 'Loyalty Isles' with a dotted line representing the track of the *Britannia*. For futher information on this point, and on the various indigenous and European names given to the three islands, see my

'La découverte par les Européens des Iles Loyauté', *Bulletin de la Société d'Etudes Historique de la Nouvelle-Calédonie*, 17(1973), 31-8.

    4 Dubois, 'L'Arrivée des Blancs à Maré', *JSO*, 25(December) 1969, 310; Fabvre, 'Notes sur le R.P. Jean-Baptiste Fabvre', n.d., TS; Fabvre Personal File, APM; T. Beckford Simpson, 'The *Strathisla*'s Voyage', *The Shipping Gazette and Sydney General Trade List*, 13 September 1845.

    5 J.J.H. Labillardière, *Voyage in search of La Pérouse*, II, London, 1800, 246-7.

    6 Patteson to Jones, 25 August 1858, JP, A399, ML.

    7 Dorothy Shineberg, *They Came for Sandalwood*, Melbourne, 1967, appendix 1.

    8 Jones, 'Shipping Intelligence', JP, A399, ML; shipping reports in *Mon.*, 1862-86.

    9 This figure is calculated from Guillain to Min., 30 September and 23 October, 1868, carton 86, ANOM; Palmer to Lambert, 22 March 1869, *RC*, 1-2; LMS and Marist missionary letters 1865-74 in LMS and APM.

    10 'South Sea Islanders in Queensland', *QVP*, III, 1876, 49.

    11 Cf. H.E. Maude, *Of Islands and Men*, Melbourne, 1968, 145-6.

    12 These names, as well as those of beachcombers etc. can be found in my 'Culture Contacts on the Loyalty Islands', 199-202.

    13 Census, 15 June 1870, carton 28, ANOM.

Rival Chiefs, Rival Faiths

    1 MacFarlane, *Story of the Lifu Mission*, 22.

    2 Jones to LMS, 18 November 1880, SSL.

    3 Gaide to ?, 10 October 1879, IV ONC.

Chapter 3

    1 M.J. Dubois, 'Les Eletok de Maré d'après la tradition. Etude d'ethnohistoire', thèse de doctorat de 3e cycle [Sorbonne, 1971]; Guiart, *Structure de la Chefferie*, chapter VII.

    2 There is some debate as to whether or not the Naisilines assumed the great chiefship before or at the time of the massacre of the *eletok*; see Guiart, *Structure de la Chefferie*, 320-8.

    3 A.W. Murray, *Missions in Western Polynesia*, London, 1863, 299-300.

    4 Murray, 'Samoa 1841 . . . Tutuila to Sydney in the "Camden" ', SSJ.

    5 Murray, *Missions in Western Polynesia*, chapter XI.

    6 Shineberg, *They Came for Sandalwood*, appendix 1.

    7 Slatyer, 'Journal of a Voyage in the *Camden* . . . 1842', MS A1770, ML.

    8 Gill and Nisbet to LMS, 28 October 1846, SSL.

    9 Ta'unga, *The Works of Ta'unga*, ed. R.G. and Marjorie Crocombe, Canberra, 1968, 79.

    10 Ibid., 80-1.

    11 George Turner, *Nineteen Years in Polynesia*, London, 1861, 404-7. Recognition of the youngest son as heir was an exception to the general rule. The reason given in this instance was that Menedoku Bula's mother was a noblewoman in the chiefdom of Losi in the south of Lifu. As the Si Gwahma tribe wished to strengthen friendly ties with Losi, Yiewene's advisers considered that the appointment of her son as great chief would ensure continued amicable relations. See Jones to Resident, 13 June 1876, JP A399, ML.

    12 Murray and Turner, 'Samoa 1845 . . . Deputation to New Hebrides', SSJ.

    13 Turner, *Nineteen Years*, 408-11. There were two more violent incidents between Europeans and Mareans. In 1849 Captain Lewis of the *Will o' the Wisp*, fearing the people of Tadine were going to attack him, shot and killed three Islanders; see Erskine, *Journal of a Cruise*, appendix B. In 1851 the cutter *Lucy Ann* was captured and the

Notes to Pages 16–34

crew of seventeen killed at Medu; see Murray and Sunderland, 'Samoa 1852 . . . Deputation from Apia', SSJ.
14   Gill and Nisbet to LMS, 28 October 1846, SSL.
15   William Gill, *Selections from the Autobiography of the Rev. William Gill*, London, 1880, 225–6.
16   Erskine, *Journal of a Cruise*, 379.
17   Beaulieu, 'Tableau de la Généalogie des chefs de Gouama', n.d., MS, AAN; Jones to Resident, 13 June 1876, JP, A339, ML.
18   Murray, *Missions in Western Polynesia*, 305–7.
19   Quoted in *Colonial Church Chronicle*, London, 7(1853–4), 276.
20   Voluminous correspondence is in SSL from 1849 until the mid-1850s, and in 'Correspondence between the London Missionary Society and the Bishop of New Zealand', folder 1, G.A. Selwyn Papers, MS 273, Auckland Institute and Museum.
21   Nihill to his father, 1 August 1852, W. Nihill Papers, MS 720, Hocken Library, Dunedin.
22   [Church of England], *The Island Mission*, London, 1869, 60–70.
23   *Report of the Melanesian Mission for the year 1857–8*, Auckland, 1858, 63.
24   [Church of England], *The Island Mission*, 148.
25   Murray, *Missions in Western Polynesia*, 311.
26   Hardie, 'Samoa 1854 . . . Voyage to New Hebrides', SSJ.
27   Creagh to LMS, February 1855; and Jones to LMS, 20 June 1855, SSL; Stallworthy and Gill, 'Samoa 1858 . . . Deputation in the "John Williams" to New Hebrides', SSJ.
28   Beaulieu, 'Tableau de la Généalogie des chefs de Gouama', AAN; Creagh to LMS, 14 December 1862, SSL.
29   Jones, 26 April 1856, Diary, JP, A399, ML; Taka to Gill, January 1864, SSL.
30   Jones to LMS, 6 June 1861, 6 May 1863, 10 September 1880, SSL.
31   F.A. Campbell, *A Year in the New Hebrides, Loyalty Islands*, Melbourne, 1873, 139.
32   Jones, 'Shipping Intelligence', JP, A399, ML.
33   B.Y. Ashwell, *Journal of a Visit to the Loyalty, New Hebrides, and Banks Islands*, Auckland, 1860, 5.
34   Creagh to LMS, 29 September 1858, SSL.
35   Jones, 4 November 1856, Journal, JP, A399, ML.
36   Jones to LMS, 20 June 1855, SSL; Jones, 9 April 1856, Journal, A399, ML; Sunderland to LMS, 16 August 1855, SSL. Sunderland took Creagh's place during his absence for a few months in 1855.
37   Jones to his parents, 25 May 1859, JP, A399, ML; Sunderland to LMS, 6 July 1855, SSL.
38   Creagh to LMS, 15 February, 7 May 1860, SSL; Jones, 9 April 1856, Journal; and to his parents, 25 May 1859, JP, A399, ML; Jones to LMS, 11 February 1856, SSL.
39   Creagh to LMS, 26 November 1860, SSL.
40   Creagh to LMS, 6 November 1861; and Jones to LMS, 6 June 1861, SSL.
41   Jones to LMS, 22 June 1864, SSL.
42   Creagh to LMS, 23 April 1863; and Jones to LMS, 22 June 1864, SSL.
43   Creagh to LMS, 14 December 1862; and Jones to LMS, 6 May 1863, SSL.
44   Goujon, 'La Mission de Maré', La Loyalty, III ONC.
45   Ibid.
46   Beaulieu, 'Notes sur l'Ile de Maré. Etat de l'Ile de Maré en 1866', n.d., MS., and 'Histoire Sommaire de Penelo', n.d., MS; PCD; Goujon, 'La Mission de Maré', III ONC.
47   Goujon to Poupinel, 14 September 1866, VMA.

Chapter 4
1. Turner, *Nineteen Years*, 396-7.
2. Cheyne, *Trading Voyages*, 103.
3. Ibid., 93-102.
4. Simpson, 'The Strathisla's Voyage', *Shipping Gazette*, 23 August 1845.
5. Ibid., 13 September 1845.
6. Murray, *Missions in Western Polynesia*, 329.
7. Turner, *Nineteen Years*, 399.
8. Ibid., 400.
9. Gill and Nisbet to LMS, 28 October 1846, SSL.
10. Erskine, *Journal of a Cruise*, 368; Murray, *Missions in Western Polynesia*, 330.
11. Murray and Sunderland, 'Samoa 1852 . . . Deputation from Apia', SSJ.
12. Murray, *Missions in Western Polynesia*, 336.
13. Hardie, 'Samoa 1854 Voyage', SSJ.
14. Murray and Sunderland, 'Samoa 1853-1854 . . . Apia to . . . New Caledonia', SSJ.
15. MacFarlane, *Story of the Lifu Mission*, 38-9.
16. Ibid., 49.
17. Jones to 'My dear friend', 16 May 1856; and Jones, 16 May 1856, Journal, JP, A399, ML.
18. Jones, 16 May 1856, Journal, JP, A399, ML. See also Jones to LMS, 21 July 1857, SSL.
19. Harbutt and Drummond, 'Samoa 1857 . . . From Apia', SSJ. See also Palazy to Colin, 10 June 1861, OP.
20. Rougeyron to Poupinel, 29 April 1858, VMA.
21. Poupinel to Germain, 5 June 1865, *AMO*, 2(n.d.), 343. See also Bernard to Fabvre, 28 August 1858, IV ONC.
22. Montrouzier to his parents, 21 May 1858, Montrouzier Personal File, APM; Montrouzier to Yardin, 8 September 1858, IV ONC.
23. Testard to Min., 23 April 1858, carton 42, ANOM.
24. Montrouzier to his parents, 21 May 1858, Montrouzier Personal File, APM.
25. Palazy to Colin, 10 June 1861, OP.
26. Ibid.
27. Montrouzier to his parents, 22 September 1858, Montrouzier Personal File, APM.
28. Palazy to Colin, 10 June 1861, OP.
29. Patteson to his sister, 4 June 1858, Patteson Papers, ANU.
30. *Report of the Melanesian Mission . . . 1857-8*, 37-8.
31. *Papers relating to the Melanesian Mission*, 1858, in *Two Letters and Melanesian Mission Reports*, ML.
32. Charlotte Mary Yonge, *Life of John Coleridge Patteson*, I, London, 1874, 369.
33. Patteson to his father, 12 May 1858, Patteson Papers, ANU.
34. Montrouzier to Fauvre, 1 January 1859, IV ONC.
35. Fabvre to Poupinel, 24 October, 18 November 1859, VMA.
36. Tidman to Creagh, 12 July 1858, '5 letters Tidman to Creagh', MS At24, ML.
37. Jones to LMS, 10 November 1859, SSL.
38. Turner, *Nineteen Years*, 507-8.
39. MacFarlane, *Story of the Lifu Mission*, 70.
40. Ibid., 72.
41. Baker to LMS, 3 January, 25 February 1861; and MacFarlane to LMS, 18 June 1863, SSL.

42 MacFarlane, *Story of the Lifu Mission*, 113-14.
43 'Notes sur le R.P. Jean-Baptiste Fabvre', Fabvre Personal File, APM.
44 Fabvre to Fauvre, 20 November 1863, IV ONC.
45 Bertrand to Poupinel, 1 June 1860, VMA; Fabvre to Yardin, March 1860, IV ONC.
46 Gaide to Fauvre, March 1864, IV ONC.

Chapter 5

1 Guiart, *Structure de la Chefferie*, 561-76, 608-13.
2 Bernard, 'Notices Historiques', AAN.
3 Innumerable nineteenth-century travellers recorded the oral traditions surrounding the migration. Among the earliest were Viard to Colin, 27 October 1845, *APF*, 18 (1846), 414; Leconte to Min., 1 April 1847, carton 40, ANOM; Erskine, *Journal of a Cruise*, 340-1; Cheyne, *Sailing Directions From New South Wales*, London, 1855, 28. The story of the migration can also be traced from the Wallis Island end, see Edwin G. Burrows, 'Ethnology of Uvea (Wallis Island)', *Bernice P. Bishop Museum Bulletin*, 145, Honolulu, 1937, 50-2.
4 Hollyman, 'Polynesian Influence in New Caledonia', 362. Using linguistic evidence, Hollyman has suggested that the Wallisian migration may have been the last, and the only one remembered, in a series of small migrations from Polynesia; see Bronwen Douglas, 'A Contact History of the Balad People of New Caledonia 1774-1845', *JPS*, 79 (June 1970), 190 n. 65.
5 Bernard, 'Notices Historiques', AAN.
6 Cheyne, *Sailing Directions*, 28; Erskine, *Journal of a Cruise*, 340.
7 Cheyne, *Trading Voyages*, 113; Murray, *Missions in Western Polynesia*, 354. See also Guiart, *Structure de la Chefferie*, 608-24. Of the Polynesian chiefs, Beka paid tribute to Bazit, but Nekelo, possibly because of his military strength, did not. There is some evidence that at the time of European contact Bazit's authority vis-à-vis Nekelo was on the wane; see Bernard, 'Notices Historiques', AAN. The situation was later reversed when Bazit associated himself with the Marist missionaries as described below.
8 Erskine, *Journal of a Cruise*, 343, 344.
9 Bernard, 'Notices Historiques', AAN.
10 Cheyne, *Trading Voyages*, 111.
11 E.g., ibid., 109-23.
12 Erskine, *Journal of a Cruise*, 343.
13 Bernard to a colleague, 28 July 1858, *APF*, 32 (1860), 447.
14 Creagh to LMS, March 1856; and Jones to LMS, 26 October 1858, SSL.
15 Evidence of Burns, *RC*, 22.
16 Ibid., 20.
17 Bernard, 'Notices Historiques', AAN.
18 *Samoan Reporter*, October 1859.
19 Commentary, *AMO*, 3(1875), 262.
20 Bernard to Fauvre, 28 August 1858, IV ONC.
21 Ibid.
22 Gabriel to Poupinel, 19 March 1860, VMA.
23 Bernard to Poupinel, 16 November 1859, VMA. See also ibid., 8 September 1858, 19 January 1859, VMA.
24 Barriol to his parents, September 1858; and Bernard to Fauvre, 14 July 1859, IV ONC.
25 Barriol to Poupinel, 15 July 1859, VMA: Bernard to Fauvre, 28 August 1858, IV ONC.

26 Barriol to his parents, September 1858, IV ONC.
27 Barriol to Poupinel, 25 December 1859, VMA.
28 Rougeyron to Poupinel, 15 June 1860, VMA.
29 Barriol to his parents, September 1858, IV ONC.
30 Rougeyron to Poupinel, 15 June 1860, VMA.
31 Jouan, 'Iles Loyalty', 373.
32 Bernard to his sister, 14 April 1861; and Bernard to Yardin, 16 November 1861, IV ONC.
33 Bernard to Fauvre, 15 April 1861, IV ONC.
34 Bernard, 'Notices Historiques', AAN.
35 Poupinel to Colin, 5 June 1865, *AMO*, 2(n.d.), 325.
36 'Etat de la Nouvelle-Calédonie' [1861], *AMO*, 2(n.d.), 8; Rougeyron to Rocher, 23 October 1862, VMA.

Chiefs, Church, and State
  1 Saisset to Min., 26 May 1860, carton 42, ANOM.
  2 Du Bouzet to Min., 5 May 1855, carton 86, ANOM.

Chapter 6
  1 Guillain to Min., 5 July 1864, carton 85, ANOM.
  2 Fabvre to Bertrand, 20 February 1864, enclosed in Guillain to Min., 5 January 1865, carton 85, ANOM.
  3 Arrêté, 1 May 1864, *Mon.*, 22 May 1864.
  4 MacFarlane, *Story of the Lifu Mission*, 129.
  5 Ibid., 133.
  6 Bourgey to Guillain, 1 June 1864, enclosed in Guillain to Min., 5 January 1865, carton 85, ANOM.
  7 Guillain to Min., 5 July 1864, carton 85, ANOM.
  8 Ibid. See also Fabvre to Poupinel, 8 September 1865, VMA: MacFarlane, *Story of the Lifu Mission*, chapter 13.
  9 MacFarlane, *Story of the Lifu Mission*, 156.
  10 Arrêté, 24 June 1864. *Mon.*, 3 July 1864.
  11 Guillain to Bula, 26 June 1864; and Guillain to Bourgey, 29 June 1864, enclosed in Guillain to Min., 5 July 1864, carton 85, ANOM.
  12 Guillain to Min., 5 July 1864, carton 85, ANOM.
  13 MacFarlane to Jeffries, 3 May 1866, SSL.
  14 'Correspondence between the Rev. S. MacFarlane of Lifu and the French Authorities', 1864-5, SSL.
  15 FO 27/1537, 1554, 1555, 1567, 1592; Océanie IV, AMAE; carton 86, ANOM.
  16 Ministre des Affairs Etrangères to Guillain, 26 October 1864; and Min. to Guillain, 13 December 1864, carton 86, ANOM.
  17 Cowley to Russell, 23 January 1865, FO 27/1567.
  18 Napoleon to LMS, 24 January 1865 (copy), carton 86, ANOM. Also reproduced in MacFarlane, *Story of the Lifu Mission*, 198. I have retained MacFarlane's translation.
  19 MacFarlane, *Story of the Lifu Mission*, 211.
  20 Douglas, 'A History of Culture Contact', 139.
  21 E.g., Testard to Min., 23 April 1858, carton 42, ANOM; Saisset to Min., 10 October 1860, BB4 1036, ANM; Durand to Min., 31 December 1861, BB4 797, ANM.
  22 'Le Guillainisme', Démêlés avec le Gouverneur Guillain, III ONC.
  23 Douglas, 'A History of Culture Contact', 172-88.
  24 Gaide to Rougeyron, 17 August 1864, IV ONC.

Notes to Pages 61–69

25 Fabvre, notes, 23 May 1866, Administration Civile II, III ONC; Poupinel to Germain, 5 June 1865, *AMO*, 2(n.d.), 347–8.
26 Gaide to Rougeyron, 17 August 1864, IV ONC; Fabvre to Poupinel, 8 September 1865, VMA.
27 Fabvre to ?, 27 July 1866, IV ONC.
28 E.g., Fabvre, 'Notices Historiques', AAN; Fabvre to Rougeyron, 13 December 1867, IV ONC.
29 Fabvre to Forestier, 6 July 1866, IV ONC; MacFarlane to LMS, 12 November 1869, SSL.
30 MacFarlane to LMS, 30 August 1869, SSL.
31 Fabvre, notes, 23 May 1866, Administration Civile II, III ONC.
32 MacFarlane to LMS, 27 May 1870, SSL.
33 Décision, 16 May 1867, AAN.
34 MacFarlane to LMS, 12 November 1864, SSL.
35 Fabvre, 'Notices Historiques', AAN; MacFarlane to Jeffries, 27 June 1867, SSL.
36 Fabvre to Poupinel, 24 November 1874, IV ONC.
37 Caillet, MS. notebook, 10–11.
38 Voluminous correspondence on the affair is in carton 86, ANOM; FO 58/117; and MacFarlane to LMS, 1865–71, SSL.
39 Caillet, Rapport politique, 15 September 1874, notebook, 53; Fabvre to Germain, 11 August 1874, IV ONC; Lifu statistics 1884, SSL.
40 Ibid.
41 Creagh, 10 year report, 25 December 1880, SSL.
42 B. Balansa, *La Nouvelle-Calédonie*, Paris, 1873, 529. See also Caillet, Rapport Politique, 15 September 1874, notebook, 53; Courbet to Min., 29 April 1881, carton 86, ANOM.

Chapter 7

1 Ella, 8 December 1864, Diary, EP, B249, ML; Poupinel to Colin, 5 June 1865, *AMO*, 2(n.d.), 327.
2 Ella, December 1864–February 1865, Diary, EP, B249, ML.
3 Ibid., 9, 10 January 1865.
4 Ibid., 23 April 1865.
5 Ella to LMS, 24 October 1865, SSL.
6 Ella to Guillanton, 11 May 1865, EP, A200, ML; Gaide to Poupinel, 8 November 1865, VMA.
7 Guillain to Min., 30 June 1865, carton 85, ANOM.
8 Décision, 17 June 1865, *Mon.*, 9 July 1865.
9 'Dispositions arrêtés à Ouvéa', 26 June 1865, AAN.
10 Ella to LMS, 24 October 1865, SSL.
11 Ella, 2 August 1867, EP, A249, ML.
12 Ella to LMS, 24 October 1865, 20 December 1866, SSL.
13 FO 58/117; FO 27/1693, 1694.
14 'Rapport de la Commission d'enquête', 1869, carton 86, ANOM.
15 Pionnier to Poupinel, 5 April, 19 May 1872, IV ONC; 'Statement Respecting the Persecution of the Protestant Converts', 2 December 1874, FO 27/2098.
16 Sleigh to Ella, 9 April 1873, EP, A205, ML.
17 Jones to Ella, 6 June 1872, EP, A208, ML.
18 Sleigh to LMS, 10 February 1873, SSL.
19 Caillet, notebook, 35–47; Creagh to Caillet, 1 July 1873, SSL; Creagh to Ella, 30 June 1873, EP, A205, ML; Pionnier to Gay, 15 June 1873, IV ONC.

20 Pionnier to Gay, 28 July 1873; and Roussel to Poupinel, January 1874, IV ONC.
21 Caillet to Richerie (copy), 18 September 1873, notebook, 40–7.
22 Ella to LMS, 10 April 1874, SSL.
23 Ibid.
24 Ella to LMS, 14 November 1874, 26 April 1875, SSL.
25 Vitte to ?, 15 March 1874, 5Ca 411, I ONC.
26 Hadfield, Uvea statistics 1884, SSR.
27 The Onyat villagers did not return to their lands until the end of the century; see Creagh to LMS, 21 January 1899, SSL.

Chapter 8

1 Beaulieu to Poupinel, 1 August 1867, and Beaulieu, 'Histoire Sommaire de Penelo', PCD; Creagh to LMS, 10 December 1869, 28 February 1870, SSL.
2 Beaulieu, 'Guerre de 1869', MS; 1878, PCD; Creagh to Guillain, 24 March 1870, SSL.
3 Creagh to Guillain, 11 February, 24 March 1870, SSL.
4 Beaulieu to Poupinel, 27 February 1871, 18 August 1872, IV ONC.
5 Creagh to LMS, 21 July 1871; and Jones to LMS, 15 October 1871, SSL.
6 Beaulieu to Poupinel, 28 December 1872; and Gaide to Mulsant, 9 March 1877, IV ONC.
7 Creagh to LMS, 12 August 1875, SSL.
8 Creagh left Mare in 1871. Jones remained the only LMS missionary on the island.
9 A copy of the Nengone texts, dated 24 November 1875, is in PCD. See also 'Rapport sur les affaires de Maré', MS., 1876, carton 86, ANOM.
10 'Rapport sur les affaires de Maré', carton 86, ANOM. A more detailed treatment of Mare tribal politics in the 1870s and 1880s is in my 'Culture Contacts on the Loyalty Islands'.
11 Pritzbuer, 'Règlement de Maré', 4 June 1876, AAN; Cave, 'delimitation', 3 August 1876, AAN; Benet to Director of the Interior, 11 December 1876, carton 86, ANOM; Dollon, notebooks, 1879, PCD.
12 Director of the Interior to Pritzbuer, 29 September 1876, carton 86, ANOM.
13 Dollon, inquiries about chiefships, 14 August 1879, notebook, PCD.
14 E.g., Gaide to Fraysse [1876], PCD; Jones to Resident, 13 June 1876, JP, A399, ML; Jones to Pritzbuer, 18 September 1876, enclosed in Pritzbuer to Min., 7 October 1876, carton 85, ANOM.
15 Jones, 'Report of the Mare Institution', 1879, SSL.
16 Gaide to ?, 10 October 1879, IV ONC. The three chiefs referred to were the Catholics Sinewami of the Si Gureschaba tribe, Andre Kawawa of the Si Medu, and Jalo of the Si Gurewoc.
17 Gaide to Resident, 7 January 1879, PCD.
18 Gaide to Poupinel, 10 July 1880, IV ONC.
19 Beaulieu to Poupinel, 4 September 1880; and Gaide to Poupinel, 3 September 1880, IV ONC; Jones to LMS, 18 November 1880, SSL.
20 Jones to LMS, 18 November 1880, SSL.
21 Ibid.
22 Beaulieu to Poupinel, 4 September 1880, IV ONC; Jones to LMS, 5 April 1881, SSL.
23 Min. to Courbet, 23 August 1882, carton 86, ANOM.
24 Courbet to Min., 13 April 1882, carton 86, ANOM.

25 Dupénil, 'Compte-rendu de ma mission à Maré', 28 September 1880, carton 86, ANOM.
26 Gouharou to Pallu de la Barrière, 4 December 1883, carton 86, ANOM.
27 E.g., Walter Coote, *The Western Pacific*, London, 1883, 155.
28 Courbet to Jones, 4 December 1880, SSL.
29 Jones to Courbet, 16 December 1880, 24 September 1881, SSL; Jones to Louis, July 1885, enclosed in Courbet to Min., 1 December 1885, carton 85, ANOM.
30 Benet, 'Note confidentielle sur le Révérend M. Jones', 12 December 1876; and Courbet to Min., 24 December 1880, carton 86, ANOM.
31 E.g., FO 27/2233, 2244, 2265; Ministre des Affaires Etrangères to Min., 28 February 1882, carton 86, ANOM.
32 Courbet to Min., 18 March 1881, carton 86, ANOM.
33 Jones to LMS, 7, 13, 19, 30 May, 3 July 1884, SSL.
34 Yiewene to Tournois, 2 January 1886, Océanie VIII, AMAE.
35 See letters of Jones, Louis, and Tournois in Le Boucher to Min., 13 January 1886, carton 85, ANOM.
36 E.g., Le Boucher to Min., 7 April 1886, carton 38, ANOM.
37 Le Boucher to Min., 5 February 1886, carton 85, ANOM.
38 There are numerous documents about the expulsion and the subsequent controversy in England and Australia. See, e.g., 'Correspondence Respecting the Expulsion of the Rev. J. Jones from Maré', *GBPP*, 109 (1888), 75–139; Océanie VIII, AMAE; FO 27/2992.
39 Rousseau to SMEP, 6 January 1896, SMEP.

Chapter 9

1 Coote, *The Western Pacific*, 154.
2 William T. Wawn, *The South Sea Islanders and the Queensland Labour Trade*, London, 1893, 7.
3 Thomas, *Cannibals and Convicts*, 165. See also H. le Chartier, *La Nouvelle-Calédonie*, Paris, 1885, 106; Jules Garnier, *Voyage Autour du Monde. Océanie. Les Iles des Pins, Loyalty et Tahiti*, Paris, 1871, 288; Jouan, 'Les Iles Loyalty', 2; de Rochas, *La Nouvelle-Calédonie*, 212.
4 Charles Pigeard, *Voyage dans l'Océanie Centrale*, Paris, 1846, 90.
5 Evidence of Burns, *RC*, 20.
6 Ibid., 21.
7 Evidence of Henry, *RC*, 45; Turner, *Nineteen Years*, 492–3; Shineberg, *They Came for Sandalwood*, 191–2.
8 Saisset to Min., 1 February 1860, MS 9448, BN.
9 E.g., Jouan, 'Renseignements Nautiques sur les Iles Loyalty', *Annales Hydrographiques*, 19(1861), 456; *Mon.*, 2 August, 11 October 1863, 24 October 1869; S.M. Vollet, 'Renseignements sur les Iles Loyalty', *Annales Hydrographiques*, 35(1872), 54.
10 Jones, 'Shipping Intelligence', JP, A 399, ML; shipping reports in *Mon.*, 1862–86. The progress of the local shipping is difficult to trace after 1886 because the *Mon.* ceased publication in that year.
11 J.M. [MacGillivray], 'A Look in at Lifu', *Empire*, 11 April 1864.
12 J.W. Anderson, *Notes of Travel in Fiji and New Caledonia*, London, 1880, 159.
13 Ella, 23–27 October 1870, 5 May 1871, 2–4 June 1874, Diary, EP, B250, ML; evidence of Burns, Merriman, *RC*, 20, 21, 23.
14 Evidence of Burns, Merriman, *RC*, 21, 23.
15 Evidence of Palmer, Wood, *RC*, 8, 13.

16 Dupénil to Courbet, 28 September 1880, carton 86, ANOM.
17 Evidence of Burns, RC, 20-1.
18 *Samoan Reporter*, October 1857; Bataillon to Directors of the Société de la Propagation de la Foi, 1 November 1861, APF, 34 (1862), 411-12.
19 FitzRoy to Grey, 24 December 1847 (and enclosures), CO 201/386.
20 Evidence of Burns, Towns, RC, 20, 26.
21 This figure is calculated from Guillain to Min., 23 October, 30 September 1868, carton 86, ANOM; Palmer to Lambert, 22 March 1869, RC, 1-2; LMS and Marist missionary letters 1865-74 in LMS and APM.
22 'Report from the Immigration Agent', QVP, 1868-9, 553.
23 'South Sea Islanders in Queensland', QVP, III, 1876, 49.
24 Report, RC, 7.
25 Jones in *The Christian World*, 11 May 1888, newscuttings, JP, ML. My underlining.
26 Peter Corris, *Passage, Port and Plantation*, Melbourne, 1973.
27 Lancaster's statement enclosed in FitzRoy to Grey, 24 December 1847, CO 201/386.
28 Erskine to Oliver, 4 March 1850, Admiralty I, 5606, Cap. E60; Oliver, 10 June 1850, *Fly* letterbook, microfilm, ANU.
29 Guillain to Min., 30 September 1868, carton 86, ANOM.
30 Ibid., 23 October 1868.
31 E.g., LMS to Granville, 6 April 1869, a printed document on behalf of Protestant missionary societies in the south-west Pacific, in Sleigh Papers, Box 1, SSO.
32 Palmer to Lambert, 22 March 1869, RC, 1.
33 Evidence of Burns, Merriman, Henry, Dawson, Row, RC, 21, 23, 45, 64, 66, 72.
34 Creagh to LMS, 14 January 1868, SSL; Creagh to Macdonald, 19 February 1869, in RC, 36.
35 Jones to LMS, 6 September 1882, SSL.
36 Gaide to Poupinel, 22 January 1873; and Pionnier to Poupinel, 23 November 1873, IV ONC.
37 Evidence of Joly, RC, 49.
38 E.g., evidence of Fangi, Watongani, Enowat, RC, 52-3.
39 Creagh to LMS, 13 October 1869, SSL.
40 Evidence of Dawson, Row, RC, 64, 72; Creagh to LMS, 13 October 1869, SSL.
41 Dupénil to Courbet, 28 September 1880, carton 86, ANOM.
42 Report, RC, 5.
43 Dupénil to Courbet, 28 September 1880, carton 86, ANOM.
44 Gaide, Rapport 1871-2, Rapports I, III ONC; Pionnier to Poupinel, 5 February 1874, IV ONC.
45 Palmer to Lambert, 22 March 1869, RC, 2.
46 Creagh to LMS, 14 January 1868, SSL.
47 Evidence of Row, RC, 72.
48 Jones to LMS, 6 September 1882, SSL.
49 Ella, June 1874, Diary, EP, B250, ML.
50 Evidence of King, RC, 12-13.
51 Erskine, *Journal of a Cruise*, 342, 366.
52 Evidence of Dawson, Burns, RC, 20, 66.
53 Bernard, 'Notices Historiques', AAN. See also evidence of Joly, Row, RC, 49, 72; Coote, *The Western Pacific*, 154; Jones to LMS, 6 September 1882, SSL; Barriol to ?, August 1858, IV ONC; Dupénil to Courbet, 28 September 1880, carton 86, ANOM.
54 Evidence of Rees, RC, 50.

Notes to Pages 97-103

55 J.M. [MacGillivray], 'A Look in at Lifu', *Empire*, 11 April 1864.
56 Gaide to Poupinel, 27 January 1873, IV ONC.
57 Evidence of Burns, Rees, *RC*, 21, 51.
58 Evidence of Henry, Hebblewhite and his son, King, Watongani, Fangi, *RC*, 12-13, 24-5, 47, 48, 52.
59 'South Sea Islanders in Queensland', *QVP*, III, 1876, 49; 'South Sea Islanders', *QVP*, II, 1878, 39.
60 MacFarlane to Ella, 11 June 1867, EP, A206, ML.
61 Evidence of Hovell, *RC*, 68.
62 Sleigh to Ella, 20 May 1872, EP, A208, ML.
63 Ella to LMS, 20 June 1874, SSL.
64 Lancaster's statement enclosed in FitzRoy to Grey, 24 December 1847, CO 201/386.
65 Kirsopp's statement enclosed in FitzRoy to Grey, 24 December 1847, CO 201/386.
66 Evidence of Burns, *RC*, 21, 22.
67 Evidence of Palmer, Hovell, *RC*, 10, 69.
68 The Loyalty Islanders' motives for travelling discussed here are similar to the reasons why Solomon Islanders signed on for work in Queensland and Fiji. However, one motive attributed to the Solomon Islanders—'pressures within their own society'—appears to have been of far less relevance to the Loyalty Islanders. See Corris, *Passage, Port and Plantation*, 59.
69 Evidence of Palmer, *RC*, 9.
70 Evidence of Henry, Hovell, *RC*, 45, 68.
71 Evidence of Henry, *RC*, 45.
72 Evidence of Joly, *RC*, 49.
73 Hadfield, Lifu Report, 29 December 1894, SSR.
74 Dollon to Beaulieu, 10 October 1882; and Salinis, Rapport, 24 February 1884, AAN.
75 Creagh to LMS, 14 January 1886, SSL; *Messager des Loyalty*, 28 August 1893.
76 *L'Océanie Française*, September 1911.
77 Fritz Sarasin, *La Nouvelle-Calédonie et les Iles Loyalty*, Paris [1917], 268.

Chapter 10

1 See above, page 8.
2 Cheyne, *Trading Voyages*, 131.
3 Turner, *Nineteen Years*, 422.
4 Hadfield, *Among the Natives*, 83.
5 Cheyne, *Trading Voyages*, 128.
6 Ibid., 116.
7 Ibid., 92-143, 150-4.
8 Gill, *Selections from the Autobiography*, 225.
9 Cheyne, *A Description of Islands in the Western Pacific Ocean*, London, 1852, 18.
10 J.M. [MacGillivray], 'A Look in at Lifu', *Empire*, 11 April 1864.
11 Erskine, *Journal of a Cruise*, 376-7.
12 MacFarlane, *Story of the Lifu Mission*, 73.
13 James Hope, *In Quest of Coolies*, London, 1872, 20-1.
14 Anderson, *Notes of Travel*, 158-9; Erskine, *Journal of a Cruise*, 380; Jules Patouillet, *Trois Ans en Nouvelle-Calédonie*, Paris, 1873, 11.
15 MacFarlane, *Story of the Lifu Mission*, 48-9.

16 Erskine, *Journal of a Cruise*, 345.
17 MacFarlane, *Story of the Lifu Mission*, 78.
18 MacFarlane to LMS, 18 June 1863, SSL; Hope, *In Quest of Coolies*, 20-1.
19 Selwyn to his father, 14 March 1850, Letters from Bishop Selwyn and Others, TS., Auckland Institute and Museum Library.
20 Jouan, 'Les Iles Loyalty', 10. See also Garnier, *Voyage Autour du Monde*, 288; de Rochas, 'Iles Loyalty', 22.
21 Henry Swainson, 'Private Journal . . . Her Majesties [sic] Ship "Havannah" ', MS., Turnbull Library, Wellington.
22 Cheyne, *Trading Voyages*, 128-9.
23 Bernard, 'Notices Historiques', AAN.
24 Evidence of Burns, *RC*, 22; Jouan, 'Les Iles Loyalty', 10.
25 Swainson, 'Private Journal', Turnbull Library.
26 Creagh to LMS, 13 June 1864, SSL.
27 Shipping reports, *Mon*.
28 Creagh, 10 year report, 25 December 1880, SSL; shipping reports, *Mon*.
29 MacFarlane to LMS, 27 May 1870, SSL.
30 Creagh 10 year report, 25 December 1880, SSL; Fabvre, 'Notes sur le R.P. Jean-Baptiste Fabvre', Fabvre Personal File, APM.
31 Hadfield to LMS, 26 April 1882, SSL; shipping reports, *Mon*.
32 Caillet, notebook, 27, 29-30; Creagh, 10 year report, 25 December 1880, SSL; Jones, 10 year report, 1881, SSL; Salinis, Rapport, 24 February 1884, AAN; shipping reports, *Mon*.
33 Caillet, notebook, 27, 29-30; Coote, *The Western Pacific*, 156; Jones, 10 year report, 1881, SSL.
34 Evidence of Burns, Merriman, Row, *RC*, 22, 32, 72.
35 Evidence of Towns, *RC*, 31.
36 Hope, *In Quest of Coolies*, 16.
37 Campbell, *A Year in the New Hebrides*, 136.
38 Le Chartier, *La Nouvelle-Calédonie*, 106. See also Creagh, 10 year report, 25 December 1880; and Jones, 10 year report, 1881, SSL.
39 Jones, 10 year report, 1881, SSL.
40 Rougeyron to Guillain, 3 May 1866, 411, I ONC; Jones to LMS, 29 March 1881, SSL.
41 Creagh to Ella, 12 June 1867, EP, A206, ML; Ella, 19 June 1867, Diary, B249, ML; Bernard to Fauvre, 14 July 1859, IV ONC; Forestier to Poupinel, 17 September 1860, IV ONC; Bernard to Rocher, 30 November 1861, VMA.
42 Evidence of Henry, *RC*, 47.
43 Caillet, notebook, 33; Montrouzier to Fauvre, 1 January 1859, IV ONC; Sleigh to LMS, 9 December 1882, SSL.
44 Palmer to Lambert, 22 March 1869, *RC*, 1.
45 Sleigh, Lifu Report, 1877, SSR.
46 Salinis, Rapport, 24 February 1884, AAN.
47 Creagh, 10 year report, 25 December 1880, SSL; Hadfield, Lifu Report, 2 January 1888, SSR.
48 Hadfield, Lifu Report, 28 December 1893, SSR.
49 Shipping reports, *Mon*.
50 Calculated from SSL, SSR, and SSO Box 11, 12.
51 Creagh, 10 year report, 25 December 1880; and Jones, 10 year report, 1881, SSL.
52 Gaide to Poupinel, 10 July 1880, IV ONC.

53 Ibid.
54 Creagh, 10 year report, 25 December 1880, SSL.
55 Hadfield, Lifu Report, 2 January 1888, SSR.
56 Pallu de la Barrière to Min., 6 December 1883, carton 86, ANOM.
57 Gouharou to Pallu de la Barrière, 4 December 1883, carton 86, ANOM.
58 Campbell, *A Year in the New Hebrides*, 135; Anderson, *Notes of Travel*, 158; Coote, *The Western Pacific*, 154; James G. Goodenough, *Journal of Commodore Goodenough*, ed.V.H. Goodenough, London, 1876, 305-8.
59 Vollet, 'Renseignements sur les Iles Loyalty', 55.
60 Campbell, *A Year in the New Hebrides*, 134.
61 Hope, *In Quest of Coolies*, 30.
62 MacFarlane to LMS, 20 June 1864, SSL.
63 Creagh to LMS 21 July 1871, SSL.
64 Creagh, 10 year report, 25 December 1880, SSL.
65 Campbell, *A Year in the New Hebrides*, 138; Evidence of Henry, *RC*, 47.
66 Creagh to LMS, 2 November 1859, SSL.
67 Jones to LMS, 20 June 1855, SSL.
68 Jones, 10 year report, 1881, SSL.
69 Ibid.
70 Annie C. Creagh, 'A Short Record of the Life . . . of the Revd. Stephen Mark Creagh', 1933, TS. in my possession.
71 Jones, 10 year report, 1881, SSL.
72 MacFarlane, *Story of the Lifu Mission*, 16; Cheyne, *Trading Voyages*, 129.
73 Creagh, 10 year report, 25 December 1880, SSL.
74 Hadfield, *Among the Natives*, 73-4.
75 Hadfield to LMS, 26 April 1882, SSL.
76 I have borrowed this term from W.H. Oliver, *Challenge and Response. A study of the development of the Gisborne East Coast Region*, Gisborne, 1971, 28.
77 Campbell, *A Year in the New Hebrides*, 136; Jouan, 'Les Iles Loyalty', 10; de Vaux, 'Les Iles Loyalty', 490.
78 Hadfield to LMS, 26 April 1882, SSL.
79 Creagh, 'A Short Record'.

Chapter 11
1 Hadfield, report, 28 December 1893, SSR.
2 Evidence of Macdonald, *RC*, 34. See also evidence of Lang, Lewers, Steel, 15-16, 38, 44.
3 See above, pages 8-9.
4 Ta'unga, *Works*, 80.
5 Turner, *Nineteen Years*, 463-4.
6 E.g., Ta'unga, *Works*, 83-4, 100-1.
7 Turner, *Nineteen Years*, 463; Bernard to his sister, 14 April 1861, IV ONC.
8 E.g., MacFarlane, December 1860, Journal, A833, ML; Baker to LMS, 16 July 1861, SSL; Ella to his wife, 24 February 1865, EP, A207, ML.
9 Creagh to LMS, 26 May 1859, SSL.
10 Ella, 20 June 1865, Diary, EP, B249, ML; Pratt to Ella, 18 September 1872, EP, A208, ML.
11 [Marist Mission], *Rapport sur les Superstitions*.
12 Jones, 'Nengone Habits, Tales, Traditions', 1863, MS., A396, ML.
13 Hadfield, *Among the Natives*, 214-17; Jones, 'Nengone Habits', A396, ML; [Marist Mission], *Rapport sur les Superstitions*, 17, 30.

14 [Marist Mission], *Rapport sur les Superstitions*, 86-7, 100.
15 Ibid., 100-1.
16 MacFarlane, *Story of the Lifu Mission*, 89.
17 Turner, *Nineteen Years*, 463.
18 Creagh, 10 year report, 25 December 1880, SSL.
19 MacFarlane to LMS, 16 October 1860, SSL. See also Jones to LMS, 20 June 1855; and Sleigh to LMS, 12 November 1886, SSL.
20 Pionnier to Gay, 13 June 1871, IV ONC. See also Guitta to Poupinel, 26 November 1873, IV ONC.
21 Fabvre to Poupinel, 8 January 1873, IV ONC.
22 Hadfield, Lifu report, 22 December 1892, SSR.
23 Jones to LMS, 20 June 1855, SSL.
24 Rougeyron to Fauvre, 16 December 1868, *APF*, 41(1869), 464.
25 Hadfield, Lifu report, 22 December 1892, SSR.
26 To be discussed shortly.
27 MacFarlane, *Story of the Lifu Mission*, 87-8.
28 MacFarlane to LMS, 14 April 1869, SSL.
29 Creagh to LMS, 2 July 1880, SSL.
30 E.g., MacFarlane, *Story of the Lifu Mission*, 83-5.
31 Jones to LMS, 11 February 1856, 23 April 1858, SSL.
32 Creagh to LMS, 8 July 1882; Hadfield to LMS, 26 October 1882; Jones to LMS, 22 February 1878, all in SSL.
33 Creagh to LMS, 8 July 1882, SSL.
34 Creagh to LMS, 23 January 1869; and Jones to LMS, 22 February 1878, SSL.
35 Creagh to LMS, 15 January 1883, SSL.
36 Creagh, Report for the Lifu Institution 1875, SSR.
37 MS. notes at Ecole Pastorale, Chepenehe, Lifu.
38 Murray and Sunderland, 'Samoa 1852 . . . Deputation from Apia', SSJ.
39 Murray, *Missions in Western Polynesia*, 315.
40 Creagh to LMS, February 1855; Jones to LMS, 20 June 1855; Sunderland to LMS, 6 July, 16 August 1855; all in SSL.
41 Jones to LMS, 20 June 1855, SSL.
42 Ibid.
43 Creagh to LMS, 3 January 1865, SSL.
44 'A list of Scriptures translated on the Loyalty Islands to Dec 1871', SSL.
45 Sleigh, Lifu report, 18 December 1878, SSR.
46 Jones to LMS, 15 October 1871, SSL.
47 Garnier, *Voyage Autour du Monde*, 302.
48 Creagh to LMS, 21 July 1971, SSL.
49 Salinis, Rapport, 24 February 1884, AAN.
50 Creagh to LMS, 8 July 1882, SSL.
51 Hadfield Lifu reports, 29 December 1894, 26 December 1901, SSR.
52 Ella to LMS, 24 October 1865, SSL.
53 Montrouzier to Fauvre, 1 January 1859, IV ONC.
54 Ibid.
55 MacFarlane, *Story of the Lifu Mission*, 77.
56 Gaide to Poupinel, 8 November 1865, VMA; Fabvre to Poupinel, 8 January 1873, IV ONC.
57 Jones to LMS, 6 September 1882, SSL.
58 Nihill, 'Journal of a Voyage to . . . the Loyalty Islands', 1850, MS., Auckland Public Library.

59 *Samoan Reporter*, October 1857.
60 Evidence of Merriman, *RC*, 23.
61 Garnier, *Voyage Autour du Monde*, 302.
62 Patteson to 'Fan', 25 August 1858, Patteson Papers, ANU.
63 Creagh, 10 year report, 25 December 1880, SSL.
64 Turner, *Nineteen Years*, 464.
65 Lewis M. Hogg, *A Letter to His Grace the Duke of Newcastle*, London, 1853, 19.
66 *Samoan Reporter*, October 1857.

Chapter 12
1 Douglas L. Oliver, *The Pacific Islands*, New York, 1961, 128. Other references are in my 'Firearms and Indigenous Warfare: a case study', *JPH*, 9(1974), 21-38, n. 1-5.
2 Guiart, *L'Organisation Sociale et Politique Traditionelle à Maré*, Noumea, 1952, 1. See also Guiart, *Structure de la Chefferie*, 649-50.
3 Saisset to Min., 10 August 1860, BB4 1036, ANM.
4 Cheyne, *Trading Voyages*, 104-5, 128; Hadfield, *Among the Natives*, 169-70; Ta'unga, *Works*, 84, 86-7.
5 Cheyne, *Trading Voyages*, 105.
6 Ibid., 106.
7 Hadfield, *Among the Natives*, 169.
8 Cheyne, *Trading Voyages*, 129; Ta'unga, *Works*, 86.
9 Garnier, *Voyage Autour du Monde*, 303; Jouan, 'Les Iles Loyalty', 11.
10 Cheyne, *Trading Voyages*, 94, 104, 129.
11 Ibid., 114-15.
12 Ibid., 100.
13 Ibid., 96.
14 Sleigh to LMS, 30 November 1863, SSL.
15 E.g., Ella to LMS, 25 February 1870, SSL.
16 E.g., Cheyne, *Trading Voyages*, 153; Testard to Bernard [1856], 5Ca 180, I ONC; Jones, 9 April 1856, Journal, JP, A399, ML.
17 E.g., Harrison M. Wright, *New Zealand 1769-1840*, 87-90.
18 Evidence of Dawson, *RC*, 64.
19 Jouan, 'Les Iles Loyalty', 9; de Rochas, 'Iles Loyalty', 22, 26.
20 Saisset to Min., 10 August 1860, BB4 1036, ANM.
21 Treve to Guillain, 10 September 1864, enclosed in Guillain to Min., 1 February 1865, carton 85, ANOM.
22 de Rochas, *La Nouvelle-Calédonie*, 210.
23 Ella, MS. notes, EP, A212, ML; Ella to Richerie, 18 July 1874, SSL.
24 Guillain to Min., 1 February 1865, carton 85, ANOM.
25 Beaulieu, 'Guerre de 1869', PCD; Creagh to Ella, 4 December 1869, EP, A206, ML.
26 Courbet to Min., 3 September 1880, carton 86, ANOM.
27 This term is from D.U. Urlich, 'The Introduction and Diffusion of Firearms in New Zealand 1800-1840', *JPS*, 79(1970), 399-410.
28 Erskine, *Journal of a Cruise*, 374; MacFarlane, *Story of the Lifu Mission*, 35.
29 Ibid., 39.
30 de Rochas, *La Nouvelle-Calédonie*, 205.
31 Sleigh to Richerie, 8 May 1872, SSL.
32 MacFarlane, *Story of the Lifu Mission*, 7.
33 de Rochas, *La Nouvelle-Calédonie*, 210.
34 Caillet, notebook, 35-47; Creagh to Caillet, 1 July 1873, SSL; Creagh to Ella, 30

June 1873, EP, A205, ML; Pionnier to Gay, 15 June 1873, IV ONC.
35   Beaulieu, 'Etat de l'Ile de Maré en 1866', PCD; Jones to LMS, 6 June 1861, SSL.
36   Beaulieu, 'Guerre de 1869', PCD; Creagh to Guillain, 24 March 1870, SSL.
37   Beaulieu to Poupinel, 4 September 1880; and Gaide to Poupinel, 3 September 1880, IV ONC; Jones to LMS, 18 November 1880, SSL.
38   A detailed investigation of each incident is in my 'Firearms and Indigenous Warfare', *JPH*, 9 (1974).
39   Hadfield, *Among the Natives*, 172-3.
40   Dorothy Shineberg, 'Guns and Men in Melanesia', *JPH*, 6 (1971), 61-82.
41   de Rochas, *La Nouvelle-Calédonie*, 209.
42   Pionnier to Gay, 15 June 1873, IV ONC.
43   MacFarlane, *Story of the Lifu Mission*, 301.
44   Bernard, 'Notices Historiques', AAN.
45   Shineberg, 'Guns and Men', 82.
46   Jones to LMS, 21 June 1866, SSL.
47   Bernard, 'Notices Historiques', AAN.
48   Pionnier to Gay, 15 June 1873, IV ONC.
49   MacFarlane, *Story of the Lifu Mission*, 7.
50   de Rochas, *La Nouvelle-Calédonie*, 201.

Chapter 13

1   F. Macfarlane Burnet, 'Impact of Disease in the Pacific', *MD Australia*, June 1972, 21.
2   McArthur, *Island Populations*.
3   John F. Kessel, 'The Ecology of Filariasis', *Studies in Disease Ecology*, ed. Jacques M. May, New York, 1961, 65; Burnet, 'Impact of Disease', 21; Isaac van der Sluis, *The Treponematosis of Tahiti*, Amsterdam [1966], 73, and *passim*.
4   James Cook, *Journals ... II The Voyage of the Resolution and Adventure 1772-75*, ed. J.C. Beaglehole, Cambridge, 1969, 540; Cheyne, *Trading Voyages*, 127.
5   van der Sluis, *Treponematosis*, 68.
6   Cheyne, *Trading Voyages*, 127; Turner, *Nineteen Years*, 401.
7   *Report of the Melanesian Mission for the Year 1857-1858*, 40-1.
8   Bernard, 'Notices Historiques', AAN; Ella to his wife, 9 December 1864, EP, A204, ML; Jouan, 'Les Iles Loyalty', 9-10; de Rochas, 'Sur les maladies des Néo-Calédoniens', *Bulletins de la Société d'Anthropologie de Paris*, 2(1861), 49.
9   Jouan, 'Les Iles Loyalty', 10.
10   M.O.T. Iyengar, 'Filariasis Investigations in New Caledonia', *South Pacific Commission Quarterly Bulletin*, 5(January 1955), 27, 34; Jean Rageau, 'Insectes et autres arthropodes d'intérêt médical ou vétérinaire en Nouvelle-Calédonie et aux Iles Loyauté', *Etudes Melanesiennes*, 10-1 (1956-7), 69.
11   Jouan, 'Les Iles Loyalty', 9-10.
12   John D. Comerie, *Black's Medical Dictionary*, 19th ed., London, 1948, 380.
13   Quoted by Ray, 'The People and Language of Lifu', 271.
14   Ibid.
15   Hadfield, *Among the Natives*, 191.
16   de Rochas, 'Iles Loyalty', 22-3.
17   Wright, *New Zealand 1769-1840*, 79-80.
18   Théophile Mialaret, 'Notes sur les Maladies cutanées à Maré', *Archives de Médecine Navale et Coloniale*, 56(1891) 59-62; Noc, 'Les Iles Loyalty. Géographie médicale', *Annales d'Hygiène et Médecine Coloniales*, 7(1904), 8-11.

19 Hadfield, *Among the Natives*, 203-4.
20 Grall, 'Contribution a l'étude de la contagiosité de la lèpre', *Archives de Médecine Navale*, 62(1894), 183-6, 345; Mialaret, 'Notes sur les Maladies', 63; Charles Nicolas, 'Etat actuel de la lèpre', *Bulletins de la Société de Pathologie Exotique*, 2(1909), 494.
21 Yaws and the primary stages of syphilis, which are superficially similar, were commonly confounded with each other. Both are caused by related spirochetes— *Treponema pertenue* and *Treponema pallidum*, respectively.
22 Noc, 'Les Iles Loyalty', 9. See also Nicolas, 'Etude des causes de la disparition', *Bulletins de la Société de Pathologie Exotique*, 21 (1928), 457.
23 Peter Pirie, 'The effects of treponematosis and gonorrhoea on the populations of the Pacific', *Human Biology in Oceania*, 1(February 1972), 196.
24 Ibid., 197, 203.
25 Ibid., 195, and see also 189; John R. Baker, 'The Northern New Hebrides', *The Geographical Journal*, 73(April 1929), 324.
26 Patrick A. Buxton, *Researches in Polynesia and Melanesia*, parts 5-7, London, 1928, 72.
27 Beaulieu, notes for the theological conference Noùmea 1890, AAN.
28 Murray and Turner, 'Samoa 1845 . . . Deputation to New Hebrides', SSJ; Ta'unga, *Works*, 80-1; Jones to LMS, 21 July 1857, SSL.
29 Creagh to LMS, 26 November 1860; and Baker to LMS, 3 January 1861, SSL; Bernard to his sister, 14 April 1861, IV ONC; Fabvre to Poupinel, 4 January 1861; and Gaide to Poupinel, 25 January 1861, VMA.
30 Goujon to Poupinel, 14 September 1866, VMA; Ella, 30 July 1866, Diary, EP, B249, ML.
31 Ella to LMS, 26 April 1875, SSL.
32 Mialaret, 'Notes sur les Maladies', 59.
33 Hadfield, *Among the Natives*, 80. See also 193-4.
34 de Rochas, *La Nouvelle-Calédonie*, 198.
35 MacFarlane, *Story of the Lifu Mission*, 14.
36 Hadfield, *Among the Natives*, 200.
37 Mialaret, 'Notes sur les Maladies', 63.
38 Jones to LMS, 26 May 1862, SSL. For further details see Ella, 'Notes for an address in England on medicinal and surgical practices in the S. Seas', EP, A212, ML.
39 Ella, 29 December 1864, Diary, EP, B249, ML.
40 Hadfield, *Among the Natives*, 199.
41 E.g., Fabvre to Poupinel, 4 January 1861; and Gaide to Poupinel, 25 January 1861, VMA.
42 Creagh to LMS, 4 June 1866, SSL.
43 Maurice Leenhardt, *Gens de la Grande Terre*, Paris, 1937, 206.
44 Hadfield, Lifu report, 2 January 1888, SSR.
45 Hadfield, *Among the Natives*, 217.
46 Felix Speiser, 'Decadence and Preservation in the New Hebrides', *Essays on the Depopulation of Melanesia*, ed. W.H.R. Rivers, Cambridge, 1922, 29.
47 Mialaret, 'Notes sur les Maladies', 59-63; Noc, 'Les Iles Loyalty', 7-17.

Chapter 14

1 *Samoan Reporter*, March 1860.
2 Jones to LMS, 15 October 1871, SSL.
3 Jones, 10 year report, 1881, SSL.

4   Ibid.
5   Le Boucher to Min., 29 October 1885, carton 85, ANOM; *L'Océanie Française*, September 1911; *Bulletin du Commerce*, 24 October 1931; Léon Collin, 'Aperçus démographiques sur les Iles de la Loyauté', *Bulletins de la Société de Pathologie Exotique*, 7(1914), 601.
6   Census, September 1866, Sleigh Papers, Box 1, SSO.
7   Sleigh to LMS, 21 December 1875, SSL.
8   Creagh, 10 year report, 25 December 1880, SSL; *Bulletin du Commerce*, 24 October 1931; Collin, 'Aperçus démographiques', 601.
9   Ella to Guillanton, 8 May 1869, EP, A200, ML; Rougeyron, Rapport 1870, Rapports I, III ONC.
10 Le Boucher to Min., 29 October 1885, carton 85, ANOM.
11 *Bulletin du Commerce*, 24 October 1931; *L'Océanie Française*, September 1911.
12 This figure is naturally tentative and given with full realisation of the limitations of early European estimates. See McArthur, 'The Demography of Primitive Populations', *Science*, 167(February 1970), 1097–101.
13 *Samoan Reporter*, March 1861.
14 E.g., Creagh to LMS, 8 January 1867, SSL.
15 Rougeyron, Rapport, 18 November 1869, Rapports I, III ONC.
16 Collin, 'Aperçus démographiques', 601; Sarasin, *La Nouvelle-Calédonie*, 266, 268.
17 Sources for the graphs to 1911 have been given in preceeding footnotes. Sources from 1911 are *Bulletin du Commerce*, 24 October 1931; *L'Océanie Française*, January-February 1922; Pierre Métais, 'Démographie des Néo-Calédoniens', *JSO*, 9 (December 1953), 117; Service de la Statistique, *Annuaire Statistique de la Nouvelle-Calédonie 1972*, Noumea, 1972. In the nineteenth century only those Islanders present were counted in censuses. Recent censuses, however, include those officially known to be on the New Caledonian mainland. At any one time up to half the total current population might be there.
18 McArthur, *Introducing Population Statistics*, Melbourne, 1961, 11.
19 Métais, 'Démographie des Néo-Calédoniens', 104.
20 Laquieze, 'Les Iles Loyauté. Etude démographique', *Bulletins de la Société de Pathologie Exotique*, 25(1932), 434–5.
21 Bernard, *L'Archipel de la Nouvelle-Calédonie*, 304; *L'Océanie Française*, September 1911.
22 Métais, 'Démographie des Néo-Calédoniens', *passim*.; Nicolas, 'Etude des causes de la disparition', 460–5.

Bibliography

Only those sources which have been cited in the notes or which gave relevant background information appear in this bibliography. For a more comprehensive list of published sources on the Loyalty Islands see Patrick O'Reilly, *Bibliographie de la Nouvelle-Calédonie*, Paris, 1955.

PRIMARY SOURCES

A. MANUSCRIPT

Official Records

FRANCE:

Archives du Ministère des Affaires Etrangères

Océanie IV. Mémoires et Documents. Nouvelle-Calédonie, Iles Loyalty 1862-5.

Océanie VIII. Mémoires et Documents. Iles Loyalty 1885-91.

Archives Nationales, section Marine

Sub-series BB4, Campagnes. Correspondence of officers commanding naval vessels. Cartons for 1853 to 1890 were examined. Those containing relevant information are: 797, 1036, 1604.

Archives Nationales, section Outre-Mer

The New Caledonian section has been described elsewhere.[1] The cartons containing relevant information on the Loyalty Islands are:

---

1 Elizabeth Scarr, 'French Government Archives', *JPH*, 5(1970), 176-94. Corrections were published in *JPH*, 6(1971), 170-9.

26. Correspondance générale 1855-71.
28. Statistiques 1865-1904.
38. Affaires de Maré 1886.
40. Correspondance générale 1842-57.
42. Correspondance générale 1856-62.
85. Iles Loyalty: Rapports Politiques 1864-6;
Correspondance générale 1885, 1886, 1887, 1888-91, 1894-5.
86. Iles Loyalty: Correspondance générale 1854-64, 1865-6, 1867-71, 1877-84.
174. Mission du Sr Caillot aux Loyalty.

Bibliothèque Nationale

Nouvelles acquisitions, 9448, Océanie et Mers australes: Nouvelle-Calédonie.

NEW ZEALAND:

National Archives (consulted on microfilm, NLA)

Royal Navy—Australia Station. Correspondence.
Vol. 21: Kidnapping, 1869-75.
Vol. 32: New Caledonia, 1870-83.

UNITED KINGDOM: (Public Record Office. Consulted on microfilm, NLA)
Admiralty

Admiralty 1. Secretaries' In-Letters 1840-1900. The volumes to 1870 were consulted. Relevant letters and reports are: 5606, Cap. E12, Cap. E60, Cap. E61.

Colonial Office

In-Letters, New South Wales series, Admiralty section, CO 201/ 386.

Foreign Office

1 France. General correspondence, FO 27, 1864-1890. Those files specifically relating to the Loyalty Islands are: FO 27/ 1537, 1554, 1555, 1567, 1592, 1670, 1693, 1694, 1701, 1798, 1801, 2063, 2064, 2090, 2098, 2108, 2146, 2160, 2161, 2190, 2233, 2244, 2265, 2328, 2337, 2336, 2992.

2 Pacific Islands. General correspondence, FO 58/ 69, 117.

Official Missionary Records

Archevêché de Noumea. Archives du Vicariat apostolique de la Nouvelle-Calédonie, Noumea.

1 Two large bundles of uncatalogued documents including Marist missionary letters and reports, and French administration regulations, letters, and reports, concerning the Loyalty Islands, and especially Uvea and Mare.

2 Bernard, Jean, 'Notices Historiques sur l'île Ouvéa et les îles Beauprés', [c. 1873], MS.

3 Fabvre, Jean-Baptiste, 'Notices Historiques sur Lifou', n.d., MS. and TS.

Archives de la Société des Missions Evangéliques de Paris, Paris.

Correspondence relating to Mare. Folders marked: Maré 1890, 1891, 1893, 1894, 1895, 1896, 1897, 1900.

Bibliography

Archivio Padri Maristi. Archives of the Marist Fathers, Rome.

I have described elsewhere the material for the Vicariate of New Caledonia (Oceania Nova Caledonia).[2] Those sections containing relevant information on the Loyalty Islands are:

I ONC. Dossiers marked:

    5Ca 180   Potestas civilis executiva.

    411   Rougeyron (correspondence).

    5Ca 411   Vitte (correspondence).

                      Fraysse (correspondence. Continues in II ONC).

II ONC.

    5Ca 411   Fraysse (continued).

                      N.C. Statistiques.

                      Goujon, 'Journal de l'Ile des Pins', October 1866–February 1867, TS.

                      Palazy, 'Mission de Kougne (Ile des Pins)', Journal, January 1865–September 1866, TS.

III ONC.

                      N.C. Rapports, 1862–1916.

                      N.C. Rapports I.

                      N.C. Rapports II.

                      N.C. La Loyalty (a large unsorted collection of notes and letters on the Loyalty Islands).

                      N.C. Administration Civile II.

                      Démêlés avec le Gouverneur Guillain, 1863–69.

IV ONC.

                      Correspondance générale. Read for the years 1848, 1855–1900.

Provincia Oceaniae

    OP 418   Letters of Poupinel, 1857–70.

    OP   Lettres des missionaires en passage 1861–94, in particular, Palazy to Colin, 10 June 1861.

Personal Files. Files of all the Marist missionaries on the Loyalty Islands were consulted.

[Uncatalogued]

    Pionnier, 'Les origines d'Ouvéa', n.d., TS.

London Missionary Society Archives, London. (Consulted on microfilm, NLA)

    South Sea Journals, 1840–66.

    South Sea Letters, 1854–1900.

    South Sea Odds, Box 1, 11, 12.

    South Sea Reports, 1866–1900.

---

2 'Further Notes on the Archives of the Marist Fathers—the Vicariate of New Caledonia', *JPH*, 7(1972), 178–81.

Villa Maria Archives. Marist Fathers. Archives of the Province of Oceania, Sydney.
    Nouvelle-Calédonie: Correspondance, 1858, 1860-9.

Private collection of Father M.J. Dubois.

    Father Dubois spent almost thirty years as a missionary at La Roche on Mare. On his return to Paris he took with him the nineteenth-century papers from the mission station, so protecting them from the ravages of time and the periodic and enthusiastic burning of accumulated rubbish (most Marist archival material on Lifu and Uvea has long since been destroyed). The extensive collection fills a trunk and consists of hundreds of invaluable notes, letters, reports, journals, diaries, and local histories written by the Marist missionaries, particularly Beaulieu. There are also many similar items written by French officials. The collection is arranged chronologically.

Unpublished Notes, Private Papers, Journals, etc.
(all are original MSS. unless otherwise stated)

Caillet, Xavier, notebook, 1871-5, in possession of R.H. Leenhardt, Paris.

Ella, Samuel, papers, Mitchell Library:

B249	Diary 1864-7
B250	Diary 1868-78
B251	Diary 1867-78
A200-2	Letterbook 1864-76
A204	Correspondence 3, 1863-4
A205	Correspondence 4, 1873-4
A206	Correspondence 5, 1867-9
A207	Correspondence 6, 1865-7
A208	Correspondence 7, 1870-2
A209	Correspondence 8, various dates
A212	Correspondence 11, various dates
A213	Correspondence 12, 1847-78

Gill, W. Wyatt, Diary of a tour of the Gilbert, Ellice, Union and Loyalty Islands in the John Williams. . . . 1872', B1444, Mitchell Library.

Jones, John, papers, Mitchell Library:

A395	Notebook 1867-77
A396	'Nengone Habits, tales, traditions', 1863
A398	'Nengone Customs, Traditions, and Anecdotes', n.d.
A399	Papers 1845-76
A400	Papers 1877-85
A401	Papers 1886-1908
	Newscuttings, 1 box.

MacFarlane, Samuel, Journal 1859-69, A833, Mitchell Library.

Marist Mission, baptismal register, Nathalo, Lifu, Loyalty Islands.

Murray, Robert, Logbook of the *Britannia*, 1792-6, Peabody Museum, Salem. Microfilmed by the Pacific Manuscripts Bureau, PMB 214, 215.

———, Logbook of the *Providence*, 1796, Peabody Museum, Salem. Microfilmed by the Pacific Manuscripts Bureau, PMB 215.

Nihill, William, 'Journal of a Voyage to the New Hebrides, New Caledonia, and the Loyalty Islands in the Bishop of New Zealand's Schooner "Undine" ' [1850], Auckland Public Library.

Bibliography

———, 'Journal of a Voyage from Auckland, N.Z. to the New Hebrides and the Loyalty Islands 1851', Auckland Public Library.

———, W. Nihill Papers, MS. 720, Hocken Library, Dunedin.

Oliver, R.A., *Fly* letterbook. Extracts on microfilm in the Department of Pacific History, Australian National University.

Patteson, John Coleridge, Patteson Papers, 1855–71, on microfilm in the Department of Pacific History, Australian National University.

Protestant Mission, notes on the Protestant Seminary, Ecole Pastorale, Chepenehe, Lifu, Loyalty Islands.

Selwyn, George Augustus, 'Letters from Bishop Selwyn and others 1842–67', TS, Auckland Institute and Museum.

———, George Augustus Selwyn Papers, MS. 273, Auckland Institute and Museum.

Slatyer, Thomas, 'Journal of a Voyage in the "Camden" from Samoa among the New Hebrides etc. June 6 1842', A1770, Mitchell Library.

Swainson, Henry, 'Private Journal Commencing June 1 1850 Ending Dec 31 1851. Her Majesties [sic] Ship "Havannah" ', Turnbull Library, Wellington.

Tidman, A., 5 letters Tidman to Creagh 1854–62, At24, Mitchell Library.

Vigors, Philip D., 'Private Journal of a Four Months Cruise Through Some of the "South Sea Islands" and New Zealand in H.M.S. "Havannah" ', 1850, TS, Auckland Institute and Museum.

Whitehouse, John Owen, notes on the Loyalty Islands based on letters sent to the London Missionary Society by its missionaries, PMB 149.

B. Printed

Official Records

AUSTRALIA:

Queensland: Votes and Proceedings of the Legislative Assembly:

'Report from the Immigration Agent on the Working of the Polynesian Act' 1868–9, 553–5.

'South Sea Islanders in Queensland', III, 1876, 49.

'South Sea Islanders', II, 1878, 39.

Report of the Royal Commission Appointed to Inquire into Certain Alleged Cases of Kidnapping of Natives of the Loyalty Islands, etc., Together with Minutes of Evidence and Appendix, Sydney, 1869 (in Royal Navy-Australia Station. Correspondence. Vol. 21: Kidnapping, 1869–75, microfilm, NLA).

UNITED KINGDOM:

Great Britain: Parliamentary Papers:

'Queensland (South Sea Islanders)'; and 'South Sea Islanders (Deportation)', 43(1868–9), 1005–168.

'South Sea Islanders (Queensland)', 48(1871), 155–551.

'Queensland (Polynesian Labourers)'; and 'South Sea Islands', 50(1873), 39–314.

'Correspondence Respecting the Expulsion of the Rev. J. Jones from Maré, one of the Loyalty Islands, by the French Authorities', 109(1888), 75-139.

Collections of Documents
(read for the years indicated)

Annales des Missions d'Océanie, 1855-99.

Annales de la Propagation de la Foi, 1857-1900.

Colonial Church Chronicle, 1852-4.

Journal des Missions Evangéliques, 1890-1900.

Missionary Magazine and Chronicle, 1842-66, thereafter *Chronicle of the London Missionary Society*, 1867-1900.

Missions Catholiques, 1868-90.

Newspapers, Journals, Reports

Annuaire de la Nouvelle-Calédonie et dépendances pour l'année 1890, Noumea, 1890.

Bulletin du Commerce de la Nouvelle-Calédonie et des Nouvelles-Hébrides, 24 October 1931.

Bulletin Official de la Nouvelle-Calédonie, 1864-90.

Messager des Loyalty, (nos. 2, 3, 5, 10) 1893-4.

Moniteur impérial de la Nouvelle-Calédonie et dépendances, 1859-86. (Known as *Moniteur de la Nouvelle-Calédonie* after 1861).

Nautical Magazine and Naval Chronicle, 1840-70.

New Zealand Church Almanac, 1852.

Océanie Française, September 1911, January-February 1922.

Report of the Melanesian Mission for the Year 1857-1858, Auckland, 1858.

Samoan Reporter, 1845-62.

Shipping Gazette and Sydney General Trade List, 23 March 1844, 12 July 1851. (See also Simpson in primary books and articles.)

Sydney Gazette, 24 May 1842.

Sydney Herald, 24, 25, 26 May 1842.

Sydney Morning Herald, 11 August 1842, 20 March 1844, 21, 27 September 1864.

Books and Articles

Alcan, Eugène, *Les Cannibals et leurs temps. Souvenirs de la Campagne de l'Océanie sous le Commandant Marceau*, Paris, 1887.

Anderson, J.W., *Notes of Travel in Fiji and New Caledonia with some remarks on South Sea Islanders and their Languages*, London, 1880.

Ashwell, B.Y., *Journal of a Visit to the Loyalty, New Hebrides, and Banks Islands in the Melanesian Mission Schooner the Southern Cross*, Auckland, 1860.

Balansa, B., *La Nouvelle-Calédonie et ses dépendances*, Paris, 1873.

Bibliography

Bernard, Augustin, *L'Archipel de la Nouvelle-Calédonie*, Paris, 1894.

Boyer, 'Quelques mots sur la pathologie indigène de la Nouvelle-Calédonie, des Loyalty, et des Nouvelles-Hébrides', *Archives de médecine navale*, 30(1878), 224-31.

Brainne, Charles, *La Nouvelle-Calédonie. Voyages. Missions. Moeurs. Colonisation (1774-1854)*, Paris, 1854.

Campbell, F.A., *A Year in the New Hebrides, Loyalty Islands, and New Caledonia*, Melbourne, 1873.

Le Chartier, H., *La Nouvelle-Calédonie et les Nouvelles-Hébrides*, Paris, 1885.

Cheyne, Andrew, *The Trading Voyages of Andrew Cheyne 1841-1844*, ed. Dorothy Shineberg, Canberra, 1971.

____, *A Description of Islands in the Western Pacific Ocean, North and South of the Equator: with Sailing Directions together with their Productions; Manners and Customs of the Natives and Vocabularies of the Various Languages*, London, 1852.

____, *Sailing Directions from New South Wales to China and Japan; including the whole islands and dangers in the Western Pacific Ocean*, London, 1855.

[Church of England], *The Island Mission: Being a History of the Melanesian Mission from its Commencement*, London, 1869.

Collin, Lèon, 'Le pian ou "Tonga" aux îles Loyalty', 180; 'Vaccine en Nouvelle-Calédonie et aux Loyalty', 503-6; 'Hygiène des indigènes des îles de la Loyalty', 598-600; 'Aperçus démographiques sur les îles de la Loyauté', 600-4; all in *Bulletins de la Société de Pathologie Exotique*, 7(1914).

Collins, David, *An Account of the English Colony in New South Wales*, London, 1798.

Cook, James, *The Journals of Captain James Cook. II. The Voyage of the Resolution and Adventure 1772-1775*, ed. J.C. Beaglehole, Cambridge, 1969.

Coote, Walter, *The Western Pacific. Being a description of the groups of islands to the north and east of the Australian continent*, London, 1883.

Cordeil, Paule, *Origines et Progrès de la Nouvelle-Calédonie*, Noumea, 1885.

Creagh, Stephen, 'Notes on the Loyalty Islands', *Report of the Fourth Meeting of the Australasian Association for the Advancement of Science*, 4(1892), 680-88.

Deniker, J., 'Les indigènes de Lifou (Iles Loyauté)', *Bulletins de la Société d'Anthropologie de Paris*, 4(1893), 791-803.

Dumont d'Urville, J.S.C., *Voyage de la Corvette l'Astrolabe exécuté par ordre du Roi, Pendant les Années 1826-1827-1828-1829 . . . Histoire du Voyage*, IV, Paris, 1832.

____, *Voyage au Pole Sud et Dans l'Océanie sur les Corvettes l'Astrolabe et la Zélée . . . Pendant les Années 1837-1838-1839-1840. Histoire du Voyage*, IX, Paris, 1846.

Ella, Samuel. 'The Action of the French towards the Protestant Mission at the Loyalty Islands', *Sydney Quarterly Magazine*, 7(March 1890), 3-16.

Erskine, John Elphinstone, *Journal of a Cruise Among the Islands of the Western Pacific Including the Feejees and others Inhabited by the Polynesian Negro Races, in Her Majesty's Ship Havannah*, London, 1853.

Gagnière, Matthieu, *Etude ethnologique sur la Religion des Néo-Calédoniens*, Saint-Louis, 1905.

Garnier, Jules, *Voyage Autour du Monde. Océanie. Les Iles des Pins, Loyalty et Tahiti*, Paris, 1871.

Gill, William, *Selections from the Autobiography of the Rev. William Gill.... Being chiefly a Record of his Life as a Missionary in the South Sea Islands*, London, 1880.

Glaumont, Gustave, 'Ethnogénie des Insulaires de Kunié (Ile des Pins)', *Revue d'Ethnographie*, 6(1887), 336-42.

———, 'Usages, moeurs et coutumes des Néo-Calédoniens', *Revue d'Ethnographie*, 7(1889), 73-141.

Godey, Charles, *Tablettes d'un Ancien Fonctionnaire de la Nouvelle-Calédonie*, Paris, 1886.

Goodenough, James G., *Journal of Commodore Goodenough ... During his Last Command as Senior Officer on the Australian Station 1873-1875*, ed. V.H. Goodenough, London, 1876.

Grall, 'Contribution à l'étude de la contagiosité de la lèpre; apparition et extension de cette maladie en Nouvelle-Calédonie', *Archives de Médecine Navale et Coloniale*, 62(1894), 161-88, 288-307, 344-53.

Hope, James L.A., *In Quest of Coolies*, London, 1872.

Hogg, Lewis M., *A Letter to His Grace the Duke of Newcastle ... on behalf of the Melanesian Mission of the Bishop of New Zealand*, London, 1853.

Inglis, John, 'Report of a Missionary Tour in the New Hebrides', *Journal of the Ethnological Society of London*, 3(1854), 53-85.

Jouan, Henri, 'Renseignements Nautiques sur les Iles Loyalty', *Annales Hydrographiques*, 19(1861), 452-64.

———, 'Les Iles Loyalty', reprinted from *Revue Maritime et Coloniale*, 1(1861).

[Jouan, Grimoult, Dutaillis, etc.], 'Les Iles Loyalty', *Annales Hydrographiques*, 29(1864), 207-22.

Labillardière, J.J.H., *Voyage in search of La Pérouse Performed by order of the Constituent Assembly during the Years 1791, 1792, 1793, and 1794*, II, London, 1800.

Lambert, Pierre, *Moeurs et Superstitions des Néo-Calédoniens*, Noumea, 1900.

Lemire, Charles, *La Colonisation Française en Nouvelle-Calédonie et dépendances*, Paris [1900].

London Missionary Society, *Statement of the Case of the Rev John Jones of Mare*, London, 1889.

MacFarlane, Samuel, *The Story of the Lifu Mission*, London, 1873.

J.M. [MacGillivray, John], 'A Look in at Lifu', *Empire*, 11 April 1864.

[Marist Mission], *Rapport sur les Superstitions Calédoniennes*, Noumea, 1891.

[Mayet, Claude], *August Marceau. Capitaine de Frégate, Commandant de l'Arche d'Alliance*, II, Paris, n.d.

[Melanesian Mission], *Two Letters and Melanesian Mission Reports etc.*, a collection of printed material relating to the Melanesian Mission, Mitchell Library.

Mialaret, Théopile, 'Notes sur les Maladies cutanées à Maré, Iles Loyalty', *Archives de Médecine Navale et Coloniale*, 56(1891), 59-63.

———, *L'Ile des Pins. Son Passé, Son Présent, Son Avenir. Colonisation et Réssources Agricoles*, Paris, 1897.

Murray, A.W., *Missions in Western Polynesia: being Historical Sketches of these Missions from their Commencement in 1839 to the Present Time*, London, 1863.

Nicolas, Charles, 'Etat actuel de la lèpre dans l'archipel desîles Loyalty', *Bulletins de la Société de Pathologie Exotique*, 2(1909), 493–7.

Noc, 'Les Iles Loyalty. Géographie médicale', *Annales d'Hygiène et Médecine Coloniales*, 7(1904), 5–17.

Patouillet, Jules, *Trois Ans en Nouvelle-Calédonie*, Paris, 1873.

Pigeard, Charles, *Voyage dans l'Océanie Centrale sur la Corvette Française le Bucéphale*, Paris, 1846.

Rivière, Henri, *Souvenirs de la Nouvelle-Calédonie*, Paris, 1881.

De Rochas, Victor, 'Iles Loyalty', *Bulletin de la Société de Géographie*, 20(1860), 5–27.

———, 'Sur les maladies des Néo-Calédoniens', *Bulletins de la Société d'Anthropologie de Paris*, 2(1861), 48–51.

———, *La Nouvelle-Calédonie et ses Habitants. Productions, Moeurs, Cannibalisme*, Paris, 1862.

De Salinis, A., *Marins et Missionaires. Conquête de la Nouvelle-Calédonie 1843–1853*, Paris, 1892.

Selwyn, George Augustus, *Two Letters from Bishop Selwyn*, Eton, 1850.

Simpson, T. Beckford, 'The *Strathisla*'s Voyage', *Shipping Gazette and Sydney General Trade List*, 9, 23 August, 13 September 1845.

Ta'unga, *The Works of Ta'unga. Records of a Polynesian Traveller in the South Seas, 1833–1896*, ed. R.G. and Marjorie Crocombe, Canberra, 1968.

Thomas, Julian, *Cannibals and Convicts. Notes of Personal Experiences in the Western Pacific*, London, 1886.

Turner, George, *Nineteen Years in Polynesia: Missionary Life, Travels, and Researches in the Islands of the Pacific*, London, 1861.

De Vaux, Le Baron L., 'Les Iles Loyalty, Les Nouvelles-Hébrides et Les Viti. Impressions et Souvenirs', *Revue d'Ethnographie*, 3(1884), 484–507.

Vollet, S.M., 'Renseignements sur les Iles Loyalty', *Annales Hydrographiques*, 35(1872), 53–6.

Wawn, William T., *The South Sea Islanders and the Queensland Labour Trade*, London, 1893.

Yonge, Charlotte Mary, *Life of John Coleridge Patteson. Missionary Bishop of the Melanesian Mission*, I, London, 1874.

SECONDARY SOURCES

Unpublished Works

Creagh, Annie C., 'A Short Record of the Life and Missionary Work of the Revd. Stephen Mark Creagh and Mrs. Creagh in the Loyalty Islands', 1933, TS, in my possession.

Douglas, Bronwen, 'A History of Culture Contact in North-eastern New Caledonia 1774–1870', Ph.D. thesis, Australian National University, 1972.

Dubois, M.J., 'Histoire Résumé de Maré à partir de 1866', TS, n.d., Archivio Padri Maristi.

———, 'Ethnologie de Maré'. Particularly useful is the section entitled 'La Société, le Clan, La Tribu'. TS. microfilm in my possession.

———, 'Géographique mythique et traditionnelle de Maré', thèse de doctorat d'état [Sorbonne, n.d.].

———, 'Les Eletok de Maré d'après la tradition. Etude d'ethno-histoire', thèse de doctorat de 3ᵉ cycle [Sorbonne, 1971].

Howe, K.R., 'Culture Contacts on the Loyalty Islands 1841–1895', Ph.D. thesis, Australian National University, 1973.

Laracy, Hugh M., 'Catholic Missions in the Solomon Islands 1845–1966', Ph.D. thesis, Australian National University, 1969.

Newbury, Colin, 'The Administration of French Oceania, 1842–1906', Ph.D. thesis, Australian National University, 1956.

Tavernier, R., 'Lifou. Une caractéristique: La "Coutume" ', n.d., TS. in my possession.

Tryon, D.T., 'The Languages of the Loyalty Islands', Ph.D. thesis, Australian National University, 1967.

Books and Articles

Baker, John R., *Man and Animals in the New Hebrides*, London, 1929.

———, 'The Northern New Hebrides', *The Geographical Journal*, 73(April 1929), 305–25.

Belshaw, Cyril S., *Changing Melanesia. Social Economics of Culture Contact*, Wellington, 1954.

Le Borgne, Jean, *Géographie de la Nouvelle-Calédonie et des Iles Loyauté*, Noumea, 1964.

Brou, Bernard, *Mémento d'histoire de la Nouvelle-Calédonie*, Noumea, 1970.

Burnet, F. MacFarlane, *Natural History of Infectious Disease*, Cambridge, 1953.

———, 'Impact of Disease in the Pacific', *MD Australia*, June 1972, 18–22.

Burrows, Edwin G., 'Ethnology of Uvea (Wallis Island)', *Bernice P. Bishop Museum Bulletin* 145, Honolulu, 1937.

Buxton, Patrick A., *Researches in Polynesia and Melanesia. An account of investigations in Samoa, Tonga, the Ellice Group, and the New Hebrides, in 1924, 1925, V–VII (Relating to Human Diseases and Welfare)*, London, 1928.

Cané, E., 'Infiltration des Polynésiens dans les îles voisines de la Nouvelle-Calédonie', *Etudes Mélanésiennes*, 3(January 1948), 14–17.

Comrie, John D., *Black's Medical Dictionary*, London, 1948.

Corris, Peter, *Passage, Port and Plantation. A history of Solomon Islands labour migration 1870–1914*, Melbourne, 1973.

Diapea, William, *Cannibal Jack: the True Autobiography of a White Man in the South Seas*, London, 1928.

Dubois, M.J., 'Les Eletoke de Maré', *Etudes Mélanésiennes*, 3(January 1948), 18–24.

———, 'Sorcelleries Maréennes: le Kaze et le Paace', *Etudes Mélanésiennes*, 4(July 1949), 5–15.

———, 'L'Origine des Eletoke', *Journal de la Société des Océanistes*, 6(December 1950), 248–50.

———, 'La Propriété Foncière Maréenne au temps du Paganisme', *Etudes Mélanésiennes*, 5(January 1951), 69–78.

———, 'L'Arrivée des Blancs à Maré. Tragiques contacts 1793–1851', *Journal de la Société des Océanistes*, 25(December 1969), 307–16.

Bibliography

———, 'Les grands refuges de guerre de Hnaened à Maré, Nouvelle-Calédonie', *Journal de la Société des Océanistes*, 26(March 1970), 55-60.

Douglas, Bronwen, 'A Contact History of the Balad People of New Caledonia 1774-1845', *Journal of the Polynesian Society*, 79(June 1970), 180-200.

———, 'The Export Trade in Tropical Products in New Caledonia 1841-1872', *Journal de la Société des Océanistes*, 31(June 1971), 157-69.

Dousset, Roselène, *Colonialisme et Contradictions. Etude sur les causes socio-historiques de l'insurrection de 1878 en Nouvelle-Calédonie*, Paris, 1970.

Fagot, 'Relations Familiales et Coutumières entre les trois îles Loyauté (Maré, Lifou, Ouvea) et en particulier entre leurs chefferies', *Journal de la Société des Océanistes*, 5(December 1949), 87-96.

Golson, Jack, 'Report on New Zealand, Western Polynesia, New Caledonia, and Fiji', *Asian Perspectives*, 5(1961), 166-80.

———, 'Archaeological Prospects for Melanesia' *Prehistoric Culture in Oceania*, ed. I. Yawata and Y.H. Sinoto, Honolulu, 1968, 3-14.

———, 'The Remarkable History of Indo-Pacific Man', *Journal of Paciic History*, 7(1972), 5-25.

Guiart, Jean, *L'Organisation Sociale et Politique Traditionnelle à Maré (Iles Loyalty)*, Noumea, 1952.

———, 'Les Origines de la Population d'Ouvea (Loyalty)', *Etudes Mélanésiennes*, 6(September 1952), 26-35.

———, 'Nouvelle-Calédonie et Iles Loyalty. Carte du dynamisme de la société indigène à l'arrivée des Européens', *Journal de la Société des Océanistes*, 9(December 1953), 93-7.

———, 'Liste par district des villages indigènes de la Nouvelle-Calédonie et dépendances', *Journal de la Société des Océanistes*, 9(December 1953), 87-91.

———, 'Histoire Mythique de l'Ile Maré', *Etudes Mélanésiennes*, 8(December 1954), 34-42.

———, *Structure de la Chefferie en Mélanésie du Sud*, Paris, 1963.

Hadfield, Emma, *Among the Natives of the Loyalty Group*, London, 1920.

Haudricourt, A.G., 'New Caledonia and the Loyalty Islands', *Current Trends in Linguistics*, 8, *Linguistics in Oceania*, ed. Thomas A. Seboek, Paris, 1971, 359-96.

Haudricourt, A.G., and Hollyman, K.J., 'The New Caledonian Vocabularies of Cook and the Forsters (Balad 1774)', *Journal of the Polynesian Society*, 69(June 1960), 215-27.

Hilliard, David, 'John Coleridge Patteson: missionary bishop of Melanesia', *Pacific Islands Portraits*, ed. J.W. Davidson and Deryck Scarr, Canberra, 1970, 177-200.

Hogbin, H.I., *Experiments in Civilization. The Effects of European Culture on a Native Community of the Solomon Islands*, London, 1939.

Hollyman, K.J., 'Polynesian Influence in New Caledonia. The Linguistic Aspect', *Journal of the Polynesian Society*, 68(December 1959), 357-89.

Howe, K.R., 'La Découverte par les Européens des Iles Loyauté', *Bulletin de la Société d'Etudes Historiques de la Nouvelle-Calédonie*, 17(1973), 31-8.

———, 'Firearms and Indigenous Warfare: a case study', *Journal of Pacific History*, 9(1974), 21-38.

Iyengar, M.O.T., 'Filariasis Investigations in New Caledonia', *South Pacific Commission Quarterly Bulletin*, 5(January 1955), 27, 34.

Keesing, Felix M., *The South Seas in the Modern World*, New York, 1946.
Laquieze, E., 'Les Iles Loyauté. Etude démographique', *Bulletins de la Société de Pathologie Exotique*, 25(1932), 431–6.
———, 'Enquête sur la lèpre aux îles de la Loyauté', *Bulletins de la Société de Pathologie Exotique*, 25(1932), 479–87.
Laracy, Hugh M., 'Xavier Montrouzier. A missionary in Melanesia', *Pacific Islands Portraits*, ed. J.W. Davidson and Deryck Scarr, Canberra, 1970, 127–45.
Laville, M.J., 'Les Trois Districts d'Ouvea', *Etudes Mélanésiennes*, 4(July 1949), 16–18.
Lawrence, P., and Meggitt, M.J., eds. *Gods Ghosts and Men in Melanesia*, Melbourne, 1965.
Leenhardt, Maurice, *Notes d'Ethnologie Néo-Calédonienne*, Paris, 1930.
———, *Gens de la Grande Terre*, Paris, 1937.
———, 'L'Archipel des Loyalty', *L'Anthropologie*, 49(1940), 833–4.
———, 'Les Chefferies Océaniennes', *Académie des Sciences Coloniales*, December 1941, 359–76.
Leenhardt, Raymond, *Au Vent de la Grande Terre. Histoire des Iles Loyalty de 1840 à 1895*, Paris [1957].
Legge, Christopher, 'William Diapea. A biographical sketch', *Journal of Pacific History*, 1(1966), 79–90.
Lenormand, Maurice H., 'The Population of New Caledonia and the Loyalty Islands', *Proceedings of the Seventh Pacific Science Congress of the Pacific Science Association 1949*, 7(1953), 609–13.
Leverd, A., 'Etude Linguistic et Ethnographique sur l'île Uvea ou Halgan (Archipel des Loyalty)', *Bulletin de la Société d'Etudes Océaniennes*, 2(September 1917), 43–53.
Maude, H.E., *Of Islands and Men. Studies in Pacific History*, Melbourne, 1968.
May, Jacques M., *The Ecology of Human Disease*, New York, 1958.
———, ed., *Studies in Disease Ecology*, New York, 1961.
McArthur, Norma, *Introducing Population Statistics*, Melbourne, 1961.
———, *Island Populations of the Pacific*, Canberra, 1967.
———, 'The Demography of Primitive Populations', *Science*, 167(February 1970), 1097–101.
Métais, Pierre, 'Démographie des Néo-Calédoniens', *Journal de la Société des Océanistes*, 9(December 1953), 99–128.
Moorehead, Alan, *The Fatal Impact. An Account of the Invasion of the South Pacific 1767–1840*, Harmondsworth, 1968.
Naisiline, Henri, 'Notes sur l'organisation sociale du district de Nece', *Etudes Mélanésiennes*, 6(September 1952), 36–44.
———, 'Histoire Mythique de l'Ile Maré', *Etudes Mélanésiennes*, 8(December 1954), 34–42.
Nicolas, Charles, 'Etude des causes de la disparition progressive d'une intéressant race d'indigènes', *Bulletins de la Société de Pathologie Exotique*, 21(1928), 453–65.
Oliver, Douglas L., *The Pacific Islands*, New York, 1961.
O'Reilly, Patrick, 'Deux Sites Fortifiés du district de la Roche dans l'Ile de Maré (Iles Loyalty)', *Journal de la Société des Océanistes*, 6(December 1950), 87–93.
———, *Calédoniens. Répertoire bio-bibliographique de la Nouvelle-Calédonie*, Paris, 1953.

Perry, William J., 'The Mosquitoes and Mosquito-Borne Diseases on New Caledonia. An historic account: 1885-1946', *American Journal of Tropical Medicine*, 30(1950), 103-14.

Person, Yves, *La Nouvelle-Calédonie et l'Europe 1774-1854*, Paris, 1953.

Pirie, Peter, 'The Effects of Treponematosis and Gonorrhoea on the Populations of the Pacific Islands', *Human Biology in Oceania*, 1(February 1972), 187-206.

Pisier, Georges, *Kounié ou l'Ile des Pins. Essai de monographie historique*, Noumea, 1971.

Poirier, Jean, 'Les mythes de Maré: I Mythes et récits maréens recueillis par le R.P.M.J. Dubois. II Sens et rôle du mythe en ethnologie', *Journal de la Société des Océanistes*, 4(December 1948), 5-47.

———, 'A propos du peuplement de Maré. Les couches ethniques des Loyauté: raciologie et paléogéographie', *Journal de la Société des Océanistes*, 9(December 1950), 247-8.

Price, A. Grenfell, *The Western Invasions of the Pacific and its Continents*, Oxford, 1963.

Priday, H.E.L., 'A Polynesian Migration circa 1765', *Journal of the Polynesian Society*, 3(September 1950), 245-60.

Rageau, Jean, 'Insectes et autre arthropodes d'intérêt medical ou vétérinaire en Nouvelle-Calédonie et aux îles Loyauté', *Etudes Mélanésiennes*, 10-11(December 1956-December 1957), 60-104.

Rau, Eric, *Institutions et Coutumes Canaques*, Paris, 1944.

Ray, S.H., 'The People and Language of Lifu, Loyalty Islands', *Journal of the Royal Anthropological Institute of Great Britain and Ireland*, 47(1917), 239-322.

Rey-Lescure, Philippe, 'Ethnographie. Maré et la Polynésie', *Bulletin de la Société des Etudes Océaniennes*, 5(1935), 443-9.

Rivers, W.H.R., ed., *Essays on the Depopulation of Melanesia*, Cambridge, 1922.

Sahlins, Marshall D., 'Poor Man, Rich Man, Big-Man, Chief: Political types in Melanesia and Polynesia', *Cultures of the Pacific*, ed. Thomas G. Harding and Ben J. Wallace, New York, 1970, 203-15.

Salisbury, R.F., *From Stone to Steel. Economic consequences of a technological change in New Guinea*, Melbourne, 1962.

Sarasin, Fritz, *La Nouvelle-Calédonie et les Iles Loyalty. Souvenirs de voyage d'un naturaliste*, (translated from the German by Jean Roux), Paris [1917].

Service de la Statistique, *Annuaire Statistique de la Nouvelle-Calédonie 1972*, Noumea, 1972.

Shineberg, Dorothy, *They Came for Sandalwood. A study of the sandalwood trade in the south-west Pacific 1830-1865*, Melbourne, 1967.

———, 'Guns and Men in Melanesia', *Journal of Pacific History*, 6(1971), 61-82.

Shutler, Richard, 'Peopling of the Pacific in the Light of Radio-carbon Dating', *Asian Perspectives*, 5(1961), 207-12.

———, 'Pacific Island Radiocarbon Dates, an overview', *Studies in Oceanic Culture History*, II, ed. R.C. Green and M. Kelly, Honolulu, 1971, 13-27.

Shutler, Richard, and Shutler, M., 'Archaeological Excavation in Southern Melanesia', *Prehistoric Culture in Oceania*, ed. I. Yawata and Y.H. Sinoto, Honolulu, 1968, 15-17.

Van der Sluis, Isaac, *The Treponematosis of Tahiti. Its origin and evolution. A study of the sources*, Amsterdam [1969].

Société des Missions Evangéliques de Paris, *Un Siècle d'Evangile à Ouvéa 1856-1956*, Noumea [1956].

Tryon, D.T., *Dehu-English Dictionary*, and *English-Dehu Dictionary*, Pacific Linguistics, Series C, nos. 6, 7, Canberra, 1967.

———, and Dubois, M.J., *Nengone Dictionary. Part I Nengone-English, Part II English-Nengone*, Pacific Linguistics, Series C, nos. 9, 23, Canberra, 1969, 1971.

Urlich, D.U., 'The Introduction and Diffusion of Firearms in New Zealand 1800-1840', *Journal of the Polynesian Society*, 79(December 1970), 399-410.

Vayda, A.P., *Maori Warfare*, Wellington, 1960.

———, 'Maoris and Muskets in New Zealand: Disruption of a War System', *Political Science Quarterly*, 85(1970), 560-84.

Wedgwood, Camilla H., 'Some Aspects of Warfare in Melanesia', *Oceania*, 1(1930-1), 5-33.

Wright, Harrison M., *New Zealand 1769-1840: Early Years of Western Contact*, Massachusetts, 1959.

Index

Admiralty Islands, 89
Adolphus Yates, 87
Akotesi, 119
Alcohol, 152-153
Aneityum, 87
Atua, 119
Australia: Loyalty Islanders go to, 90, 94, 97. *See also* Labour recruiting
Awi, 71, 75

Baker, William, 43, 45
Banner, Captain, 89
Banut, 66, 70
Barriol, Eugène, 50, 51, 65, 68
Bazit: attacks Owa, 52; exploits Christianity, 51; in tribal fighting, 65, 66, 67, 68, 140; invites Marist missionaries, 49; political position, 46-47; possesses firearms, 138, 140; supports Marist missionaries, 50; success of, 70, 80
Beachcombers, 16
Beaulieu, François, 34; besieged at La Roche, 71, 75; long stay, 121
Beka, 46, 47, 50, 70
Belep Islands, 89
Bernard, Augustin, 158

Bernard, Jean, 65, 122, 142; involved in tribal politics, 50-52; lands on Uvea, 49-50; recalled, 68
Bertrand, Jean, 57
Bible: translated, 126
Blue Bell, 89
Books: Loyalty Islanders' desire for, 125-127
Boyd, Benjamin, 90
Bridget, Charles, 35, 38, 98
Brigand, 24
Britannia, 13
British Foreign Office, 56, 60, 68, 76
Bula: accepts LMS teachers, 36; death of, 38; encourages LMS, 38; fights Ukeneso, 139; welcomes Europeans, 35
Bula (son of above), 40, 49, 58, 64, 80; assumes leadership, 38; exploits Christianity, 44-45; invites LMS, 38; persecutes Catholics, 57; punished by French, 59, 62
Burns, Henry: employs Loyalty Islanders, 87; evidence to Royal Commission, 92, 93; forced to leave Uvea, 87; house used by Ella, 65; on Loyalty Islanders' keenness to travel, 97; on Uvean politics, 49; regent on Uvea, 49; stations on

Aneityum, Uvea, 15, 49, 87; takes Loyalty Islanders to Sydney, 90; Uveans request he relocate them, 98
'Bush party', *see* Si Gwahma

Cahaze, 119
Caillet, 63
California: Loyalty Islanders visit, 89
Camden, 22
Cannibal Charley, *see* Bridget, Charles
Canton: Loyalty Islanders visit, 87
Cargo cults, 116
Castlereigh, 16
Catholicism, *see* Marist missionaries
Cheetah, 87
Chepenehe, 4, 36, 39, 40, 43, 55, 57, 58, 59, 63, 108, 111, 112, 122
Cheyne, Andrew: cannon fire, 136-137; in Sandalwood Bay, 36; involved in tribal politics, 36; on diseases, 145-146; on Mareans, 7; on sexual customs, 104; on tribal fighting, 135; on Whenegay, 47; trading difficulties, 102; trading prices, 102
Christianity: Loyalty Islanders' interpretation of, 118-124; on Lifu, 36-45 *passim*; on Mare, 25-34 *passim*; on Uvea, 49-52 *passim*; reasons for acceptance of, 19, 55, 117-120; social influence of, 128-129. *See also* LMS and Marist missionaries
'Civilisation', 30, 38, 44, 104, 110-111, 114
Cloth/clothing: and health, 147; Loyalty Islanders' desire for, 103-104, 106, 115, 137
Cochin-China: Mare chiefs exiled to, 75
Coconut oil, 105, 109
Commandants (French), 57, 58, 60, 61, 62, 66, 71, 72, 92, 98
Cook, James, 13, 145
'Conversion', *see* Christianity
Convicts, 16, 24
Copra, 105-106
Coquette, 87
Corvées, 62, 63, 80, 98
Cotton, 105, 109, 113
Creagh, Stephen, 38, 44, 49, 64, 110, 123; amongst enemy tribes, 30-31; amongst Si Gwahma, 27-29; lands on Mare, 27; long stay, 121; on Islanders as workers, 112; on Islanders being recruited, 93, 95; on Islanders' Christianity, 120; on Islanders' education, 125; on Islanders' houses, 111; on literacy, 126; on population, 149; supports Si Gwahma conquests, 31-32
Cru, Jean-Pierre: rebellion against, 77; removed by French, 78; sent to Mare, 76; supports Yiewene, 77

Dawson, Lancelot, 92, 97
Dehu, 9, 127
D'Entrecasteaux, Joseph, 13
Depopulation, 154-158 *passim*
De Pritzbuer, Leopold, 72
De Rochas, Victor: on diseases, 146; on firearms and fighting, 140, 141, 143; on medicine, 150
Diseases, 145-153 *passim*; effects on population, 155, 157; endemic, 145-146, 148-149; epidemic, 24, 118, 119, 149-150, 151. *See also* individual illnesses
Dueulu, 4, 36, 41, 45, 63, 80, 112
Dumai, 65, 67, 70; attacks Pumeli, 66, 68; from Wallis Islands, 46; political position, 47; supports Marist missionaries, 51
Dumont d'Urville, Jules, 13
Dysentery, 149

Eacho, 4, 40, 41, 43, 45, 63, 80, 87, 112
Edwards, Charles, 87
Elephantiasis, 47, 145, 146
Eletok, 21, 35, 73, 149
Ella, Samuel: arrives on Uvea, 65; commission investigates, 68; conflicts with Catholics, 66, 68, 69; leaves Uvea, 70; on defeated Protestants, 69; on firearms, 138; on Islanders' health, 150; on Islanders sailing away, 98; on trepanning, 151; relations with English traders, 96; relations with Guillain, 66, 67, 68
Enehmu, 6, 22, 35, 58
English influences on Loyalty Islanders, 40, 41, 49-50, 55, 56, 58, 61, 63, 76, 88, 96, 107, 111, 127
English language/words: spoken by Loyalty Islanders, 22, 41, 58, 91, 127-128
English traders: accused of introducing

Index

firearms, 138; dominate New Caledonia commerce, 15; employ Loyalty Islanders, 86-89, 91; French restrictions on, 88; licensed by French, 15, 88; relations with LMS, 96; take Loyalty Islanders to Sydney, 96; trading routes, 88-90. *See also* Traders
Enu, 58
Eoche, 112
Epidemics, *see* Diseases
Eromanga, 87
Erskine, John Elphinstone: describes Nekelo and Bazit, 47; describes Yiewene Kicini Bula, 25; on civil war in Losi, 139; on Islanders' bartering, 102; on Islanders' desire for cloth, 103; on Islanders' love of travel, 96-97; visits Mare, 25; visits Uvea, 47
Europeans resident on Loyalty Islands, 15-16, 108
European trade goods, tools, technology: consequences of, for Islanders, 106-107, 113-116; introduced by missionaries, 29-30, 122; Islanders responses to, 101-106. *See also* individual items

Fabvre, Jean-Baptiste, 44; death of, 63; difficulties on Lifu, 43; hostile to Guillain, 61; on religious divisions, 121
Fancy, 13
Fao: accompanies Bula's warriors, 139; influence at Mu, 38; leads Polynesian teachers on Lifu, 39
Fayawe (district), 46, 47, 49, 51, 52, 65, 69
Fayawe (village), 46, 47, 49, 50, 51, 52, 66, 68, 70, 136; seige of, 69, 140-141
Feillet, Jacques, 158
Filariasis, 145, 146, 148, 149
Firearms: introduced to Loyalty Islands, 136-139; no general demand for, 105; role in fighting/warfare, 139-144 *passim*
Fly, HMS, 91
French ambassador in London, 60
French authorities/government/administration in Noumea: accuses LMS missionaries of teaching Loyalty Islanders English, 127; annoyed that Loyalty Islanders speak English, 126; approached by Yiewene for assistance, 77; bans importation of firearms to Loyalty Islands, 138; blames Jones for problems on Mare, 76; builds leper camps on Loyalty Islands, 148; confiscates firearms on Loyalty Islands, 138; declares Loyalty Islands 'native reserves', 81; difficulties on Mare, 76; exiles Gocene to Isle of Pines, 78; exiles Mare chiefs to Cochin-China, 75; expels Jones from Mare, 78; forced to intervene on Loyalty Islands, 55; gains Yiewene's support, 76; imprisons Naisiline Nidoish, 73; influence on Loyalty Islands chiefships, 80; inquiry on Uvea, 68; investigates problems on Mare, 72-73; military expedition to Lifu, 57-64 *passim*; on Loyalty Islanders' keenness to travel, 94, 97; opposed to English labour recruiters at Loyalty Islands, 89, 90, 91, 99; opposed to missionaries trading, 107; policy for Lifu, 63; policy for Loyalty Islands, 14, 81; policy for New Caledonia, 81, 158; prohibits LMS fibre trade, 105; recruits Loyalty Islands labour, 99, 100; relations with Marist missionaries, 60-61; removes Cru from Mare, 78; sends doctors to Loyalty Islands, 152; sends French Protestant missionary to Mare, 76; takes censuses of Loyalty Islands, 154-155; trading regulations for Loyalty Islands, 88-89; transports Mare Catholics to Isle of Pines, 72; treats leprosy on Loyalty Islands, 152; tries to teach French on Loyalty Islands, 128; wary of LMS diplomatic pressure, 76. *See also* Guillain, Governor Charles
French government in Paris, 56, 61, 68, 71, 76
French language on Loyalty Islands, 128
French soldiers, 64; fight Lifuans, 58-59; Lifuans labour for, 61, 62; sent to Lifu, 57-63 *passim*; withdrawn from Lifu, 62-63

Gaide, Lubin, 44; on death of Naisiline Nidoish, 75; on fighting on Mare, 73; on Islanders being recruited, 93, 94; on opposition to Ukeneso, 45; on poverty of Marist mission on Mare, 110
Gaitcha, 35, 36, 40, 44, 46, 57, 64

Gocene: defeated by Naisiline Nidoish, 31-32; leads 'bush party', 78; leads rebellion against Yiewene, 77
Gonorrhoea, *see* Sexual diseases
Goujon, Prosper, 33
Guillain, Governor Charles: accuses missionaries of involvement in labour recruiting at Loyalty Islands, 92, 94, 95; argues with MacFarlane, 60; arrives with soldiers on Lifu, 58; as anti-cleric, 61; censured by Napoleon III, 60; closes LMS mission on Lifu, 59; closes Marist mission on Lifu, 61; complains about English labour recruiters at Loyalty Islands, 92; confiscates firearms on Lifu, 138; declares state of seige on Lifu, 59; dislike of English influences on Loyalty Islands, 96; has MacFarlane recalled from Lifu, 63; his Lifu expedition worries Ombalu, Naisiline Nidoish, 65, 71; hostile to missionaries trading, 107; imposes *corvées* on Lifu, 62; interviewed by Palmer, 92; lands on Uvea, 66; leaves Lifu, 59; leaves Uvea, 67; opposed to Naisiline Nidoish, 72; regulations for Uvea, 66-67; reinstates chiefs on Lifu, 59; relations with Marist missionaries, 60-61; returns to Paris, 62; Royal Commission does not support his accusations of kidnapping at Loyalty Islands, 94; sends commission to Uvea, 68; sends military expedition to Lifu, 57; trouble with Lifu chiefs, 62
Guillanton, Commandant on Lifu, 62
Guitta, Jerome, 34, 71, 73
Gwiet, 35, 36

Hadfield, Emma: on alcohol, 153; on clubs, 141; on Islanders' medical techniques, 150; on trepanning, 151; on yaws, 148
Hadfield, James: at Fayawe, 70; magic lantern shows, 122; on Islanders' literacy, 126-127; temperance societies, 153
Havannah, HMS, 25, 104
Haze, 8, 119, 150
Health, *see* Diseases
Henry, Andrew: employs Loyalty Islanders, 87; evidence to Royal Commission, 92; on Loyalty Islanders unwilling to work for French, 99; supplies labourers for New Caledonia, 99
Heo (or St Joseph), 47, 49, 50, 136
Hnaened, 136
Hovell, Albert, 98, 99
Hydrocele, 145, 146

Iai, 9, 50, 119, 127
Imwene, 47, 50, 70
Inangod, 112
Influenza, 149
Iron: Loyalty Islanders' desire for, 101-103. *See also* European trade goods
Island produce trade, 15, 16, 30, 88, 102-103, 105-109 *passim*, 113-114
Isle of Pines: Gocene exiled to, 78; Isle of Pines people on Mare, 24; Mare Catholics transported to, 72; Mare pastors exiled to, 77; on island produce trade routes, 88; prehistoric links with Loyalty Islands, 6, 8, 13, 101; sacking of *Star*, 24; social ties with Loyalty Islands, 106; visits to and from Mare by chiefs and Marist missionaries, 32-33
Iwateno, 9, 10

John Williams, 43
Jokwie, 49
Joly, Claudius, 93, 99
Jomae, 32, 33
Jones, John, 38, 44; amongst enemy tribes, 30-31; and LMS mission press, 126; and Naisiline Nidoish's constitutional convention, 72; arrives on Mare, 27; as trader, 108; blamed by French for troubles on Mare, 76; builds huge church, 111-112; 'conversion' of Si Gwahma, 27-28; expelled from Mare, 78; French thoughts on expelling him, 76; gives Mare church its independence, 77; grows cotton, 105; long stay, 121; on Islanders' desire for travel, 93; on Islanders finding 'liberty' in Australia, 95; on Islanders reading English, 128; on Naisiline Nidoish's death, 73; opposes Cru, 77; outcry against his expulsion from Mare, 78; relations with Si Gwahma chiefship, 28-32 *passim*, 34; supported by Gocene and 'bush party', 78; supports

Naisiline Nidoish against Si Achakaze, 31-32; supports use of violence against Catholics, 68; supports Yiewene's attack on Mare Catholics, 75; visits England with Yiewene, 75; visits Lifu, 39; Yiewene breaks friendly ties with him, 76

Jouan, Henri, 146

'Kidnapping', *see* Labour recruiting
Kirsopp, Edward, 90-91, 98
Kone, 47
Kong, 119
Kumo, 112

Labour recruiting: accusations of kidnapping at Loyalty Islands, 91-92; Boyd's scheme, 90; by Kirsopp, 90-91; by Lancaster, 90-91; for New Caledonia, 15, 99-100; for Queensland, 15, 90; Henry as recruiter for French, 99; inquiry into by NSW authorities, 91; Loyalty Islanders' attitude to French recruiting, 99-100; Loyalty Islanders employed as crews on recruiting vessels, 89, 97; Loyalty Islanders' profits from, 97, 106; Loyalty Islanders' responses to, 90-100 *passim*; missionaries accused of assisting, 92, 95; Oliver investigates, 91; Palmer investigates, 92; Royal Commission investigates, 92-94 *passim*

Lancaster, George, 90, 91, 98
La Perouse, 13
La Roche, 4, 33, 34, 71, 75, 76, 77, 80, 112, 122
Leenhardt, Maurice, 152
Leprosy, 148, 150, 152
Lewin, Ross, 87, 89
Lifu: becomes arrondissement, 62-63; communications on, 112; cotton growing on, 105; demand for LMS missionaries on, 38-40; diseases on, 146, 148-149; English influences on, 40; English spoken on, 128; European 'discovery' of, 13; firearms introduced to, 136-139; French administration of, 55-56, 63; French miliatry expedition to, 57-62 *passim*; geography of, 3-6; health on, 153; Islanders leave for New Caledonia, 100; Islanders leave to escape *corvées*, 98; labour recruiting at, 90, 92-93; languages on, 9, 10; literacy on, 126-127; LMS missionaries on, 43-45 *passim*; LMS teachers landed on, 36; map of, 37; Marist missionaries on, 40-45 *passim*; Melanesian Mission school on, 42; methods of warfare on, 134-136; mission schools on, 124-125; peace on, 62-64; population of, 155, 156, 157; prehistory of, 35; Protestants versus Catholics on, 55, 57; religious divisions of, 79; resident traders on, 108; sandalwood traders at, 35-36; tribal divisions on, 35; tribal fighting on, 35-36, 139-140; wealth of, 110; whalers at, 87

Lifu Resident (French), 63, 69, 81, 108
Literacy in Loyalty Islanders' languages, 26, 125-128 *passim*
London Missionary Society missionaries, 13-14, 19-20, 46; and 'conversion' of Si Gwahma, 25-28 *passim*; anger at return of Mare Catholics, 72; areas of influence on Loyalty Islands, 79-80; as traders, 107; church activities, 123; contributions to, 109; demanded by Lifuans, 38-40; education policies, 124-128 *passim*; encouraged by Bula chiefship, 38; explain Christianity to Islanders, 118-120; export coconut fibre, 105; forbidden on Mare by French, 78; give details of tribal fighting, 139, 141; give Mare church independence, 77; hope for Islanders' moral 'improvement', 129; identified with European technology, 122; improved relations with French government and Marist missionaries on Lifu, 63-64; influence on Islanders' commerce, 108; influence on Islanders' political structure, 80; influence on Uvea, 70; land missionaries on Lifu, 43, Mare, 26-27, Uvea, 52; land Polynesian teachers on Lifu, 36, Mare, 22, Uvea, 50; medical care for Islanders, 151; mission on Lifu closed by French, 59; on Islanders' overseas experience, 89; on labour recruiting, 95-96; opinion of Islanders' Christianity, 121; opinion of Noumea, 100; opposed by Cru on Mare, 76-77; opposed to *corvées* on Lifu, 62; opposed to

French administration on Lifu, 62; protest against French military expedition to Lifu, 60; relations with French government in Noumea, 55-56; relations with Melanesian Mission, 26, 43; relations with traders, 96; sell cotton, 105; support Bula and Wainya on Lifu, 44-45; support Jones through British FO, 76; support Naisiline Nidoish on Mare, 28-34 *passim*, 71-72; support Uvean Protestants against Uvean Catholics, 65-68 *passim*; take censuses of Loyalty Islands, 154-155; teach Islanders to read and write, 125-128; transfer Mare to SMEP, 78; visits to Mare, 21, 24; Yiewene breaks friendly ties with, 76. *See also* individual missionaries, Christianity

London Missionary Society teachers, *see* Polynesian teachers, Loyalty Islands teachers

Losi, 35, 38, 39, 135, 136, 139

Loyalty Islanders: alleged treachery of, 102; 'civilisation' of, 110-111; considered 'superior', 86; early descriptions of, 6-7; languages, 9; lifestyles and economic activity, 7-8, 113; origins and prehistory, 6; religious beliefs, 8-9; settlement patterns, 112; sexual customs, 104-105; social structure, 9-12; socio-economic changes, 111-116; socio-political changes, 79-81; summary of European contact with, 13-16; trade and migration routes, 6, 8. *See also* Lifu, Mare, Uvea, and specific subject references

Loyalty Islands, *see* Lifu, Mare, Uvea

Loyalty Islands teachers (LMS), 124, 125

Luengoni, 4, 108, 112

MacFarlane, Samuel: accused of trading, 108; alleged ruler of Lifu, 57, 58; arrives on Lifu, 43; barters with Lifuans, 102-103; confined to his house by French, 59; describes tribal fighting, 140, 143; establishes seminary, 124; hears of Fao's influence in tribal fighting, 139; hostile to Lifu commandants, 62; ignores Guillain's regulations, 61; leads LMS protest against Guillain, 60-61; on exploiting Islanders' 'superstition', 120; on Islanders' desire for church membership, 122; on Islanders' fear, 123; on Islanders' use of firearms, 142; on Losi civil war, 139; rapid success at Lifu, 44-45; recalled by LMS, 63; rummages in Catholic church, 63

Mair, Hugh, 87

Maize, 113

Maoris and health, 147

Mare: Catholics move to Isle of Pines, 72; chiefs exiled to Cochin-China, 75; communications on, 112; cotton growing on, 105; diseases on, 24, 118, 148, 149, 150; English influences on, 76; English spoken on, 76, 128; European 'discovery' of, 13; firearms introduced to, 136-139; geography of, 3-6; health on, 153; labour recruiting at, 93; languages on, 9, 10; literacy on, 125-126; locust plague on, 110; LMS departs, 78; LMS missionaries on, 26-34 *passim*; LMS teachers on, 22, 25; LMS visits to, 21-22, 24; maize growing on, 110; maps of, 23, 74; Marist missionaries on, 32-34; Melanesian Mission on, 25-26; methods of warfare on, 135-136; mission schools on, 124-125; overseas travel from, 95; peace on, 75-76, 78; population of, 154-155, 156, 157; poverty of, 110; prehistory of, 21; printing press on, 125-126; Protestants versus Catholics on, 70-72, 75; religious divisions of, 79; reputation as 'massacre island', 24; sandalwood traders at, 22, 24; sandalwood vessels attacked at, 24; supplies women, sailors and labourers for traders, 86; tribal divisions on, 21; tribal fighting on, 31-32, 70-72, 75, 141; troubles with Cru and Yiewene, 77-78; war damage on, 110; whalers at, 87

Mare pastors (LMS): attacked by Yiewene, 77; exiled to Isle of Pines and New Caledonia, 77; rebel against Cru, 77

Mare teachers (LMS): landed on Uvea, 49, 50

Marist missionaries (French Roman Catholic), 14, 19-20, 32, 46, 55; and coconut oil trade, 105; and cotton trade, 105; as traders, 107; beseiged at

Index

La Roche, 72, 75; church activities, 123; difficulties on Lifu, 41, 43–45; difficulties on Uvea, 50; difficulties teaching Islanders to read and write, 127; difficulties teaching French, 128; education policies of, 124–128 *passim*; explain Christianity to Islanders, 118–120; gain support on Mare, 33–34; gain support on Uvea, 50–52; give details of tribal fighting, 139, 141; improved relations with French government and LMS on Lifu, 63–64; influence on Loyalty Islands, 79–80; influence on Uvea, 70; invited to Lifu, 40, Mare, 32–33, Uvea, 49; leave Mare for Isle of Pines, 72; medical care for Islanders, 151–152; mission on Lifu closed by French, 59; on Islanders' overseas travels, 89–90; on Islanders' sexual customs, 104; on Isle of Pines, 32; on labour recruiting at Loyalty Islands, 93–95; on Mare politics, 73; opinion of Islanders' Christianity, 121; opposed by Naisiline Nidoish on Mare, 71; opposed to *corvées* on Lifu, 62; opposed to MacFarlane on Lifu, 57; organise peace feast on Lifu, 76; poverty on Mare, 110; relations with French authorities, 60–61; support Uvean Catholics against Protestants, 65–69; take censuses, 155. *See also* individual missionaries, Christianity

Mebuet, 4, 21

Medical treatment: as practised by Loyalty Islanders, 150–151, 152; as practised by missionaries, 150–152. *See also* Diseases

Medu, 80, 112

Melanesian Mission: on Mare, 25, 26–27; plans of, 14; relations with LMS, 26, 43; school on Lifu, 42. *See also* Nihill, Patteson, Selwyn

Melek, 112

Menaku, 31, 77, 112

Menedoku Bula, *see* Naisiline chiefship

Merriman, William, 89, 92

Metaris, 89

Mialaret, Théophile, 147–148, 150, 153

Mining on New Caledonia: Loyalty Islanders as labourers, 90, 99, 100

Miny, 9, 10, 119

Missionaries, *see* LMS, Marist, and individual missionaries

Money: Loyalty Islanders' desire for, 106

Montrouzier, Xavier, 45, 50; meets Patteson, 42; mission to Lifu, 40–42; sceptical of Protestants being literate, 127

Mu, 4, 35, 36, 37, 41, 43, 57, 58, 108, 112, 122

Muli, 46, 47, 51, 52, 66, 67

Murray, A.W., 6–7

Muskets, *see* Firearms

Naisiline chiefship:
   Menedoku Bula: killed in explosion, 24
   Naisiline Alakuten: as regent, 25, 28; dies, 32; supports Polynesian teachers, 25
   Naisiline Nidoish: as regent, 25, 32; attacks Catholic tribes, 71, 141; authority over Si Gwahma, 28–30; becomes great chief of Si Gwahma, 32; close relations with LMS, 28–32, 34, 71, 72; crowned king of Mare, 32; defeats Gocene and Si Achakaze, 31–32, 141; dies, 73; extends influence on Mare, 32; fearful of French, 71; French try to limit his authority, 72–73; imprisoned in New Caledonia, 73; imprisoned on Lifu, 72; involved in tribal politics, 72–73; Jones supports his war policies, 68; opposed by other chiefs, 31; opposes Marist missionaries, 33; organises constitutional convention, 72; overshadows Naisiline Alakuten, 28; supports Polynesian teachers, 25
   Yiewene Dokucas Naisiline: attacks Catholic tribes, 75; attacks Mare pastors, 77; causes schism in Si Gwahma, 77; changes allegiance to French, 76; great chief of Si Gwahma after Naisiline Nidoish, 75; leads 'sea party', 78; rebellion against by Gocene, 77; supports Cru, 77
   Yiewene Kicini Bula, 25, 28
   Yiewene Naisiline: adopts Taufa as *enehmu*, 22; attacks sandalwood vessels, 24; conquers Si Waeko, 21; dies, 25; exploits sandalwood trade, 22; ignores LMS teaching, 22, 25

Napoleon III: censures Guillain, 60
Nathalo, 39, 41, 45, 59, 63, 80, 108, 110, 112, 122
Nekelo: arrives on Uvea from Wallis Islands, 46–47; described by Erskine, 47; dies, 49
Nekelo (son of above): dominated by Bazit, 70; invites Marist missionaries, 49; supports Marist missionaries, 50, 52
Nengone, 9, 125, 127
Netche, 4, 21, 25, 26, 27, 29, 30, 31, 72, 108, 112, 122, 149
New Caledonia: alcohol on, 152; and island produce trade, 15, 88; annexed by France, 14, 55; declining population of, 158; diseases on, 145, 148; European population on, 99; government policy on, 81; Loyalty Islanders recruited for, 90, 99, 100; Loyalty Islands pastors sent there, 125; Mare pastors exiled there, 77; migration to Uvea from 46–47; Naisiline Nidoish imprisoned there, 73; prehistoric links with Loyalty Islands, 6, 8, 101; settlement of, 6; social links with Loyalty Islands, 106–107. *See also* Noumea
New Forest, 87
New Guinea, 15, 125, 148
New Hebrideans, 42, 100, 106
New Hebrides, 9, 19, 42, 86, 87, 88, 89, 97, 99, 124
Nihill, William: mission on Mare, 26; on Loyalty Islanders speaking English, 128; on Melanesian mission scholars returning to Islands, 129; translates and prints in Nengone, 125–126
Noc, Dr, 147–148, 153
Node ri kurubu, 32
Northern Bay, 21, 30
Noumea, 55, 57, 59; and island produce trade, 15, 88, 107, 108–109; Loyalty Islanders enjoy, 100; Loyalty Islands chiefs at, 62, 68

Ohwen, 46, 47, 49, 51, 52, 70
Oliver, Captain, 91
Ombalu: as regent, 49, 51; attacks Uvean Protestants, 66, 68; authority of, 70, 80; imprisoned in Noumea, 68; returns from Noumea, 69; supports Marist missionaries, 65

Onyat, 47, 51, 67
Owa: political position, 47; rebels against Bazit and is defeated, 51, 52, 70; supports Marist missionaries, 50

Paddon, James, 98
Palazy, François, 40, 41, 49, 50
Palmer, George, 92, 95, 98, 99, 107
Paris, *see* French government in Paris
Patteson, John Coleridge, 14, 41; and Melanesian Mission school on Lifu, 41–42, 43; meets Montrouzier, 42; on Loyalty Islanders' diseases, 146; on Loyalty Islanders social habits, 128
Penelo, 71, 75, 80, 112
Peng, 112
Peorawa, 3
Pionnier, Jean Nestor: attitude to labour recruiting, 94–95; describes tribal fighting, 143; on defeated Uvean Protestants, 69; on firearms, 141; on Uveans wanting to leave, 93
Polynesian Labourers Act of 1868, 90
Polynesians: influence on Loyalty Islands, 6–7, 9, 13, 22
Polynesian teachers (LMS): adopted by Yiewene Naisiline, 22; expelled from Lifu, 59; explain Christianity to Loyalty Islanders, 118–119; extend their influence on Lifu, 39, 40; houses of, 111; influence on Mareans, 25–26; influence on tribal fighting on Lifu, 139; in tribal fighting on Uvea, 51–52; landed on Lifu, 36, Mare, 22, Uvea, 50; LMS plans to introduce them, 14; lose Ombalu's allegiance, 65; oppose Marist missionaries on Lifu, 41; supported by Naisiline chiefship, 25
Population of Loyalty Islands, 7, 154–158
Port de France, *see* Noumea
Portenia, 90
Poupinel, 40
Presbyterian missionaries in New Hebrides, 95
Printing press on Mare, 125–126
Protestantism, *see* LMS missionaries
Protestant teachers, *see* Polynesian teachers, Mare teachers
Providence, 13
Pumali: fights Dumai, 66, 68; from Tonga, 46; on Muli, 47

Index

Queensland: Loyalty Islanders recruited for, 15, 16, 90-97 *passim*, 117

Rarotongan teachers, *see* Polynesian teachers
Rawa, 3, 112
Reece, James, 38
Rees, Captain, 97
Richerie, Eugène Gaultier de la, 69
Ro, 4, 25, 27, 29, 31, 108, 111, 112, 122
Roman Catholicism, *see* Marist missionaries
Rotuma, 90
Roussel, Jacques, 69, 70
Row, James, 92-93
Royal Commission of 1869 to investigate rumours of kidnapping, 90, 92-94. *See also* Labour recruiting.

St Johns College, Auckland, 14, 27, 42
St Joseph, 50, 108, 122. *See also* Heo
Saisset, Jean, 138, 143
Salinis, 126
Samoan influence on Loyalty Islands, 6. *See also* Polynesian teachers
Samoan teachers, *see* Polynesian teachers
Sandalwood Bay, 4, 35-36, 87
Sandalwood traders, 13, 15, 22, 35-36, 47, 49, 86-87, 101
Sarah, 16
Scarlet fever, 149, 157
Schools, *see* LMS, Marist missionaries, Melanesian Mission
'Sea party', *see* Si Gwahma
Selwyn, George Augustus: attempts school at Lifu, 41-42; lands Nihill on Mare, 26; on Loyalty Islanders' craving for tobacco, 104; plans for Melanesian Mission, 14; visits Mare, 25
Seminary at Chepenehe, 124, 125
Sexual diseases, 148-149
Sexual relations: Loyalty Islanders' customs, 104-105
Si Achakaze: attacked by Naisiline Nidoish, 31, 141; rebels against Yiewene Naisiline, 77
Si Gureschaba, 33-34
Si Gurewoc, 32, 33
Si Gwahma: and literacy, 125; 'Christian soldiers' of, 76; growing influence of, 21; LMS missionary influence on, 25-32 *passim*; reconciliation amongst,

78; split into 'bush party' and 'sea party', 77-78. *See also* Naisiline chiefship
Si Med, 32
Si Medu, 32, 33, 34
Simpson, Thomas Beckford, 36
Si Nerech, 32
Sinewami, 33
Si Ruemec, 32
Sisters, 24
Si Waeko, 21, 77
Sleigh, James, 45, 63, 121, 147
Smallpox, 149
Société des Missions Evangéliques de Paris, 78
Solomon Islands, 9, 15, 19, 90, 91, 97
Star, 24
Streeter, Captain, 87
Styx, 40, 50
Swainson, Henry, 104
Sydney: Loyalty Islanders visit, 89, 90, 93, 96, 97, 129
Syphilis, *see* Sexual diseases

Tabe, 33
Tadine, 4, 21, 87, 112
Tahiti: Mare chiefs exiled there, 73
Tanese influence on Lifu, 38
Taufa, 22
Taume, 46, 47
Ta'unga: on epidemic on Mare, 118; on warfare, 135; on Yiewene's attitude to Christianity, 22-23; translates into Nengone, 125
Tawained, 112
Telegraph, 89
Tene dosinoe, 150
Tene haze, 150
Testard, Jules, 40, 50
Titi, 4, 33; Marist missionaries take refuge on, 71, 75
Tobacco: Loyalty Islanders' desire for, 103, 104, 106, 115, 137; effects of, 146
Tomahawks: as weapons, 141; Loyalty Islanders' desire for, 137
Tongan influence on Loyalty Islands, 6-7, 22, 35, 38, 46
Torres Strait, 89
Towns, Robert, 90
Traders and trading relations, 15-16, 101-116 *passim*. *See also* English traders, European trade goods, individual traders, Island produce trade,

Labour recruiting, Sandalwood traders, Whalers
Traders resident on Loyalty Islands, 16, 108
Travel overseas by Loyalty Islanders, 86–100 *passim*
Trepanning (skull operations), 150–151
Tribal fighting, *see* Warfare
Tuberculosis, 145–149 *passim*
Turner, George, 120

Ukeneso: appeals to French authorities, 57; attacked by Protestant Lifuans, 57; blames Fao for his defeat, 139; greets French soldiers, 58; invites Marist missionaries, 40; lacks authority, 43; meets Jones, 39–40; opposed by Bula, 44; opposed by Wainya, 39; opposes LMS teachers, 39, 40; reinstated by Guillain, 59; supports Marist missionaries, 41, 63; troubles with Guillain, 62
Undine, 25
Uneis, 46, 47
Uvea: Burns's station on, 49, 87; coconut oil produced on, 105; diseases on, 146, 148, 149; English spoken on, 128; firearms introduced to, 136, 138; French government inquiries on, 68; geography of, 3–6; Guillain visits, 66–67; labour recruiters at, 90, 93–98; languages on, 9; literacy on, 126–127; LMS missionary lands, 52; LMS teachers on, 49–50; map of, 48; Marist missionaries on, 49–52; methods of warfare on, 136; mission schools on, 125; peace on, 69–70; population of, 155, 156; prehistory of, 46–47; Protestants versus Catholics on, 51–52, 65–69; religious divisions of, 79; sandalwood traders at, 47, 49, 87; seige at Fayawe, 69, 140–141; trepanning on, 150–151; tribal divisions on, 46–47; tribal fighting on, 49, 140–141; war damage on, 110
Uvea (language), 9

Velocity, 90
Vitte, Bishop, 69

Vulture, 87

Wadrilla, 52, 66, 67, 70
Waesolot, 69
Waikosone: defeats Waitheane, 33; supports Marist missionaries, 33–34 *passim*
Wainya, 40, 49, 64; accepts LMS teachers, 39; deposed by French, 59; house described, 111; persecutes Lifu Catholics, 57; rebels against Ukeneso, 39, 45
Waitheane, 33
Wakat-Lekin, 51, 52, 66, 70
Wallis Islanders: language of, 9; migration to Uvea, 6, 46–47
Wanakami, 32
Warfare, 31–32, 35–36, 49, 51–52, 65–69, 70–72, 75; examples of battles, 139–144; mortality in, 139–141; pre-European methods of, 134–136; role of firearms in, 139–144 *passim*
We, 4, 39, 41, 112, 135, 139
Weneki, 46, 47, 136
Wet, 35, 39, 44, 46, 57, 59, 64, 135, 136, 139
Whalers, 15, 87
Whenegay: and cannon fire, 136; death of, 49, 140; described by Cheyne, 47; political position, 47
Whenegay (grandson of above), 65, 66, 67, 70, 98; beseiged at Fayawe, 69; requests Ombalu's release, 69; takes over chiefship, 68
Whooping cough, 149

Yaws, 145, 146, 148, 149
Yiewene Dokucas Naisiline, *see* Naisiline chiefship
Yiewene Naisiline, *see* Naisiline chiefship

Zeula: dies, 40; opposes LMS teachers, 39; political position, 35; rivalry with Gwiet, 35–36
Zeula (son of above): opposed by Bula and Lifu Protestants, 45, 57; supported by French, 59; supports Marist missionaries, 63; trouble with Guillain, 62

About the Author

Dr K.R. Howe is Lecturer in History at Massey University in New Zealand. This book is based on extensive travel and research in libraries, archives and private collections not only in Australia and New Zealand but also in Rome, Paris and Noumea. In addition the author spent some time in the Loyalty Islands.

⼈ Production Notes

The text of this book has been designed by Roger J. Eggers and typeset on the Unified Composing System by the design & production staff of The University Press of Hawaii.

The text typeface is California and the display matter is set in Korinna.

Offset presswork and binding is the work of Vail-Ballou Press. Text paper is Glatfelter P & S Offset, basis 55.